MAKING VALUE

TIMOTHY D. TAYLOR

Making Value

Music, Capital, and the Social

DUKE UNIVERSITY PRESS
Durham and London
2024

Project Editor: Livia Tenzer
Designed by A. Mattson Gallagher
Typeset in Untitled Serif by Copperline Book Services

Library of Congress Cataloging-in-Publication Data
Names: Taylor, Timothy Dean, author.
Title: Making value : music, capital, and the social /
Timothy D. Taylor.
Description: Durham : Duke University Press, 2024. |
Includes bibliographical references and index.
Identifiers: LCCN 2023033162 (print)
LCCN 2023033163 (ebook)
ISBN 9781478030355 (paperback)
ISBN 9781478026143 (hardcover)
ISBN 9781478059349 (ebook)
Subjects: LCSH: Music—Economic aspects. | Music—
Social aspects. | Music—Labor productivity—History. |
Value. | BISAC: MUSIC / Ethnomusicology | SOCIAL
SCIENCE / Anthropology / Cultural & Social
Classification: LCC ML3916 .T3905 2024 (print) |
LCC ML3916 (ebook) | DDC 338.4/778—dc23/eng/20231103
LC record available at https://lccn.loc.gov/2023033162
LC ebook record available at https://lccn.loc.gov/2023033163

Cover art: Illustration using "Treble Clef Musical Note
with Keyboards," color lithograph, American school, 1946.
Photo © GraphicaArtis/Bridgeman Images.

For Sherry

CONTENTS

ACKNOWLEDGMENTS

Some years ago, I asked Steve Feld to read something I had written, and he kindly obliged. The only comment I now remember was that while he thought what I had written was good, it would benefit from a reading of Fred Myers's introduction to his edited volume *Empire of Things*. I made a mental note but that's as far as it went. A while later, Steve again generously agreed to read something, and again he said that while what I had written was good, it would (also) benefit from reading Myers's introduction. Which I finally did. That was the beginning of my venture into anthropological value theory. So, first thanks go to Steve, as well as Fred, whose book, along with his monograph *Painting Culture*, have become essential texts.

I will let the existing acknowledgments in the publications collected in this volume stand, but I would like to thank, and in some cases rethank, people who have been helpful to me in the work collected here: Hannah Appel, Giorgio Biancorosso, Jessica Cattelino, Hauke Dorsch, Shannon Garland, Brent Luvaas, Louise Meintjes, Anna Morcom, David Novak, Ana-María Ochoa Gautier, Ron Radano, and Markus Verne. The previously unpublished chapters were auditioned at a couple of places, so I would like to thank the audience in the Music Department at the University of California, Santa Barbara, for offering comments on chapter 2, and the audience in the Department of Communication, Culture, and Media at Drexel University, which heard chapter 3.

Thanks also go to the anonymous reviewers of this manuscript. Sincerest thanks also go to Ken Wissoker at Duke University Press for his enthusiastic support of this book, as well as to others at the press: Kate Mullen, Chad Royal, and Livia Tenzer. I would also like to thank indexer Diana Witt.

I would like to express my gratitude to Shelina Brown, Erin Estrada, and Maya Gutierrez for transcribing interviews. Interviews and other ethnographic research for this book were approved by UCLA's Institutional Review Board (IRB 14-000223 and IRB 15-000426).

As always, deepest thanks go to Sherry B. Ortner, whose love, encouragement, sharp intellect, and critical eye I value more than anything else.

Introduction

Theorizing Value in Practice

This book collects some of my recent writings that draw on anthropological value theory in the study of cultural production and consumption. I first forayed into this territory in *Music and Capitalism* (2016b) and in the concluding chapter of *Music in the World* (2017), and I continued this line of inquiry in my most recent monograph, *Working Musicians* (2023), but these chapters flesh out my interest in value in greater breadth, depth, and detail, covering the creation and exchange of value in a wide range of contexts: an indie rock scene; an Irish traditional music session; supply chains as sites for the creation of not just capitalist but also other forms of value; the value-seeking and -creating practices of trendspotters; musical performance as a medium of value; the work of music managers; and more. The chapters not only offer ethnographic and historical treatments of various conceptions of value but also extend anthropological value theory into considerations of cultural production and consumption.

Why value theory? What people value shapes their actions as they promote and defend what they value against those who value something else, in a ceaseless social dynamic. Conceptions of value are everywhere, not just in the political or cosmological realms. As I argued in *Music in the World* (2017), focusing on value is a way of considering meaning, as urged by Clifford Geertz (1973)—that is, concentrating our attention on what is meaningful to the people we study. I view value as a variation of the idea of meaning, though broader, in that it includes "the economic" (where "meaning" tends to be more idealist). In an era when so many fields are internally fragmented, splintering, and moving in different directions, the example of Geertz—who provided no conceptual model other than this concern for meaningfulness for social actors—has not lost its utility nor been rendered passé, even if Geertz's influence isn't what it once was. Models come and go; meaningfulness does not.

Value Theory

Neither does value. There are various ways of considering the question of value. Marxists have debated the labor theory of value for, it seems, generations (e.g., Steedman et al. 1981). Humanists have contemplated how to value aesthetic works (Smith 1988 is probably the best-known example; see also Fekete 1987); Simon Frith's *Performing Rites* (1996) draws in part on this literature to wonder about value judgments in popular music. *Making Value*, however, is less concerned with consumption of works or value judgments about them and instead considers the production of value. I draw mainly on the anthropological literature on value, in which there have been two historical trajectories.[1] One stems from Karl Marx's writings on forms of capitalist value, and the other from Marcel Mauss's classic *The Gift* (2016), on gift exchange. Writings by anthropologists have tended to veer toward one or the other, viewing them as essentially dichotomous until fairly recently.

Marx famously argues that commodities have a dual character, the aspects of which he called "use-value," the utility of a thing, and "exchange-value," the amount of one commodity required to exchange for another. And there is the famous labor theory of value, the amount of "socially necessary" labor time required to produce a particular commodity. The addition of the phrase "socially necessary" is Marx's innovation, an advance on Adam Smith and David Ricardo that understands labor not simply in an abstract, calculable, rational way, but raises questions about what is socially necessary and who decides what is and isn't (see Harvey 2010). Marx isn't concerned with other sorts of value beyond these (as he was, according to Keith Hart,[2] playing a kind of intellectual game with Adam Smith in attempting to devise a science of capitalism). Nonetheless, Marx's tools continue to be powerful if one is concerned with conceptions of value produced in capitalist exchange.

Until fairly recently Mauss was usually seen as the antithesis of Marx, at least with respect to questions of value, but some anthropologists have offered readings that interpret his work in *The Gift* and beyond as providing a more capacious conception of the value of goods (Graeber 2001, and Hart 2014 in particular). These interpretations move beyond a fairly strict functionalist orientation (that gift giving and reciprocity bind societies together) to argue that Mauss recognized that all societies practice gift exchange, and at the same time, all societies employ something that could be considered to be exchanges with money. Rather than viewing Mauss as the non-Marx (or anti-Marx), David Graeber (2001), Hart (2014), and others see his work as encompassing both capitalist exchange and gift exchange and emphasize how Mauss viewed capitalism as engendering an extreme form of exchange that casts all of the other sorts in its shadow. Mauss in effect attempted to de-focus us on the commodity in order to throw into relief other forms of the production of value and its exchange.

I said earlier that Marx wasn't really concerned with conceptions of value other than capitalist forms, which in part explains why Mauss was seen for a time as offering a clear alternative. Others have explored the sorts of value that can be produced that aren't capitalist. A major advance was the intervention by feminist scholars who challenged the Marxian, patriarchal, notion that the labor performed by men outside the home, in factories that produced commodities, was productive (i.e., generative of surplus value for capitalists), while the labor performed by women in the home was unproductive, or merely "reproductive." J. K. Gibson-Graham (2006) and others argued for breaking down the capitalist–productive labor/noncapitalist-unproductive labor dichotomy and offered ways of thinking about how noncapitalist labor could be considered to produce value (see Bear et al., 2015). This perspective was influential on Graeber's (2001) theorization of the production of value as stemming not (merely) from what could considered productive labor, but from action more generally, a perspective that I have linked to Geertz's insistence on the importance of meaning to social actors and theorized as "meaningful action" (Taylor 2017).

Apart from feminist scholars and Graeber, probably the most influential author on the question of noncapitalist and nongift conceptions of value has been Arjun Appadurai, in his introduction to his edited volume *The Social Life of Things* (1986a), which advances the term "regimes of value" to describe the various sorts of value that social actors can devise and employ. Appadurai implicitly rejects Marx in favor of an approach derived from Georg Simmel in *The Philosophy of Money* (1990), which characterizes value as defined by an object's resistance to our desire to possess it (a position critiqued in Graeber 2001). This has been a useful move, for it allows for forms of value that Marx's labor theory of value, or even Graeber's expanded action theory of value, cannot, such as luxury goods (which Appadurai considers, drawing on Mukerji 1983 and Sombart 1967), and, as I have argued (Taylor 2017), artworks—two categories of goods that can be thought to possesses values that are seemingly irrational—unrelated to the amount of socially necessary labor time expended in their production—but more comprehensible in Simmel's and Appadurai's terms.

Following Appadurai and Igor Kopytoff (1986), subsequent anthropologists emphasized that goods have careers—that they can be placed in different regimes of value, and that these regimes can be short- or long-lived. I can purchase food as a commodity at my local grocery store, then cook a nice meal as a gift for my wife. Or a commodity can become an heirloom for a generation, then become a gift or a commodity again. And Anna Tsing (2015) has theorized how a good in a noncapitalist regime of value can be "translated" into a capitalist good.

Graeber was also deeply indebted to the writings of Terence Turner, some of which were unpublished but were in circulation among graduate students in the Anthropology Department at the University of Chicago, where Graeber earned his PhD. Graeber's 2001 book on value is essentially an extensive working out of a 1979 article by Turner, "Anthropology and the Politics of Indigenous Peoples' Struggles," which takes the encounter between native peoples and colonizers (or other intruders) to fashion an argument that moves beyond a binarized conception of the extinction or preservation of traditional ways of life. Turner argues instead for a more complex consideration of how dominated peoples can continue to practice and believe what they value from their own point of view, rather than regarding them as victims whose culture has seemingly been obliterated. An example for students of music would be the (common) adoption of Western instruments tuned in equal temperament, which would seem to eradicate indigenous tuning systems—and may in fact do so. But this doesn't mean that indigenous peoples cannot and do not make music with Western instruments that is still meaningful to them, that still articulates what they value, musically, culturally, and socially.

Anthropological perspectives on value have continued to expand more recently, following not only Graeber but also Fred R. Myers (2001, 2002); Tsing (2015); and the authors included in a 2013 special double issue of *Hau: Journal of Ethnographic Theory*, titled "Value as Theory" (Otto and Willerslev). In 2023 a special issue of *Economic Anthropology* titled "Value and Change, Value in Crisis" and a special issue of *Ethnos: Journal of Anthropology* titled "Infrastructures of Value" brought together new contributions to this field (Souleles, Archer, and Thaning; Lammer and Thiemann). The authors collected in these special issues and others have helped reinvigorate studies of value, building on some classic earlier publications (e.g., Gregory 2015; Munn 1992).

In addition to Graeber, this book is perhaps most indebted to Tsing, whose work has been the most influential on my own in recent years (see Taylor 2023). She has fruitfully combined Marxist, feminist, and other bodies of work into a bold and compelling interpretation of capitalism as global yet patchy, hegemonic yet not ubiquitous—theorizing how noncapitalist forms of value can be "translated" into capitalist forms, and how the workings of supply chains create value; analyzing the scalability (and nonscalability) of production; and offering still other critical perspectives that help us understand not only today's capitalism in the present but also how it came to be.

Value Theory in Ethnomusicology

Ethnomusicological readers may recall that a classic in the field, David P. McAllester's *Enemy Way Music* (1954), participated in mid-twentieth-century anthropological conversations about value (the subtitle of his monograph is *A Study of Social and Esthetic Values as Seen in Navaho Music*). McAllester's book appeared in a series edited by anthropologist Clyde Kluckhohn—the main driver of anthropological studies of value in this period—entitled "Reports of the Rimrock Project Values Series."

McAllester drew on Kluckhohn's work, clearly summarized by Florence Kluckhohn (Clyde's wife, also an anthropologist), who wrote with a collaborator that variation in "value orientation" was the most important type of cultural variation and thus the main feature in the structure of culture; they clarify this point by equating value with meaning (which provides a link from Kluckhohn's work to his student Geertz): "The 'system of meanings' of a society, its ethos, is more realistically and adequately derived from an analysis of the dynamic interrelationships of the variations in its value orientations than it is from a study of only the dominant values" (Kluckhohn and Strodtbeck 1961, 28).

Graeber discusses Kluckhohn and his colleagues at some length, writing that Kluckhohn's overall project was to recast anthropology as the comparative study of values. He observes that Kluckhohn's definition of value changed over time, but he focuses on what he says was Kluckhohn's central assumption, that values are "conceptions of the desirable" that shape the choices made by social actors (Graeber 2001, 3). But, as Graeber writes (2001, 5), the Kluckhohns' values project fizzled, despite whatever promise it might have shown in its time (though I have written elsewhere [2017] that I thought Graeber was mistaken, or at least not wholly correct, for it is clear that Geertz's insistence that the anthropologist/ethnographer focus on what is meaningful to the people they study is a refinement of the theory of values advanced by his graduate school advisor Kluckhohn).

Kluckhohn provided a foreword to McAllester's book that, while brief (less than a page), nonetheless makes his case for the centrality of the study of values to ethnographic work (though employing the notion common at the time that "cultures" were bounded, coherent, systematic):

> Dr. McAllester has treated music for what it is: an aspect of culture which can be fully understood only if its manifold and often subtle overflows into other aspects of culture are grasped. The music of a culture, in its turn, as David McAllester so brilliantly shows, reveals many hitherto hidden or half-hidden facets of the rest of the culture and gives excellent clues to the underlying premises that give cultures their systematic quality. This leads immediately into the realm of values. (Kluckhohn 1954, v)

Kluckhohn acknowledges (as does Graeber later [2001]) that practitioners in many fields articulate conceptions of value, mentioning economists, philosophers, social scientists, and aestheticians, but, he writes, McAllester's study is "the first empirical and detailed exploration of the interconnections between esthetic values and the more pervasive standards and value-orientations of a particular culture," calling it "a pioneering study in esthetic values and their relations to the total value system of a culture." And he writes that McAllester's work "greatly strengthens the hypothesis that values give the key to cultural structure and that values of all types must be investigated—not just those ordinarily designated as 'moral' and 'religious.'" Kluckhohn's final sentence announces a paradigm shift initiated by this book: "With this monograph musicology appears for the first time as a highly significant social science" (Kluckhohn 1954, v; the claim is disputed by Nettl in one of his reviews [1956a]).

McAllester's brief book states its Kluckhohnian position clearly in an introduction entitled "Music and the Study of Values": "The research described on the following pages is an attempt to explore cultural values through an analysis of attitudes toward music and through an analysis of the music itself" (1954, 3). McAllester writes that through his ethnographic studies of various events, he "made observations and asked questions with the aim of discovering what the musical dimensions of social behavior could contribute to the study of values and value theory" (1954, 4).

McAllester draws on Evon Z. Vogt, Kluckhohn's colleague in Harvard's Department of Social Relations, for his presentation of the theory of values, quoting Vogt: "A value is a conception, explicit or implicit, distinctive of an individual or characteristic of a group, of the desirable which influences the selection from available modes, means, and ends of action" (Vogt 1951, 6). Vogt's overall characterization of values and value-orientations includes a classificatory scheme: values and value-orientations are

> what is or is believed to be (existential)
> what one wants (desire)
> what one ought to want (the desirable). (Vogt 1951, 7)

McAllester takes these categories and employs them with some refinements and modifications to analyze his ethnographic and musical data. His book is in general a description accompanied by musical transcriptions of a ceremony that rids the afflicted of maladies brought on by their contact with others (a white person or other non-Navajo), followed by a discussion of values at the end. Existential values, for his purposes, concern what people conceive music to be, but an investigation of existential values, he says, leads to a consideration of normative values—what one ought to want. This in turn generates a discussion of the category of aesthetic values, which McAllester considers at some length in the course of his book, devising "a construct of Navaho musical esthetics" (1954, 73) with respect to various musical parameters. And he describes other cultural values, concerning competition, self-expression, quietness, the prestige that derives from musical knowledge, humor, women in religion, individualism, provincialism, formalism, and what he terms "music as an aid to rapport in field work" (1954, 84). These are then discussed further as Navajo values in the next chapter, following the framework established at the beginning, as things that "are" (existential values) and statements using "should" (normative values), thus concluding the book.

What is striking to readers conversant with subsequent anthropological value theory—which encompasses both the sorts of value succinctly described by Michael Lambek (2013) as economic and "ethical" (noneconomic)—is the absence of a consideration of "economic" forms of value, even though there are several descriptions of episodes in which McAllester's interlocutors clearly think of their music in terms of ownership, exchange, and as a good or a gift. Here, however, McAllester is simply following Kluckhohn and Vogt. For Kluckhohn, "the economic," and money in particular, is an expression of some other value beyond his interest or classifications.[3]

McAllester's interlocutors' actions and statements about forms of exchange and economic value are frequent and worth considering; the description of the enemy way ceremony, for example, headed "Preparation," says, "Tentative explorations sound out the clansmen who will be expected to share in the expense. If family support is forthcoming, the decision is finally reached," and preparations for the ceremony can commence (1954, 8).

McAllester's discussion of the enemy way ceremony is peppered with descriptions of money and various exchanges, as are other descriptions of encounters with his interlocutors. We learn of conceptions of ownership, exchanges of gifts and money, and these reveal, and generate, value as much as any other actions and tokens. The world of the Navajo studied by McAllester is not wholly apart from the market economy of the surrounding United States, and it is significant that McAllester (like Vogt before him) spends considerable time discussing the changing values of the Navajo, both with respect to musical aesthetics and more generally, but not about the inroads made by the market economy and the coexistence and interpenetration of this money system of value with others.

McAllester also provides interesting ethnographic observations about conceptions of song ownership, teaching and learning, and exchange. One description, albeit brief, considers how learning is akin to purchasing, even when no such act is involved: "A man who has learned a chant has 'bought' it not only by his effort and mastery but also by actual payment. This feeling of transfer for value received is important in all Navajo ceremony. The patient must pay for the ceremony in order for it to be effective. Similarly, the neophyte must have the ceremony performed over him for pay as part of his training" (1954, 66). And occasionally, straightforward exchanges of money would, or could, occur. McAllester quotes one of his key interlocutors, Eddie Cochise, who sang some Moccasin Game songs, which he described as "rare songs," but he told McAllester, "I'll teach you those for a dollar an hour." This would have been a profitable endeavor, for, Cochise said, "It takes a whole day to learn one of those, or we should get together in the night, that's the way you should learn a song. . . . " (1954; 73, ellipsis in original). Clearly, the money economy had entered Navajo life, though sometimes money was used as a universal equivalent, and sometimes employed as a token to be exchanged for another in the course of the enemy way ceremony.

Enemy Way Music received only two substantial reviews, both proclaiming its significance.[4] The review in *American Anthropologist* is prefaced by a note from the editor informing readers that since the book "combines two divergent areas of anthropology into a single whole," two reviews were necessary, "one from the interest of cultural values, the other from musicology" (Merriam and Moore, 1956, 219). Alan P. Merriam goes first, referring to the book as pioneering: "What McAllester has done, quite simply, is to relate music to culture and culture to music in terms of the value system of the Navaho; the idea of doing such a thing has occurred to ethnomusicologists with surprising infrequency" (1956, 219). Merriam provides a quick gloss of McAllester on value, but that is the extent of his contribution. Harvey C. Moore (an anthropologist at American University), for his part, essentially provides a summary, having left the discussion of values to Merriam.

Bruno Nettl's review characterizes the musical presentation and analysis as "relatively conventional" but says that the portion of the book devoted to the discussion of values "lends the entire study the status of a landmark in ethnomusicology." He notes that earlier observations about Native Americans' attitudes towards music had been presented before, but that "McAllester, for the first time devotes an entire book to the problem of the attitudes of a culture towards music, and he indicates methods which, we hope, will be followed by many scholars in case studies of other cultures" (1956b, 27).

The paradigm shift predicted by Kluckhohn in his foreword to McAllester's book never happened—the road not taken. McAllester's focus on value has gone virtually unnoticed by music scholars (though there is a sympathetic mention by Alan Merriam in *The Anthropology of Music* [1964, 249]). I would contend, however, that McAllester's study could be considered a "musical anthropology" (Seeger 2004) avant la lettre.[5] Recently, however, a few music scholars have begun to engage with this body of theory. Early in the game was Jayson Beaster-Jones's work on conceptions of musical value in the field of ethnomusicology (e.g., Beaster-Jones 2014), followed by, among others, Shannon Garland (2019) on music and value in indie rock scene in Santiago, Chile; Deonte Harris (2022), who introduces race into considerations of value; Anna Morcom (2020) on value in Hindustani music; and Eric J. Schmidt (2020) on the circulation of Tuareg recordings.

Value in Action, Value in Practice

As much as I have learned from these and other anthropological writings on value, there is still the risk that whatever one means by "value" can appear nebulous. If it is action, according to Graeber (2001) that reveals and creates value, then we also need to attend to how value is made, unmade, contested, and defended through the various practices in which social actors engage. It is necessary to ground theories of value in theories of what social actors actually do.

Curiously, Graeber didn't really provide any.[6] The essays collected in this book not only draw on and extend anthropological value theory but join them together with practice theory, which remains the most thoroughgoing and useful way to theorize how individual social actors devise projects, make plans, and attempt to carry them out in the face of social, historical, cultural, economic, and other constraints (see Ortner 2006). Theorizing how social actors act with/against such constraints—conceptualized as "structures"—was the basis of practice theory, which was mainly advanced at first by Pierre Bourdieu in France (1977, 1990), Anthony Giddens in the United Kingdom (1979), and Marshall Sahlins in the United States (1981).

Bourdieu has been the main proponent of practice theory, along with Sherry B. Ortner and William Sewell (2005) in the United States, finding a way between the extreme objectivism of Lévi-Straussian structuralism and the extreme subjectivism of Jean-Paul Sartre, which were the main paradigms circulating in France when Bourdieu entered the scene. The practice theory approach, as Bourdieu puts it, "offers perhaps the only means of contributing, if only through awareness of determinations, to the construction, otherwise abandoned to the forces of the world, of something like a subject" (1990, 21). This rather grudgingly articulated project nonetheless produced an immense and elaborate theoretical system that, while not explicitly dealing with questions of value, nonetheless employs concepts and theoretical tools that are useful in attempting to understand how social actors conceive of value and act on those conceptions as they simultaneously act against others' conceptions.

Ortner best articulates the practice theory approach, starting from a Geertzian appreciation for culture but with greater sympathy for, and attention to, social actors. I can think of no better summary of the practice theory perspective than Ortner's response to critiques of her influential article "Theory in Anthropology since the Sixties" (1984):

> Practice theory always has two moments, one largely objectivist and one largely subjectivist. In the first, the world appears as system and structure, constituting actors, or confronting them, or both, and here we bring to bear all our objectivist methodologies. But in the second, the world appears as culture, as symbolic frames derived from actors' attempts to constitute that world in their own terms by investing it with order, meaning, and value. (Ortner 1989, 112–13)

Ortner has been instrumental not just in de-hermeticizing Bourdieusian iterations of practice theory by culturalizing them (e.g., 2006), she has also brought practice theory into meaningful dialogue with feminist theory (e.g., 1996), all as part of a broader project of attempting to take seriously, as she writes, both of the perspectives she outlined above. But, she says, practice theory's

> special contributions lie in the ways in which it plays on the margins between them, examining those processes by which the one side is converted into the other. Thus we watch actors in real circumstances using their cultural frames to interpret and meaningfully act upon the world, converting it from a stubborn object to a knowable and manageable life-place. At the same time we watch the other edge of this process, as actors' modes of engaging the world generate more stubborn objects (either the same or new ones) which escape their frames and, as it were, re-enter ours. Here subjective and objective

are placed in a powerful and dynamic relationship, in which each side has equal, if temporary, reality, and in which it is precisely the relationship between the two that generates the interesting questions. (Ortner 1989, 113)

One of Bourdieu's overall aims was to combine perspectives from Marx on social class with Max Weber's writing on status and status groups into a single theoretical system that explained how certain groups achieved and maintained dominance over others. If groups are united by what they value and by their opposition to others' values, then we need to pay attention to issues of group formation and coherence. Weber thought that status groups were connected to the group's conception of honor, which could be anything to which a plurality of the group agreed. And he recognized that class and status were complexly intertwined: "Class distinctions are linked in the most varied ways with status distinctions" (1946, 187). Weber thought that people with and without property can coexist in the same status group. "Status honor," he writes, "need not necessarily be linked with a 'class situation.' On the contrary, it normally stands in sharp opposition to the pretentions of sheer property" (1946, 187). And Weber realized that economic capital supersedes everything else: "Property as such is not always recognized as a status qualification, but in the long run it is, and with extraordinarily regularity" (1946, 187). Weber understood that "both propertied and property-less people can belong to the same status group," as we also understand from Bourdieu: the dominant group in a society is composed of both people with large amounts of economic capital but not cultural capital and people with less economic capital and more cultural capital.[7]

Bourdieu offers several ways of talking about what people value: there are forms of capital in society in the broadest sense, forms of capital in particular fields and social spaces, and position takings that reveal actors' conceptions of value (the last I have elaborated on in Taylor 2017). Let me explore a bit more Bourdieu's (1986) influential articulation of the forms of capital, which seems to come closest to theorizing how social actors conceptualize value. Bourdieu famously posited several types of capital, all of which could be expressed in terms of symbolic capital, and he thought that all noneconomic forms could, in certain situations, be converted into economic capital. Bourdieu's theorization of the forms of capital is well-known but it is worth revisiting briefly to address the question of value. Here is Bourdieu's initial sorting out of the forms of capital:

Capital can present itself in three fundamental guises: as *economic capital*, which is immediately and directly convertible into money and may be institutionalized in the form of property rights; as *cultural capital*, which is convertible, on certain conditions, into economic capital and may be institutionalized in the form of educational qualifications; and as *social capital*, made up of social obligations ("connections"), which is convertible, in certain conditions, into economic capital and may be institutionalized in the form of a title of nobility. (1986, 47; emphases in original)

Convertibility matters; Graeber's critique of Bourdieu is that he is economistic—everything turns back into economic capital, or is always a form of it (2001, 26–30), which I think is a misunderstanding or even a misreading of Bourdieu. These conversions don't always occur—they require social actors making decisions based on their habitus, their location in social space. And, anyway, if something can be converted into something else, then they're not the same thing. Bourdieu's noneconomic forms of capital aren't the same as economic capital; they can be considered forms of noneconomic value, though, like the forms of value theorized by Graeber (and Geertz before him [1973, 127]), they need to be presented or stored as tokens—in this case, symbolic capital. Graeber likens convertibility to equality, but Bourdieu makes it clear that noneconomic forms of capital don't begin as economic capital and can't always be converted into it. Ultimately, I am considering Bourdieusian forms of capital to be a way of understanding how social actors conceptualize value and how they act on those conceptions. Viewing value thus is a way of particularizing it, making it less amorphous, analyzing it as a way to try to understand what particular social actors are doing in particular times and places.

And what they are doing includes the production and consumption of culture. While most anthropologists—with the most salient exception being Myers (2002; though see also Shipley 2013 and Trapido 2016)—haven't employed theories of value in studies of cultural production and consumption, I have found such theories to be enormously useful in this endeavor. The essays collected in this book draw on these recent writings by anthropologists to understand the production of value and the value of production of cultural goods, particularly music. I am concerned with the myriad ways that value is produced and consumed, how it travels, and how it is actively maintained, contested, and transformed by social actors—what one could characterize as the social life of value in the production, marketing, and consumption of goods, cultural and otherwise.

Understanding conceptions of value to be in motion, in progress, helps us better comprehend how commodities are produced, marketed, and consumed. It has become all too simple to assume that popular music is a commodity and not much else; or that classical music (or other music in what Bourdieu called a restricted field of production) is anything but a commodity. But if one pays attention to what people actually are doing with these and other cultural forms, it becomes clear that something that is produced as a commodity can be more than just that; or something not produced as a commodity can also be just that. Cultural goods, like all things, have social lives (Appadurai 1986b), cultural biographies (Kopytoff 1986).

Focusing on value also provides a way out of the endless taxonomizing that seems to plague many academic discussions of just about anything. We think we know what labor is, but what about immaterial labor, affective labor, creative labor, musical labor? I think such questions should be less about the nature of labor itself and more about how particular groups of people value particular forms of labor, and why some of these forms are valued more than others. The same goes for the products of labor. Instead of considering, say, cultural commodities to be special types of commodities (or not even commodities at all), let's ask instead: How are particular commodities valued? By whom? Why are some commodities valued more than others?

Some sorts of valuations are clearly economic, even though that category isn't separate from the rest of social life. Yet, as Lambek observes in a useful comment, there's a difference between playing the violin for pleasure and playing it to make a living (2013, 142). How do we talk about these divergent sorts of value? At least with respect to the second, studies of "the economic," and capitalism in particular, have proliferated in recent years, perhaps most significantly marked by the unlikely success of Thomas Piketty's massive *Capital in the Twenty-First Century* in 2014. Publications in the music fields that consider issues considered to be economic—whether about capitalism and the cultural industries, music as a commodity, musicians' labor, or other related matters—have greatly expanded our understanding of music as it is caught up in various social aggregations and processes. We are beginning to gain clearer pictures of how cultural producers conceptualize their work as an economic endeavor, how they attempt to make a living in various sorts of systems, be they capitalist, patronage, gift-exchange, informal economies, or other forms of exchange and reciprocity.

If "the economic" is everywhere, embedded, as we know from Karl Polanyi (2001) and many others (e.g., Appel 2017) in the fabric of social life (hence my enclosure of the term in quotes), how do we think about the particular social formation and system for the production of value known as capitalism? There seem to be two main ways that observers view today's capitalism. According to the first, capitalism is hegemonic and ubiquitous—what I would consider to be the classic Marxist position, adopted and updated by Foucault, Wendy Brown, and many others. Such studies have made much of the idea that under today's capitalism, everything is—or can be—commodified, that the logic of the market has infiltrated every aspect of life. According to Brown (2005, 39–40), "Neoliberal rationality, while foregrounding the market, is not only or even primarily focused on the economy; it involves *extending and disseminating market values to all institutions and social action*, even as the market itself remains a distinctive player" (emphasis in original). This position is, to recall the practice theory orientation, one that is more objectivist, concerned with capitalism as a structure.

Advocates of the second view—more subjectivist—prefer to focus more on actors' points of view, what is left out of, overlooked, or abandoned by this capitalist structural hegemony, a preference forwarded (or implied) by Gibson-Graham (2006), Graeber (2001), Lambek (2013), Maurer (2006), Sanyal (2013), Tsing (2015), Zelizer (2011), and others. While I find the former position to be extremely useful in understanding how capitalism functions as a hegemonic social formation, the arguments of the latter group are compelling as well, especially if one is concerned with finding ways of moving beyond or around capitalism. The difficulty in studying a social form—a "structure"—like capitalism stems from these two vantage points. If one is concerned with capitalism as a global system, then that's what one sees (as we know from Ortner): all of the aspects of it that help us understand it as system and structure. But if our focus is on social actors, then our work reveals all of their practices, their forms of complicity and resistance, their conceptions of their own culture—in short, the production, reproduction, and transformation of capitalism itself. A theory of practice helps to keep both perspectives in view.

What I take away from these two orientations, however, is not that capitalism has limits, for it seems not to. There are simply places it hasn't gone yet, and places it has visited and quit, as evidenced, for a quick example, by the many musicians whose popularity has waned and whose music no longer appeals to mass audiences—reproducing, inversely, the beginnings of many a career. Capitalism is everywhere capitalists have figured out where to take it, but that is not everywhere, always. And there are places where capitalism is resisted, such as the world of independent film (see Ortner 2013) and independent music (Taylor 2016b; chapter 3, below). There are plenty of goods that aren't (yet) commodified or that have lost their potential to be commodified; most of the musicians I know are desperate for the opportunity to commodify their music so they can hope to make a living (see chapter 5). Film and television composers work as merchants in Marx's sense, selling their work for a one-time fee (and perhaps royalties, depending on the medium). Almost never, however, do they own the copyrights to their music (copyrights are owned by producers), so the opportunities of rentier capitalism are denied them (see Taylor 2023 and n.d.).

Let me continue a bit on this question of capitalism's reach and our perspectives on it in a practice theory framework. Capitalism is hegemonic but not total; there is no "outside" of it, at least in the so-called developed world (and increasingly the rest). But there are areas of concentration of capitalist projects such as factories or banks, places where the pursuit of capitalist value—and surplus value in particular—is paramount. Such enterprises compete internally and externally to discover or create and promote the next big thing, whether it's a musician or a kitchen gadget or a soft drink. Speaking of "insides" and "outsides" of capitalism is a matter of where our attention lies—focusing on where capitalist activity occurs and where it doesn't, what sorts of entities that are dedicated to the generation of surplus value and which are not. But capitalist projects, while not ubiquitous, are nonetheless so present, so dominant, that they condition all other forms of the production of value and exchanges of value.

But how? Appadurai's theorization of what he called "tournaments of value" can be useful here. He wrote of such tournaments as comparative rarities in social life, events that happen periodically and that are distinct from everyday occurrences. Participants are privileged and are caught up in status contests through these tournaments. Appadurai also observes that "what is at issue in such tournaments is not just status, rank, fame, or reputation of actors, but the disposition of the central tokens of value in the society in question" (1986a, 21). From here, Appadurai theorizes (via Edmund Leach on the kula and Jean Baudrillard) the art auction as a tournament of value perhaps more familiar to nonanthropological readers.

The point I would like to make is that tournaments of value are extreme forms of the sorts of daily contests that occur in countless places; fields and social spaces, to recall Bourdieu, are battlefields (Weber famously observed that in the United States, capitalism had taken on the character of sport [2001, 124]). Appadurai's concept can be greatly expanded beyond the kula or art auction to theorize how capitalism can be both hegemonic and not total. Any capitalist enterprise is a tournament of value with its own playing field, players, and rules of the game. Tokens of value here are more obviously money than status, as in Appadurai's tournaments, but status in particular fields does matter.

By extending what Appadurai meant by tournaments of value to most forms of capitalist concentration and organization and bringing it into a practice theory orientation—which makes ample use of metaphors of sport and games (e.g., Bourdieu 1990; Ortner 1996) and conceptions of fields as battlefields—I am not minimizing the importance of the sort of elite tournaments of value he theorized, for they can still be considered to be events distinct from the quotidian events in which tokens of value are as much the expenditure of money as the display of status. My point here is that such competitions in more mundane form are common in social life when conceptions of value are at stake and as such allow us to comprehend the hegemony of capitalism. Tournaments—or, less grandiose, contests—are everywhere, though in different social spaces, different fields, and with different players, different rules, different forms of capital. One can be "outside capitalism" or in its margins if one is, say, struggling to make a living at music while trying to enter the capitalist music business, but this doesn't mean that one is "outside" capitalism; one is simply outside a particular capitalist tournament or battlefield or game, while at the same time participating in all sorts of other capitalist—and noncapitalist—exchanges. As do we all.

Emphasizing the actor's point of view and experience is not to reject the more objectivist perspective. But I do think that claims such as Brown's lack potency unless we examine what this capitalist penetration looks like in practice. Ideologies need to be instituted in practices, ways that people produce and reproduce themselves, their universes. The logic of the market may have infiltrated everything, but it is not until social actors act that we know what particular forms this capitalist logic takes and where it is inactive, however temporary that may be. In this sense I lean more toward the second perspective, seeking some of the ways that capitalism appears to be patchy and contingent, ubiquitous though it may be.

The Chapters

The first chapter argues that that one of the ways that capitalism operates, at least in the realm of cultural goods, is by disciplining, or creating, forms of value that exist alongside it; these are forms of value that might be viewed culturally as something other than capitalist forms but actually are part of capitalism—camouflaged and stored forms of capitalist value that I theorize, following Bourdieu, as symbolic capital. Three case studies help make this argument: the rise of the virtuoso music performer in western Europe in the late eighteenth-early nineteenth centuries as a new social personality, giving profit-oriented concerts managed by concert agents; the history of provenance as a form of value in the visual arts; and the process of designating a local cultural practice as a Masterpiece of the Oral and Intangible Heritage of Humanity by the United Nations Educational, Scientific and Cultural Organization (UNESCO), which shows how bureaucracies create a form of value that becomes linked to the value of traditional cultural practices but that is also a stored form of capitalist value as symbolic capital.

Chapter 2 employs Tsing's work on scalability to examine the music manager, a kind of popular-music analog to the nineteenth-century concert agents discussed in the previous chapter. Today's music managers act as chiefs of staff for musicians, helping them build their team of lawyers, publicists, agents, and more, and attempting to make what is nonscalable—a musician (who can only write so many songs, give so many concerts, make so many recordings)—as un-nonscalable as possible. Music managers attempt to transform their clients into productive laborers whose work can be scaled through building and maintaining an audience and loyal fanbase, which must be constantly cultivated, through the unceasing labors of musicians on social media.

My interest in anthropological value theory has taken me occasionally away from a focus on music. Chapter 3 is an example, though music as a lens through which to understand consumer tastes is important here. This chapter examines some of capitalism's agents by exploring the practices of trendspotting, carried out by people in advertising agencies and all sorts of consumer research companies that employ different methods, including ethnography, to learn more about consumers. These workers act as agents of capitalism in several ways: by making their clients' quantitative data more qualitative through ethnographic studies; by educating clients about their markets; by ethnographically describing consumers in order to improve their clients' products; and by identifying markets and helping to make a product appeal to that market. Trendspotters take the preferences of consumers segmented into particular groups and regularize them as "values," which are then employed to market products.

Chapter 4 considers how musicians and others create or increase the economic value of cultural commodities in the capitalist marketplace. For Tsing, supply-chain capitalism creates value at various nodes of a supply chain through processes of translation and purification that appear to strip away the noncapitalist social relations and noneconomic forms of value that went into the production of a particular good. While Tsing views various forms of promotion simply as different ways to create value, I argue that capitalist supply chains that generate what Tsing calls inventory frequently necessitate other means of the creation of value. These include processes of consecration and promotion (broadly understood as advertising, marketing, and branding) that reanimate cultural commodities with values that masquerade as noneconomic forms of value—firms need to claim that their inventory is superior to others'. In essence, this chapter argues that, through supply-chain capitalism and processes of translation, capitalist practices appear to take the gift out of the commodity by alienating labor and masking social relations, but, through more capitalist processes of advertising, marketing, and branding, insert representations of unalienated labor and social relations to make the commodity seem like a gift again.

If capitalism creates other forms of value that accompany it, there remain still other forms of value that can exist apart from it. Chapter 5 is based on an ethnographic study of the independent (indie) rock scene in the east Los Angeles neighborhood of Echo Park. There is very little money generated from music circulating in this scene (musicians are routinely paid only thirty-five to forty dollars for a show), and musicians, indie label owners, and others attach symbolic values to certain amounts of money, which are viewed in terms of what they can help the musicians purchase, such as gas for the band's van. People in the scene also produce and exchange value in a number of ways that aren't capitalist, from generalized reciprocity to several forms of patronage. This chapter ultimately argues that scenes such as this are simultaneously maintained and destroyed by capitalism: maintained because capitalism needs a reserve army of those who operate outside of it, but destroyed because such scenes are deprived of their ability to reproduce themselves given how little money circulates.

Chapter 6 attempts to understand the value of a particular traditional music, constructed as "world music" in a capitalist marketplace. It is not a matter simply of the commodification of something previously uncommodified but rather of the shift from one regime of value to another. Taking the Irish traditional music session as a case study, I argue that, while some Irish traditional music today can be understood as a commodity, most of the music occupies another regime of value in which it is sociality that matters to participants. This conception of sociality includes the practice of many musicians posting photographs of sessions on social media and participants sharing memories of tune sources, teachers, and other sessions.

Chapter 7 draws on theories of value, mainly from Turner and Graeber, to argue that musical performances, and those that are caught up in broader contexts such as festivals, rituals, or ceremonies, play important roles in realizing, consummating, establishing, and reinforcing values held by communities that engage in such performances. I define performance as something that takes place with an audience and that is culturally and socially understood as a performance. Value is built up privately in preparations for performances but is only realized or consummated in the moment of performance, with the presence of and interactions with audience members. South African *isicathamiya* music serves as a case study of how a community-defined value of excellence in performance is cultivated.

The final chapter moves beyond the common metaphor of "flows" to describe how music moves in an era commonly thought of as globalized. "Circulation" today refers to people as well as goods, and it labels an idea with a long history, going back to Marxian conceptions of the movement of money, and still useful with respect to cultural goods such as music. Drawing on Marx and anthropologists who have studied value and exchange such as Jane Fajans and Gabriel Tarde, this chapter argues that things circulate because they have value, and circulation therefore manifests as constant exchange—of time, money, goods, and more—that constantly (re)makes social life and relations. Radio serves as a case study in this chapter, especially as it plays an important role in the indie rock scene in Southern California. Returning to classic theories of the audience as commodity from Dallas Smythe (1977), which are still useful if liberated from a strict Marxian framework and applied to broader conceptualizations of value, I argue that Smythe's conception is predicated in the idea of exchange, and that his insights can be extended from radio and other broadcast media to the circulation of digital media today.

Taken together, I hope that these contributions not only help to bring anthropological value theory and practice theory closer together but also demonstrate how cultural goods, whether or not they are commodities, are meaningful and valuable to those who make and consume them.

1

Supply Chains and the Production of Value of Cultural Goods

This chapter considers how capitalism, as a mode of the production of capitalist forms of value, creates some other forms of value that appear to be something other than capitalist value and that coexist with the more obvious capitalist forms. The argument here is that in capitalist cultures, the production of cultural goods (and perhaps more) is accompanied by forms of value that exist alongside it. These forms of value might be viewed culturally as something other than capitalist forms but actually are part of capitalism— disguised forms of capitalist value. Anna Tsing has usefully argued that noncapitalist forms of value produced outside of capitalism, in spaces she labels "pericapitalist," can be converted into capitalist value through processes of "translation," achieved in part through what she calls supply-chain capitalism (2015). Here, I take up Pierre Bourdieu's theorization of symbolic capital to argue that supply chains can produce these seemingly noncapitalist forms of value that coexist with capitalist forms.

Whether one subscribes to one or the other of the main views of capitalism outlined in the introduction—which I characterized in practice theory terms as objectivist (emphasizing the structural aspects of capitalism) and subjectivist (more attuned to social actors' perspectives and experiences)—it is clear that capitalism exercises what David Harvey has referred to as a disciplining effect on other forms of value creation:

> Under capitalism, the money-form has to be . . . such that the money-form reflects the needs of a system of proliferating exchange relations. But by the same token . . . it is the proliferation of commodity exchange relations that disciplines any and all preceding symbolic forms to the money-form required to facilitate commodity-market exchange. The precursors of the money-form, which can indeed be found in the archaeological and historical record of coinage, have to conform to this logic to the degree that they get absorbed within capitalism and perform the function of money. At the same time, it should be clear that the market could not have evolved without that disciplining taking place. (Harvey 2010, 32)

According to Harvey's reading of Marx, then, there is no "outside" of capitalism—it "disciplines" all other symbolic forms, all forms of exchange with which it comes into contact. But I would still agree with Tsing and others by saying that dominance does not mean totality. Capitalism is dominant, but the seeming patchiness that Tsing identifies is not capitalism itself but a sign of its disciplining practices: some forms of the production of value are disciplined by capitalism and others not (though they could be), leaving these pericapitalist patches.

The disciplining effect of capitalism can cause the creation of new sorts of value that accompany capitalist forms of value or can take older forms and translate them into capitalist value. Both processes work through supply chains and how they "translate" value from one regime to another, to use Arjun Appadurai's famous formulation (1986a). Tsing's point is that supply chains translate from a noneconomic regime to a capitalist regime, though I think that supply chains can work in a number of ways, at least for cultural goods: supply chains don't only translate something from a noneconomic regime of value to a capitalist regime; they can also work more broadly to move something from one noneconomic regime to another—as in the number of hands artworks pass through in accruing value as part of their provenance (which, of course, has economic implications, as I will discuss)—or to move something from an economic regime of value to a non-economic regime. Or supply chains can appear to move something outside of capitalism, yet it remains connected, as symbolic capital.

This chapter sets out to theorize modes of the production of symbolic capital and the ways that they operate through supply-chain capitalism and, sometimes, processes of translation from noncapitalist into capitalist forms of value, as well as supply chains that create other sorts of value. I argue that supply chains can produce other forms of value apart from capitalist forms and that, in the realm of cultural production, unquantifiable forms of value usually coexist with (quantifiable) capitalist forms. I should note before proceeding that this division between "noneconomic" and "economic" regimes of value is heuristic, since, with capitalism as the dominant mode of production, everything is potentially shaped by it. Nonetheless, it is analytically useful to make a distinction between the two in order to see how various processes of translation might work.

I will argue that capitalism creates and maintains modes of the production of value that are related to it, forms of value that appear to be noneconomic, are culturally thought to be noneconomic, but that actually support capitalist forms. This argument is thus rather Bourdieusian, in that I am asserting that capitalism creates and stores seemingly noneconomic values in other systems of value, just as the various forms of economic capital—symbolic, cultural, social, and more—theorized by Bourdieu, could be amassed and "reconverted" back into economic capital. Here, I am concerned with Bourdieu on symbolic capital. Bourdieu developed his conception of symbolic capital through his research in Kabylia, where, he argued, economic interest was hidden behind cultural conceptions of debt, reciprocity, and honor. Bourdieu writes that in an economy such as that of the Kabyles,

> which is defined by the refusal to recognize the "objective" truth of "economic" practices, that is, the law of "naked self-interest" and egoistic calculation, even "economic" capital cannot act unless it succeeds in being recognized through a conversion that can render unrecognizable the true principle of its efficacy.

Bourdieu calls this converted capital symbolic capital, and he maintains that this denied capital, recognized as legitimate, that is, misrecognized as capital (recognition acknowledgement, in the sense of gratitude aroused by benefits can be one of the foundations of this recognition) which, along with religious capital . . . is perhaps the only possible form of accumulation when economic capital is not recognized. (1990, 118)

Bourdieu carried over this theorization of symbolic capital into capitalist societies, where the denial of economic interest was hidden in the world of art and culture:

> The denial of the economy and of economic interest which, in precapitalist society, was exerted first in the very area of "economic" transactions, from which it had to be expelled in order for "the economy" to be constituted as such, thus finds its favoured refuge in the domain of art and "culture," the site of pure consumption—of money, of course, but also of time. This island of the sacred, ostentatiously opposed to the profane, everyday world of production, a sanctuary for gratuitous, disinterested activity, offers, like theology in other periods, an imaginary anthropology obtained by denial of all the negations really performed by the "economy." (1990, 133–34)

My approach here relies on this theorization of symbolic capital up to a point but departs from it to argue that symbolic capital isn't just created as a hidden form of economic capital to which it can be "reconverted"; it can also be created through people's meaningful actions and "translated" into economic value.

Where Tsing considered how matsutake mushrooms were turned into commodities through their traversal of a supply chain, processes of value creation or transformation can work similarly with respect to cultural goods as they pass through a supply chain, in which they begin as one kind of cultural good and end up as another, with a different conception of their value. Three case studies help make this argument: the rise of the concert agent in western Europe in the late eighteenth and early nineteenth centuries as a new node in the supply chain, helping musicians give profit-oriented concerts, illustrating a Tsingian sort of value creation; the history of provenance in the visual arts (drawing in part on Fred R. Myers's [2002] seminal work to make a related case); and the process of designating a local cultural practice as a Masterpiece of the Oral and Intangible Heritage of Humanity by the United Nations Educational, Scientific and Cultural Organization (UNESCO), which shows how bureaucratic chains can create a form of value that is linked to the value of traditional cultural practices but is a camouflaged form of economic value.

Virtuosi and Money in the Nineteenth Century

Let me begin with a historical case study of this disciplining process, which is at the same time a case study of how a regime of symbolic capital began to emerge, one that was perceived as being different from a capitalist form of value but was a disguised form of it. The creation of capitalist forms of value alongside forms that appeared to be antithetical to it but in fact were part of the process of the creation of capitalist value itself is perhaps nowhere more evident in the practices surrounding concert tours in the nineteenth century (see W. Weber 2004). Changes in the practice of concert tours began in that century with the entry of music into the capitalist marketplace. Historian William Weber writes of how before this period musicians managed all aspects of their careers themselves, making important professional connections. Musicians weren't proffering a musical commodity, they were simply selling a good—their performances—and they did so personally, carrying letters of introduction from established musicians and patrons and participating in local musical communities as guests. Local musicians aided visitors in putting on concerts in the expectation that they would be similarly assisted when they toured (W. Weber 2004, 107; I will rely heavily on Weber in what follows). Essentially this was a system of generalized exchange (Lévi-Strauss 1969) in which musicians expected tours to enhance them professionally; they were not profit-oriented activities. But this shift to the modern concert tour was a slow process, which I will detail below.

Marx recognized that a musician who simply sings is not a productive worker, but if she is "engaged by an entrepreneur who makes her sing for money, then she becomes a productive worker, since she *produces* capital directly" (Marx 1990, 1044; emphasis in original). The building and expansion of the railroad in the nineteenth century made it increasingly possible for musicians to tour further afield, in the process increasingly becoming productive workers, which marked the beginning of the end of the older system and necessitated the concert agent (W. Weber 2004, 107). By the middle of the century, it was common for musicians to engage a number of others to further their professional lives. Weber writes of the tour of England by the piano virtuoso Johann Nepomuk Hummel (1778–1837) in 1825, who was aided both by his publisher, Maurice Schlesinger, and a piano manufacturer, this new node in the supply chain going hand-in-hand with processes of promotion. The publisher advertised Hummel's concerts, offering the sort of promotion that would become the norm by the end of the century. Weber writes that in the 1830s Schlesinger and other publishers, as well as piano manufacturers, began offering concerts themselves to promote their music and their instruments. Such promotional activities formed, Weber writes, "the foundation upon which the profession of the concert agent was built" (2004, 110). But, he cautions, in this early period performers continued to perform many duties themselves.

Weber observes that Hummel's and others' activities occurred in a moment in western European history when increasing numbers of people were purchasing music to perform at home, noting that the market grew considerably in several periods between about 1815 and 1850, the result of new techniques in printing and marketing and the increasing popularity of the piano (2004, 110). This expansion of home music-making seems to have boosted concertgoing as well, so that by the middle of the century, some type of concert manager had appeared in most European cities (2004, 110). These individuals had different origins, as musicians, theater directors, or owners of music stores—anyone who was in the local music network who could facilitate a visiting musician's appearance.

The first major musicians to employ a manager were the violin virtuoso Niccolò Paganini (1782–1840) and pianist and composer Franz Liszt (1811–86). Paganini was the first virtuoso musician to make concert tours a capitalist enterprise (W. Weber 2004, 111), giving many more concerts than had been the norm. Weber writes that Paganini relied on many different people for the management of his tours: theater impresarios, managers from outside musical networks, even financial speculators (2004, 112). Paganini and his associates employed his virtuosity, showmanship, and popularity to charge more for concerts.

For his part, Franz Liszt invented the solo piano recital and created an inner circle of wealthy women listeners at concerts. A Russian observer witnessed Liszt's first Russian performance on April 20, 1842, and describes it thus:

Liszt . . . descended from the gallery, squeezed through the crowd, and walked quickly towards the stage. Instead of climbing the steps, however, he gave a sideways leap straight on to the platform. Then, after tearing off his white kidskin gloves and tossing them on to the floor beneath the piano, and bowing low in all directions to such a thunder of applause as had surely not been heard in Petersburg since 1703 [the year of the founding of the city], he took his seat at the instrument. (Quoted in A. Williams 1990, 187)

And Hans Christian Andersen describes Liszt in recital:

As Liszt sat before the piano, the first impression of his personality was derived from the appearance of strong passions on his wan face, so that he seemed to me a demon nailed fast to the instrument whence the tones streamed forth—they came from his blood, from his thoughts; he was a demon who would liberate his soul from thralldom; he was on the rack, his blood flowed and his nerve trembled; but as he continued to play, so the demon vanished. I saw that pale face assume a nobler and brighter expression: the divine soul shone from his eyes, from every feature; he become as beauteous as only spirit and enthusiasm can make their worshippers. (Quoted in Walker 1983, 290)

As a result of these and other sorts of theatricalities and the hype surrounding his concerts, Liszt was subjected to the kind of frenzied adulation that one associates with rock musicians today; Heinrich Heine coined the term "Lisztomania" in 1844.

The previous social relations of production and consumption, in the era of generalized exchange, became exaggerated with the rise of the concert agent and the flamboyant, virtuosic displays by musicians such as Paganini and Liszt. This is how, I am arguing, an older form of value was disciplined into a capitalist form, albeit a form not thought to be capitalist. These musicians and their audiences understood that showmanship could command high ticket prices. No less an observer than Heine, who heard Paganini play in Hamburg in 1830, wrote at length of the concert: "Is that a man brought into the arena of the moment of death, like a dying gladiator, to delight the public with his convulsions? Or is it one risen from the dead, a vampire with a violin, who, if not the blood out of our hearts, at any rate sucks the gold out of our pockets?" (quoted in Stratton 1907, 44). The power of the virtuoso could not obscure the power of the pocket. Heine's language captures the two forms of value at play here, the one economic, the other—aesthetic, experiential—symbolic capital.

Mesmerizing as Paganini seems to have been, he was nonetheless criticized for charging more than the norm. Weber quotes the influential Belgian musicologist and critic François-Joseph Fétis:

> The high prices of admission charged for his concerts drew down the reprobation of the English journals, as if the artist was not privileged to put what price he pleased upon his talent. . . . [The concerts] produced an enormous amount of money; this was a large fortune, to which he added considerably afterwards. . . . He has been reproached with having sold himself to an English speculator for a certain time and a definite sum: a system which many artists have since adopted, though it is repugnant both to art and the dignity of the artist. Yet the great care necessary for the organization of concerts, and the difficulties encountered by an artist in England, certainly offer some apology for its adoption. (Quoted in W. Weber 2004, 111; ellipses and bracketed passages in original)

This was the beginning of the end of one system of the presentation of music based on generalized reciprocity and the beginning of a capitalist system in which musical goods were increasingly translated into commodities, alongside another system of value—of the deification of the performer or composer-performer, represented in part by their flamboyant behavior onstage.

According to Weber, while Paganini experienced difficulties with some of his associates, Liszt's relationships were more stable. Some of his contacts were more professional, and his publisher, Schlesinger, played an even more significant role in publicity and press relations than Paganini's (W. Weber 2004, 112–13). Liszt and his associates made concert tours profit-oriented activities, unlike musicians earlier in the nineteenth century, with the exception of Paganini. Weber implies a shift from one form of social relations to a newer one, much more shaped by capitalism, by emphasizing Liszt's and his managers' relationships with people on his tours to England, relationships that were "brief, impersonal, and commercial," rather than the "relaxed, highly collegial" relationships of the earlier era (2004, 115). By the middle of the nineteenth century, the musicians' direct role in economic matters was limited, and the concert agent's role was that of a capitalist manager seeking to generate profits (2004, 115), because, I would argue, with the rise of art existing in an "economic world reversed" (Bourdieu 1993), musicians needed to disguise their connection to capitalist forms of value, the artist standing aloof from such quotidian matters as money or the day-to-day business of managing tours; these activities were part of the realm of the production of symbolic capital.

By the 1860s, writes Laure Schnapper (2004), artists were not expected to trouble themselves with the demands of entrepreneurship; that was left up to their agents or managers or impresarios. Artists were thus expected to remain "natural" purveyors of their gift—their "talent" or "genius," terms that increasingly found currency in this era (see Battersby 1989). Artists were anything but sellers of commodities. As part of the ideology of the "economic world reversed," which could have a promotional effect, impresarios helped create and maintain the impression that musicians were not engaged in capitalist activities by taking on those tasks themselves and rendering themselves invisible. But musicians had to learn how to obey their agents. Schnapper's study of the mid-nineteenth-century travels in the United States of the Parisian pianist Henri Herz (1803–88) and his particularly canny impresario, Bernard Ullman, is instructive, for it shows how this musician, and professional performing musicians generally, were in the process of learning how to separate musical and nonmusical activities into what I am characterizing as symbolic and economic forms of capitalist value. Herz wrote (misspelling his collaborator's name),

> One day Ulmann came to tell me that we were to leave for Philadelphia, where *we* were to give a concert the next day, that the hall was rented, that the posters were up, that all the seats were sold in advance, that our trunks were closed, that our railroad tickets were bought, and that a carriage awaited us at the door to take us to the station. . . . I had made it a rule always to obey Ulmann. Without a word I followed him, and an hour later we were on the rails. (Quoted in Schnapper 2004, 138; emphasis and ellipsis in original)

Herz summed up what he took to be Ullman's overall philosophy or strategy thus: "Music is the art of attracting to a given auditorium, by secondary devices which often become the principal ones, the greatest possible

number of curious people, so that when expenses are tallied against re-
ceipts the latter exceed the former by the widest possible margin" (quoted
in Schnapper 2004, 138).[1] This quote is particularly useful for my purposes.
The "secondary devices"—presumably everything related to the deification and mystification of the performer—can become primary; that is, the
seemingly noneconomic system of value coexists with the economic system, and can even take over, but only because it is in fact an economic system of the production of symbolic capital. As Weber, notes, concert agents
became crucial in the development and expansion of a worldwide business
(W. Weber 2004, 117).

In the realm of music performance in the nineteenth century, the processes of the separation of musicians from anything to do with the business
of performance was an important way that musicians were alienated from
their own labor in the process of the creation of symbolic capital. By the
mid-nineteenth century, performing musicians were cordoned off from the
logistics of touring, which also alienated their labor. One could interpret
the sorts of flamboyant behaviors onstage as heroic but desperate efforts
to overcome this alienation.

Herz characterized Ullman's formula for what the pianist called "financial music," music presented at concerts designed to maximize profit. "For
Ullman," writes Herz, "financial music was music arranged for 8 or 10 pia-
nos, which everywhere in America has the gift of drawing crowds, especially
when the theme of the concert consisted of national airs. We had to give in
to my intelligent secretary [Ullman], and financial music, arranged for eight
or sixteen pianists recruited among the young ladies of Louisiana society,
produced its customary results. There was a crowd to hear this harmonious
squadron of fashionable ladies, all of them pretty and roundly applauded,
as one would expect" (quoted in Schnapper 2004, 139).

What I have been describing here is the production of both economic and
symbolic forms of capital of live concerts. The advent of the concert agent,
a new node in the supply chain, coincides with the entry of music into the
marketplace and the rise of aesthetics, the idea of "art for art's sake" (see
Bourdieu 1993, 1995; Taylor 2016b). That is to say, economic and these
symbolic forms of capital emerged together. Capitalism disciplined earlier
modes of the production of value into the production of the alienated but
flamboyant virtuoso. Aesthetics, the ideology of art for art's sake, is not a
reaction against the market or just an effect of it, but, I am arguing, a camouflaged and coequal part of it.

Provenance as Supply Chain of Symbolic Capital

Thus far I have considered the sort of capitalist supply chain theorized by Tsing. But one of the main points of this chapter is that supply chains can create value in other ways as well. Let me now turn to the world of visual arts in roughly the same period, which was not much different from the musical world just discussed, in that economic and symbolic forms of capitalist value emerged together. Early in her study of the art market, Sarah Thornton observes, "The artist is the most important origin of a work, but the hands through which it passes are essential to the way in which it accrues value" (2008, 9–10). One way to understand this process is by an examination of the history of provenance. Art historians Gail Feigenbaum and Inge Reist, in an exceptionally useful edited volume *Provenance: An Alternative History of Art*, write that interest in provenance emerged with the rise of the art market and collecting in the eighteenth century; a particular artwork could gain economic value simply because it had been part of an important collection. Researching the previous ownership of an artwork became an important aspect of assessing the object's value; published in museum collection catalogs and catalogues raisonnés (2012, 1), provenance became a kind of Maussian perpetuation of ownership of the object in which, "even when it has been abandoned by the giver, it still possesses something of him" (Mauss 2002, 15). And it became part of the long-term enlightenment project of cataloging and classification (Raux 2012, 87). Recounting a work's provenance served as a means of asserting its originality, an idea that seems to have been established already in the 1720s in France (Raux 2012, 89).

Art historian Sophie Raux writes in *Provenance* that the market for paintings boomed between the 1730s and 1780s, which made the question of provenance crucial, and the number and variety of works changing hands meant that provenance became more refined (Raux 2012, 91, 94). The first repertory on provenance, *Répertoire de tableaux, dessins et estampes, ouvrage utile aux amateurs*, was published in France in 1783 by a dealer, François-Charles Joullain (and was updated three years later as *Réflexions sur la peinture*). In *Répertoire*, for the first time, Raux writes, the prices of works in successive sales were presented in a manner that emphasized the relationship between provenance and value (2012, 94–95). *Répertoire* was evidently controversial in its time, with one observer criticizing it as a "'tariff' that provided a range of prices for everyone's knowledge" (quoted in Raux 2012, 97). The dealer Joullain defended himself: "Everyone knows that all the productions of the scenes and of the arts are not in the least subject to an intrinsic value, and that their more or less price depends on the competition between art-lovers and on the distinction of the object" (quoted in Raux 2012, 98). The prestige of a work's provenance is part of this "distinction."

Raux writes that a catalog for a sale published in 1780 was the first instance of a dealer mentioning the last provenance and the previous purchase price of artworks at an auction (2012, 97). But, she says, finding a relationship between provenance and commercial value is difficult; there were many discussions in France in the mid-eighteenth century about the criteria for judging an artwork, with recurrent criteria being the aesthetic quality of a painting and the trustworthiness of its attribution (2012, 98). Employing a statistical approach, Raux and a colleague determined that by the eighteenth century, provenance could clearly be seen to be one of the most significant factors contributing to the value of works of art (2012, 103n33).

It seems that in this period it wasn't so much the fame or social importance of the previous owner(s) that conferred value, but their taste. The mention of previous owners, particularly those who were renowned for their taste, meant that the painting had undergone several processes of selection and verification, which created the impression of a consensus that the painting was valuable, raising its prestige (2012, 100). Raux notes that provenance, since it can be verified, became a guarantee of the originality of the work, which is otherwise a quality that is less certain because it relies on judgment and expertise (2012, 100).

While the French in Raux's study understood provenance of artworks as contributing to the value of a work through its inclusion in prestigious collections and, later, as a guarantee of originality, in the United States art dealers systematically employed provenance as a guarantee of aesthetic authenticity (Pergam 2012, 116). One dealer in particular marketed British portraits based on the strength of the matchless pedigrees of the subjects; this operated on two levels, appealing to both the history of the work's ownership and its desirability in art-historical terms (Pergam 2012, 116–17). After World War I and the Great Depression, art institutions in the United States focused much more on aesthetic criteria as the basis of value (Pergam 2012, 117); in other words, aristocratic provenance mattered less.

In her afterword to the *Provenance* collection, Anne Higonnet emphasizes what other authors in the book observed, that ownership by a famous or powerful person adds value to the art object, sometimes so much so that the added value surpasses the original value of the object. In considering

Raux's article, Higonnet writes, "I would argue that the discourse of provenance and the money value of paintings were in a dialectical relationship with each other, and neither the money value of paintings nor their ownership could be created except through their exchange. The pace of paintings being sold was tied to the acceleration of exchange between forms of knowledge and wealth. Both provenance and money were currencies of artistic value" (2012, 206–7). Or, in the language I am employing here, artworks came to be viewed as possessing economic and symbolic forms of capital, both of which are dependent on supply chains.

The point here is that artworks in general must undergo all sorts of histories and studies to verify their provenance—to the extent that it is impossible to understand capitalist value of artworks without consideration of their accompanying forms of symbolic capital. Provenance is an ancillary way of creating economic value, coinciding with but not equivalent to capitalist forms of value. It may be that such forms of symbolic capital and supply chains are necessary for cultural commodities—or, at least, more necessary than for other sorts of commodities—though any commodity could have value added to it through advertising, marketing, branding, or more organic processes such as word-of-mouth practices that confer conceptions of hipness and coolness.

I wrote "forms" (plural) above because there is more than one sort of value-as-authenticity (see Taylor 1997)—one of the many great insights in anthropologist Fred R. Myers's discussion of the change in regime of value of the paintings of Central Australian people, from what could be characterized as a "folk" to a gallery regime. This involves a complex set of processes of documentation to establish provenance, which is required of gallery art. Myers writes of his own efforts to help document the stories behind the paintings: "Glosses of such stories typically have accompanied the works in sale, proving their 'authenticity' to Western buyers by defining the painters' mythological base and showing that the forms are more than arbitrary, pretty designs. This selection of significance, which allows some Westerners to focus on the 'spirituality' or 'religiosity' of the paintings, is actually a rather complex and ironic construction that reflects in part the Aboriginal claim of why their paintings are valuable" (2002, 18).

And Myers details the work of the art advisor, usually a "whitefella" who helps local artists in their endeavors to sell their paintings. A significant part of their job, writes Myers, is "annotating the paintings, or documenting them ethnographically" (2002, 158). Such documentation adds to the value of the paintings because it guarantees their authenticity and uniqueness (2002, 158). Myers's interlocutors support these conclusions: "When I asked Daphne Williams and Dick Kimber in July 1991 about the Australian Museum's acquisition of the Papunya Tula Collection in 1979, they emphasized the lengths to which the museum had gone to reconstruct documentation. Indeed, when Williams defended the sale, which some have criticized, she argued that the company could not have expected top price for these paintings anyway, since they lacked appropriate documentation" (2002, 158). This documentation can take a good deal of time to pull together and can slow down the flow of paintings to market.

This is a different kind of authenticity than in fine arts, but it is similar as a system of the creation of symbolic capital. Provenance here is about establishing ethnographic authenticity, a form of symbolic capital required by consumers in this art world. Whether in the realm of fine arts or that of Australian aboriginal art transitioning from the regime of the ethnographic to that of the gallery, the establishment of provenance constitutes another set of hands (or many sets) that works must traverse in order to accrue value.

Bureaucracy as a Symbolic Capital Supply Chain: UNESCO and Intangible Cultural Heritage

Another supply chain that creates symbolic capital is the sort of consecration of cultural practices that occurs through the UNESCO intangible cultural heritage process. Countries can nominate an "intangible" cultural practice, such as music, dance, or a cuisine, for consideration as a Masterpiece of the Oral and Intangible Heritage of Humanity.

As I have written elsewhere, the idea of intangible cultural heritage has clear origins in romantic, nineteenth-century notions of genius and the masterpiece; the language of the convention that established the program is replete with romanticizing language of art, as well as the idealization of relatively unscathed local identities in a modernizing world. The proclamation of something as a masterpiece has a "halo effect" and can also have economic repercussions, in the form of increased tourism to a particular region, increased consumption of the particular form of intangible cultural heritage, and more (Taylor 2017). The UNESCO intangible cultural heritage arena is complicated with respect to the question of value, I think, because a practice could be a commodity before it is formally recognized as a masterpiece; something could be a commodity and be consecrated as intangible cultural heritage and gain a "halo" while not only retaining its status as a commodity but also having its economic value increase. Or something may not be a commodity (though still with an economic value) and then become a commodity in a tourist economy.

That a UNESCO or another designation of a traditional practice as valuable cultural heritage confers value is well known in the literature (see Kirshenblatt-Gimblett 1995, 2006; Bendix 2009, 2018). I argue here that that part of this valuation is derived from the fact that nomination and adjudication are bureaucratic processes, another sort of supply chain that creates, or translates, value. Translations are not just from noneconomic to capitalist or economic regimes but can be extremely complex. Perhaps this is how value is created everywhere: a good, intangible or not, must pass through many hands. And sometimes the hands are those of bureaucrats.

The application to UNESCO for "urgent safeguarding" of intangible cultural heritage demands copious information to nourish a bureaucratic machine. Applicants must demonstrate that "the element" (whatever is being nominated) "constitutes intangible cultural heritage as defined in Article 2 of the Convention" (UNESCO 2017, 5), which says:

> The "intangible cultural heritage" means the practices, representations, expressions, knowledge, skills—as well as the instruments, objects, artefacts and cultural spaces associated therewith—that communities, groups and, in some cases, individuals recognize as part of their cultural heritage. This intangible cultural heritage, transmitted from generation to generation, is constantly recreated by communities and groups in response to their environment, their interaction with nature and their history, and provides them with a sense of identity and continuity, thus promoting respect for cultural diversity and human creativity. For the purposes of this Convention, consideration will be given solely to such intangible cultural heritage as is compatible with existing international human rights instruments, as well as with the requirements of mutual respect among communities, groups and individuals, and of sustainable development. (UNESCO n.d.)

As part of the nomination process, the urgent necessity of safeguarding must also be demonstrated and a plan proposed, with objectives and expected results. Applicants must also provide a timetable and budget, and there must be monitoring, reporting, and evaluation of the proposed plan. One or more inventories of "the element" must be compiled. Nominations are reviewed by an evaluation body that forwards its recommendations to a committee that makes the final decision (see Seeger 2009 for a longer description and evaluation of the process).

For a particular example of how all this works and how different conceptions of value are at play, I turn to the case of Sardinian *a tenore* singing, unaccompanied male quartets, which was proclaimed a Masterpiece of the Oral and Intangible Heritage of Humanity in 2005. Italian ethnomusicologist Ignazio Macchiarella (2011, n.d.) writes perceptively of this process and the reaction of local musicians, who were, to put it mildly, perplexed and not a little suspicious. The proclamation seems to have been mainly organized by a local politician (the president of the provincial administration of Nuoro, in central-eastern Sardinia), who was attacked by the media and public once it became known that the designation process was costly. Macchiarella says that there was no community discussion or participation before the UNESCO application, the expertise of scholars or singers was not sought, and, in general, there was a fair amount of public confusion about what the designation meant (n.d., 1). Political and media treatments of *a tenore* singing emphasized its ancient history in the most romanticizing and exoticizing terms ("the song of the stones of Sardinia" [quoted in Macchiarella 2011, 171]), rather than its status as a current activity, and no attempts were made to explicate UNESCO's language of "safeguarding" "authentic" traditions.

According to Macchiarella, although the musicians knew little of the process of the designation, they were interested in the events surrounding the UNESCO proclamation, especially the musicians he calls "semiprofessional," those who aren't necessarily traditional village singers but are more likely to appear on stages in more formal contexts. In January 2006, over eighty quartets founded the Associazione Tenores in response to the politicians' requests for a census of the *a tenore* musicians so that "'the true tradition'" could be "safeguarded" and "valorized" (n.d., 5). This association was composed only of these semiprofessional groups, and its first president was someone who had collaborated with Peter Gabriel, who had first brought the music to popular attention with a 1996 recording on his Real World label (Tenores di Bitti, *S'amore 'e mama*). Another set of semiprofessional groups formed their own association, Consulta del Tenore, in consultation with other local politicians. Both associations met and debated themes concerned with UNESCO's proclamation, being told by the politicians that UN-ESCO required efforts to demonstrate the "authenticity of the tradition" (n.d., 6). Someone suggested compiling a catalog of "authentic" groups or listing the villages where *a tenore* music was sung, suggestions rejected by these semiprofessional singers because they did not consider village song to be the foundation of the tradition (n.d., 6; see also Macchiarella 2011).

Macchiarella writes that due to the efforts of those with more cultural capital, the Associazione Tenores broke with the politicians. The then-president told Macchiarella, "We became conscious that we did not have to wait for uncertain initiatives from outside, and we understood that the destinies of our tradition were in our hands." They redirected their attention toward the music in village life. For this group, "safeguarding the tradition" meant focusing on and attempting to improve village *a tenore* practice, organizing an annual event in which some nontraditional practices nonetheless occurred. Contentious public discussions of the question of "safeguarding" were held, which included scholars and a UNESCO representative from Paris (n.d., 6–7).

Macchiarella sensitively captures the great complexity of such questions of "authenticity" and "safeguarding," even in a fairly small space and with a small number of participants. How could compiling inventories, establishing authenticity, be accomplished? "At the moment," Macchiarella writes,

> I know of about one hundred Sardinian villages where performances of multipart singing by chording called *a tenore* song have been recorded, but no singer would agree to include all these villages in an hypothetical list of the *a tenore* song diffusion. Everyone has a list of his own. Many singers told me that I waste my time listening to the performances of some villages where—they are sure!—there was not "the tradition" in ancient time! (but the "new invented" local traditions list changes according to each individual opinion). (n.d., 9)

Macchiarella also notes that for the musicians, UNESCO was a distant and largely unknown entity, but they do have the idea that it has something to do with politics, which, for them means the "'economic interest of someone'" (n.d., 10). As one musician told Macchiarella after the debate mentioned above, "We expected to discuss with some of UNESCO's delegates but nobody came. We know that someone from Paris met our politicians in

Nuoro, but how do they think to safeguard the tradition if they are not on the field?'" (n.d., 10).

Macchiarella concludes by saying that, according to the musicians, nothing much has changed since the UNESCO proclamation, but he notes that there has been a negative impact, in that some traditional singers believe that the semiprofessional singers are getting paid, creating a rift between these two groups of musicians (n.d., 11–12).

The point of examining the aftermath of a UNESCO proclamation is to emphasize that UNESCO's regime of value is not the same as local regimes, and so represents an imposition of value as defined by an international bureaucracy; it is not the value(s) surrounding this music held by local musicians and listeners that are at play, but the bureaucratic values that are the province of politicians and UNESCO bureaucrats, though these values continue to be contested after the UNESCO proclamation. Musicians' valuation of their own music became charged and volatilized after the UNESCO proclamation, as Macchiarella convincingly shows.

It might appear obvious that a UNESCO proclamation is in itself prestigious, and that's where its value lies. But bureaucracies create value incrementally, through their own sorts of supply chains, as anybody who has had to deal with them knows. A form or forms must be signed, after which the applicant must go through steps of varying (and usually frustrating) lengths. David Graeber's recent writings on bureaucracy, reflecting his continuing interest in value, help address questions of value and bureaucracy in this context. He argues that in the mid-nineteenth century, most Americans subscribed to a kind of folk version of the labor theory of value, that capital comes from labor. Such a belief, Graeber writes, probably stemmed from living in a world where one could observe people making and doing things in processes that resulted in the exchange of capital. But with the rise of a new financialized capitalism in the Gilded Age, which Graeber calls "bureaucratic capitalism," those in power desired to dispel this idea, hoping that Americans would come to view the labor that they, the rich, performed as productive: capital produces value, not the other way around. Their essential argument was, Graeber writes, "that the very efficiency of the new giant firms these men directed could produce such a material bounty it would allow Americans to realize themselves through what they consumed rather than what they produced. In this view, value was ultimately a product of the very bureaucratic organization of the new conglomerates" (2015b, 38).

Graeber made the same point in his book on value (2001) when he writes that things that bureaucracies do in the name of measuring value seem to become the source of value: "From inside the system, the algorithms and mathematical formulae by which the world comes to be assessed become, ultimately, not just measures of value, but the source of value itself" (2015b, 41). Graeber likens this to a form of Marxian fetishism: "Much of what bureaucrats do . . . is evaluate things"; they "are continually assessing, auditing, measuring, weighing the relative merits of different plans, proposals, applications, courses of action or candidates for promotion" (2015b, 41). A successful UNESCO intangible cultural heritage nomination confers upon the practice an internationally sanctioned and recognized bureaucratic stamp of authority, which is earned through having satisfied the bureaucracy. As Graeber writes,

> Since what is the world of securitized derivatives, collateralized debt obligations, and other such exotic financial instruments but the apotheosis of the principle that value is ultimately a product of paperwork, and the very apex of a mountain of assessment forms which begins with the irritating caseworker determining whether you are really poor enough to merit a fee waiver for your children's medicine and ends with men in suits engaged in high-speed trading of bets over how long it will take you to default on your mortgage. (2015b, 41)

Anthropologist Michael A. Di Giovine's consideration of intangible cultural heritage offers a discussion of valorization not dissimilar from mine and Graeber's. Intangible cultural heritage, in his thinking, is conferred by a museum or what he terms the "heritage-scape" (an Appadurai-esque adaption), in the process adding "value to an object by virtue of the fact that it has been specifically identified and chosen to exist in a particular collection for a specific reason" (Di Giovine 2009, 208). This recalls the discussion of the value that accrues to artworks that pass through prestigious collections, as reflected in the work's provenance. Di Giovine writes of how a locally valued practice becomes elevated to something of "universal value" through bureaucratic processes (2009, 209).

And anthropologist Akhil Gupta, in his work on bureaucracy in India, identifies writing as the main way the Indian bureaucracy expresses itself, for it is through literacy that domination is established and perpetuated, both by bureaucrats over others, but also by those higher in the bureaucracy over those beneath. Value inheres in written documents, documents that are portable (2012, 195).

Bureaucracies, therefore, produce their own form of value through their own supply chains, even as some, such as UNESCO, can confer a prestigious form of value that creates a halo effect over a particular cultural practice or, as in the Sardinian case, leads to contestation over what value is. This, as Terence Turner once pointed out, is the real struggle (Turner 1979). Economic and symbolic forms of capital are not always easy bedfellows. In this case, the UNESCO proclamation appears to have created a reasonably compatible system of symbolic capital for the more commercial *a tenore* groups, whereas the more traditional groups resisted, preferring to attempt to maintain their local conceptions of value for their musical practice.

Conclusions

I have been concerned in this chapter with the particular question of how forms of value that might not be (or might not appear to be) products of capitalism have nonetheless been disciplined by it. The origin of aesthetic values, or performativity, or provenance, or other sorts of values becomes disguised by capitalism, but these origins have nonetheless been shaped by it. A key dividing line appears to be the distinction between forms of value that can be quantified as economic capital and those that cannot—symbolic capital. Economic forms are quantifiable, whereas symbolic capital resists quantification, though it can still be spoken of in relative terms (Bourdieu, for example, talked about the "volume" of forms of capital amassed by social actors). I would go so far as to say that it is its unquantifiability that makes symbolic capital value appear to be noneconomic or noncapitalist. If something is quantifiable, it can be made to be commensurable with capitalism (see Lambek 2013).

At least with respect to cultural goods—whether or not they are considered to be "art"—the advent of a capitalist marketplace for them not only helped usher in aesthetics—the idea of "art for art's sake"—but also gave rise to systems of symbolic capital, or disciplined such preexisting systems. For workers in fields of cultural production, their reversed economic world can only appear to be so because they pay someone to handle the business side of their activities. The seemingly noneconomic world coexists with symbolic capital, which accompanies the economic world. Every field of cultural production I can think of that exists in the capitalist market creates systems of symbolic capital that are designed to be unquantifiable, yet these systems would not exist without capitalism and its quantifiable systems of value. They are capitalism's reserves. The legacy of the nineteenth century weighs like a nightmare on the brains of the living, with its discourses and systems of symbolic capital proclaiming that this or that field of cultural production produces something, anything, other than a capitalist good. Workers in artistic and other fields of cultural production can claim to inhabit "the economic world reversed" only because workers in these fields devised ostensibly noneconomic forms of value to accompany economic forms of value from the beginning.

2

Making Musicians
into Productive Laborers

This chapter continues my interest in the problem of how capitalists venture into spaces "outside" of capitalism and how things "outside" of capitalism are brought into it, whether via a supply chain, as examined in the previous chapter, or, as taken up here, an agent. In the introduction, I addressed the question of social actors' location with respect to capitalism, drawing in part on Arjun Appadurai's theorization of "tournaments of value," arguing that capitalism in the United States, as Max Weber once observed, had taken on the character of sport. Here, I would draw on another aspect of Appadurai's work, the idea of a good existing in a "commodity situation" (1986b). This is an observation stemming from his concern with the social life of things, but we can also use it to think about how value is produced—the situation of commodity production. It's not simply a question of value production occurring in the factory and the home, as David Graeber writes (2001, 78–83), and not just a matter of patches where capitalism has come and gone, like Anna Tsing (2015) says. Value is created wherever there are people, and sometimes it's capitalist value, sometimes it's other kinds. The production of capitalist value is concentrated in places like factories, banks, the music business, and so on; the production of value outside of such places and social aggregations varies tremendously.

In this chapter, I'm concerned with how cultural producers attempt to move into a wider field of popular music. My approach, as in all these chapters, is to understand and theorize capitalism not as a monolith or an agent but as a social form, a "structure" that is produced through social actors' intentions and actions as it simultaneously shapes social actors' intentions and actions.

The subject here is the music manager (sometimes referred as a talent or artist manager), the contemporary popular-music equivalent to the concert agents discussed in chapter 1—the person responsible for "building" a band or artist. Music managers have not been the focus of much scholarly attention, but they perform a number of important tasks.[1] They take people who are outside a capitalist business but want to make a living in it, educating them about the workings of the business, finding other members of a team (lawyers, publicists, agents, photographers, videographers, etc.), and helping them cultivate an audience and fan base of loyal listeners. In other words, music managers take artists as raw material and transform them as much as possible into productive laborers, akin to the process of turning Weber's "traditionalist worker" into a laborer who produces surplus value for a capitalist (M. Weber 2001, 30) through processes of organization, rationalization, and standardization. The point is not that managers help make musicians more efficient workers, but that they attempt to turn musicians into productive laborers as producers of goods that managers hope can be scaled into commodities for mass consumption.

The problem for people seeking to realize surplus value in the cultural businesses is that it is very difficult to increase the scale of production, to turn musicians or other workers into abstract laborers (though see Taylor 2023 on film and television music workers): musicians can only write so many songs, give so many concerts, make so many recordings. (The strike of the Writers Guild of America that is concluding as I write raised this very issue of management's demands for increased productivity.) The history of the record business contains many tales of attempts to manufacture a star or a hit, usually without much success, but I would be remiss not to mention such efforts as the songwriters forced to work under factorylike conditions in New York City's Brill Building in the 1960s (see Inglis 2003) or the fabrication of the Monkees the same decade (see Lefcowitz 2013). Occasionally such contrivances find success, but not so often that attempts like these have become a dominant model in the record business (except, perhaps, in Korea; see H. Lee 2012; Kim 2019).

The labor in cultural production is thus nearly always concrete labor—that is, labor directed toward a particular activity resulting in a specific use-value (see Chanan 1994, 146–47). To scale up production, cultural businesses mainly rely on increasing the number of laborers, not on increasing the efficiency of the labor itself, which is very difficult to achieve.[2] The first strategy, of course, was the dominant one of the major record labels for years—sign many musicians and hope that one would make enough to offset the costs of producing the others and generate profits (a strategy that has largely been replaced by a blockbuster model, in which the smallest number of artists are employed to maximize the number of tickets purchased or recordings sold or streamed; see Meier 2017). As Nicholas Garnham succinctly puts it, "It is cultural distribution, not cultural production that is the key locus of power and profit" (Garnham 1990, 161–62). But to have something to distribute, artists need to be made into laborers who produce something that people want to purchase or stream. Hence the many functions performed by music managers.

Scalability

I have written elsewhere that Marx's specific discussions of cultural goods aren't particularly useful in understanding such commodities (Taylor 2016b; see also R. Williams 1977, 93, for a similar critique). But Marxism is, and so, in this context it's worth remembering Marx on producers of cultural commodities. This is a reasonably well-known passage, but what interests me is not the apparent dichotomy of unproductive and productive worker, but the fuzzy border between them.

> Milton, who wrote *Paradise Lost*, was an unproductive worker. On the other hand, a writer who turns out work for his publisher in a factory style is a productive worker. Milton produced *Paradise Lost* as a silkworm produces silk, as the activation of *his own* nature. He later sold his product for £5 and thus became a merchant. But the lit-

erary proletarian of Leipzig who produces books, such as compendia on political economy, at the behest of his publisher is pretty nearly a productive worker since his production is taken over by capital and only occurs in order to increase it. (Marx 1990, 1044; emphasis in original)

"Pretty nearly." I like this hedge, which registers the complexities of scaling up cultural production; a cultural good becomes a commodity once it is produced at scale. And scalability is the question here: how does a music manager take an artist, who isn't scalable, and turn them into a productive laborer who can attract a fan base that is potentially scalable? There are thus two sets of efforts that are directed at the problem of scalability of musicians: one concerns transforming an artist into someone who can produce work that can be scaled, generating commodities that can appeal to a broad audience, and the second concerns the cultivation of that audience, determining ways to make it scalable. Both of these tasks are the province of music managers.

Questions of scale are at the heart of Marx's investigation of capitalism, as the above passage implies; Tsing has argued that Marx's labor theory of value is a theory of the scalability of work: "The commodification of 'labor power' means that workers become interchangeable and self-contained elements of the factory, since only then are they able to sell their abstract labor—that is, their ability to work in standardized conditions" (2012, 513). Tsing therefore believes that the scalability of labor lies at the foundations of capitalism (2012, 513–14). Cultural workers are somewhat, but only somewhat, different: their work is mainly concrete labor, but its products can be endlessly reproduced and distributed—scaled.

In examining the scalability of cultural production, I am not making a kind of Adornian argument that is premised on the idea that all "mass culture" is an ocean of identical commodities produced by a monolithic "culture industry." The "cultural industries" aren't really industries in the sense that they churn out identical commodities—each one is different (*pace* Horkheimer and Adorno 1990), produced by different groups of people who assemble to produce a particular cultural good through the expenditure of concrete labor. It's more useful to think of the cultural businesses as businesses (Taylor 2023).

Nonetheless, turning musicians into laborers whose products can be distributed to a scalable fan base includes a set of processes that involves different strategies of standardization, broadly understood: creating a recognizable sound for an artist and stabilizing it; deciding on an artist's look and capturing it with a particular photographer and videographer to stabilize it; assembling a team of professionals who are in agreement with the musicians about their career goals and who can help with the first two tasks; and in general, turning artists into brands, sonically and visually recognizable entities to whom fans feel a connection that makes them want to purchase or stream recordings, or purchase tickets or merchandise repeatedly.

Let me say a bit more about scalability, since it defines the main theoretical approach of this chapter. For Tsing, scalability refers to the possibility of expanding without changing the basic structure or premise, the main elements of an enterprise (2012, 505). She considers scalability in terms of production—first on colonial plantations, and later in Western factories, influenced by what was learned on plantations. Cultural production, however, is obviously different; a single musician or a band isn't a factory or plantation. Tsing thinks that a theory of nonscalability is necessary because it is important to attend to the growing pile of ruins in the landscape of neoliberal capitalism: "Nonscalability theory makes it possible to see how scalability uses articulations with nonscalable forms even as it denies or erases them" (2012, 506). Employing a theory of nonscalability can reveal scalability in action, Tsing argues (2012, 510). Since cultural producers aren't easily scalable, we need a theory of nonscalability as much as one of scalability: how do workers try to make what is nonscalable into something that is more productive of what is scalable? What are the nonscalable elements that get in the way of projects of scalability? Who are the agents of scalability?

It is the manager who is mainly in charge of the transformation of musicians into brands/productive laborers—they are the agents of scalability, of capitalism. Theirs is a fairly recent occupation. Michael L. Jones offers a useful capsule history and overview (at least in the British context) of the rise of artist managers, which occurred, he says, in the postwar era with the growth of rock and roll and its youth market. Youths couldn't attend bars to see their favorite bands, which meant that, instead of hearing the music they desired in person, they listened on jukeboxes, television, and recordings they purchased for themselves (2012, 85).[3] Jones discusses what he characterizes as a consolidation of the recording business as the dominant force in a music business that was newly distinct from the older configuration of industries collectively understood as the entertainment business, a shift that was driven in part by the success of the Beatles in the United Kingdom and Elvis Presley in the United States (2012, 84). This transformation necessitated figures such as the artist manager, someone who could mediate between musicians and the record business in the absence of an infrastructure of live performances suitable for young listeners (2012, 86). At first, it was assumed that new, young, rock-and-roll musicians were a passing fad, but with the success of the Beatles, it became clear that a someone was required to steward the hoped-for longer careers of such musicians. Managers needed to learn how to work in the environment of a newly reconfigured music business whose primary focus was recording artists, not necessarily live performers. Enter the managers who, Jones writes, "were expected to . . . 'square' the industrial 'circle'"—that is, somehow make their artists compatible with a capitalist business (2012, 88).

Jones doesn't rely much on primary sources (and none of his own interviews are included), and, I think, he oversimplifies in his portrayal of musicians as simply cogs in an industrial-capitalist machine, so in the end he offers a rather abstract account of what artist managers do, portraying them as eternally stuck between musicians and the record business, not making allowances (as my interlocutors did), for how manager-musician relations differ. But his conception of how managers "square the circle" is the concern of this chapter—how musicians outside the capitalist music business are borne into it and turned into productive laborers.

Overcoming Nonscalability: Building Artists' Commercial Potential

I now want to offer more specifics about how managers handle the nonscalability of their clients and the scalability of their clients' audiences. Managers don't simply attempt to make an artist popular so that they attract a fan base, they try to make their clients unique but still legible as brands in a vast popular music landscape, and thus, they hope, recognizable and appealing to a broader and broader and more loyal audience. There are, however, strategies that managers and musicians employ to make musicians' products scalable—this is the manager's other task. There is thus a difference between making something less unscalable and scaling something up; some managers are more focused on the former than the latter, which is increasingly left to musicians themselves, as I will discuss.

Toward a Theory of Scalability of Musical Production

Most musicians who engage a manager are outside the capitalist music business and trying to get in. We need Tsing's ideas to understand nonscalability on the cultural production side and how managers attempt to address that, and a theory of scalability to understand the production of consumption side. The difficulties artists encounter when they change style, image, or band personnel can be understood as revealing their nonscalability.

Tsing writes that for capitalists seeking scalability, there are questions of keeping "project inputs standardized," self-contained, and "unable to form relationships." Relationships, she says, "are potential vectors of transformation. Only without the indeterminacy of transformation can you nest scales—that is, move from small to large without redoing the design" (2012, 507). For Tsing, scalability necessitates more than stable project elements: "A scalable business does not change its organization as it expands. This is possible only if business relations are not transformative, changing the business as new relations are added. . . . Scalability requires that project elements be oblivious to the indeterminacies of encounter; that's how they allow smooth expansion. Thus, too, scalability banishes meaningful diversity, that is, diversity that might change things" (2015, 38).

What the nonscalability of cultural production means for musicians is that all possible elements in the artist's brand and team must be standardized and stabilized, legible to consumers who are accustomed to think of cultural products in terms of particular genres and styles; meaningful diversity is disallowed. All this involves a good deal of work and coordination, but it's not the same for each artist. All the managers I spoke to emphasized that theirs is not a one-size-fits-all profession; trying to "build" an artist so that their audience is scalable isn't the same process in each instance, so managers need to treat each client differently. Larry Little managed dozens of artists before leaving management not long before our second conversation in 2020, and he said that each is different and therefore so is his relationship to them; some of his artists are on the smallest indie labels, some on major labels (Little, interview, 2014).

In what follows, I will concentrate on those aspects of the manager's job that are most directly related to questions of scalability. Essentially, it is a process of musicians deciding to enter the capitalist music business, demonstrating that intention to a potential manager, and then following that manager's advice about how to make themselves compatible with the business and generative of a loyal (and, it is hoped, expanding) audience.

Managers perform many tasks for their clients; one guidebook calls them an artist's chief of staff (Thall 2016, 186), another, the "general manager and chief operating officer of your enterprise" (Passman 2015, 86), and still another says that managers "create, maintain and secure a career for their client" (Davison 1997, 312). But most of what they do is make their clients into productive laborers, as brands whose output can be sold or streamed at greater and greater scale, which in this context means generating, holding on to, and building a loyal fan base. Managers groom and calibrate their artist-clients to work in the capitalist music business by transforming them into brands that are legible both to people in the business and to fans. Managers engage artists as clients if they think they can deliver value; they work with their clients on their music both to locate and refine their unique sound and to find their niche in the market of recorded music; managers work with their artists on their image, and how it is represented in photographs, videos, and in social media; and managers are responsible for assembling a team of other professionals (agents, lawyers, publicists, etc.) who are compatible with their clients (the word that most of my interlocutors used was "aligned").

Paul Allen, in a guidebook for musicians, emphasizes that the first thing an "income-earning artist" needs to understand is that they are attempting to forge a career in the music business and that all their artistic efforts should be directed toward the goal of making money. A manager won't want to work with an artist unless they think they are committed to a career in the music business, he writes (2018, 44). Some young musicians might view this as selling out, but Allen says that record labels sign musicians because think that those musicians have commercial potential. Some labels might try to mold musicians to be more commercial in such a way that they are no longer true to themselves as artists, but, he says, musicians should rely on their managers to demand that they do not compromise the artists' unique sound or concoct an image that doesn't represent who the artists believe themselves to be (2018, 45).

Because the manager's role is to navigate this road into the music business in order to facilitate or enhance the scalability of their clients' work, they seek musicians who are amenable to their advice, those who are willing to enter the commercial world of the music business. The music business press and my interviews with managers are in accord that artists should seek a manager when they have decided to attempt to break into the music business, which insiders describe in different ways. According to Allen, "In today's business world, artists should get a manager when they are prepared to become competitive commercial artists" (2018, 43). David Baskerville and Tim Baskerville write, in a guidebook for musicians, that artists need a manager at the time they start earning more than union scale, at which point they need someone to take care of their business and develop their careers (2018, 155).

Managers and all the others who attend to musicians' careers—agents, business managers, road managers, attorneys, publishers, publicists, and more—work, Baskerville and Baskerville say, "to maximize artist earnings and relieve the artist from directly overseeing complex financial and business activities" (2018, 139). The Baskervilles point out that a record label will prefer an artist who has good management, judging that "it is not cost-effective to invest time and money in an artist whose career is not thoughtfully planned." They also say that labels believe so strongly in the importance of competent management that some will help some artists find a good manager (2018, 155). In other words, labels want to sign musicians who are already on the road to being as un-nonscalable as possible.

Squares and Circles

Larry Little described to me the old days (before the importance of social media), trying to find a band outside of the music business and attempting to bring them into it.

> I might keep my ear to the ground, or have scouts in places, or read blogs or magazines or local music websites in the various towns. And if somebody's getting a little bit of action but they're still local and they're still playing their first few gigs but there was a review, then, as a manager, if I found their site—back then it would have been either Myspace or Facebook, and then people started to go to Bandcamp— you would sign in to their profile page, find the songs that they were offering. And if there was a connection and you saw something or heard something in them that you think could be developed into a commercial—or just even culturally relevant—act, you'd reach out. (Little, interview, 2020)

It's noteworthy, though not surprising, that commercial potential comes before cultural relevance.

Today, those who offer advice to artists say that they need to understand that the manager's role is to build on their clients' commercial potential. Paul Allen says that when musicians ask him how they can win the attention of a music manager, he offers a stock answer that is meant to educate musicians about what a manager does, a response that emphasizes the commercial nature of the musicians' work and the musicians' need to acknowledge this. Allen's speech encapsulates the manager's goal of educating their clients about the music business and the commercial savviness (and willingness) that musicians must possess or learn to cultivate.

> Briefly, understand that a manager is primarily interested in the commercial viability of your creative work. There are a lot of truly creative people who write, sing, and perform very well but their work doesn't have the commercial potential to make it worth the investment of time of an artist manager to try to develop. What is commercial potential? Having the likelihood that a lot of people will pay to see you perform, and purchase and stream your music. So the artist who can say to an artist manager, "Listen to my music because I play to rooms of 250 people many weekends and I sell 6,000 CDs and album downloads a year," is the kind of artist who will get an artist manager's attention. It shows that you know how to make money with your music, and when you make money your manager does too. So, a potential artist manager needs to know that your creative work attracts paying customers, and that's really the starting point for you to make the case for artist management. (2018, 46)

Allen says that he doesn't downplay the importance of an artist's music but emphasizes that it is their commercial viability that attracts a manager's attention first; artists need to convince the potential manager that they understand the "basic drivers for management," which are, he says, the business aspects of music (2018, 46). Artists today need to be nearly ready to launch a career before a manager will take them on; they must already have a fan base and show that they are willing to exploit it (2018, 47).

Greg Katz, who has held different positions in the music business and runs the indie label New Professor, said that it's difficult for artists to attract a manager until they "have the ball rolling in some way," that is, they are already forging a career, building their fan base, making some money. "Then," he said, "once you're popping, once you've gotten that one song that starts to do its thing," not necessarily a smash, "just a song that starts to move the needle, then a bunch of people are going to swarm on you—it could be three people, five people, ten people, fifty people, depending on what kind of music you're making—and ask, 'Do you need a manager?'" (Katz 2019 [lecture]).

The importance placed on musicians' building of their audience through various social media platforms is such that labels today seek artists who already have a social media following. Jeffrey Evans, who manages Andra Day, said that labels are "more interested in a decent artist that has a real social engagement—the ability to push music to fans who'll receive it—than they are in an artist that is world-class but has no following, because the hard work of building that following is what they don't want to do. They'd rather pour fuel on a fire that's already burning, not try to start one" (Evans, interview, 2020).

But Katz said that in the indie music world, where there is less money involved than with major labels, it's a somewhat different story. Since he's not a major corporation, he said, he is not able to compete for musicians who have already proven their value, so he seeks instead talented people whose careers he can enhance. Katz said he must employ different criteria when signing an artist, since they're not already making a lot of money: he needs to like the music and the person. From the artist's perspective, he said, it must be clear that the manager really cares about them and that "they can deliver value to you" (Katz 2019 [lecture]).

Managers say that it is important for them to understand what their clients' career goals are, in part, I think, to ensure that their clients are sufficiently ambitious with respect to earning an income and in part so that they know who else to attempt to recruit onto their clients' team—lawyers, publicists, and others—who will be compatible. Katz said that it's the artist's job to delineate what they want for their career and ask how a particular manager can help. Artists need to see demonstrations of the potential manager's interest in them sufficient to help them achieve their career goals (2019). Christian Stavros, cofounder of the music management firm Other Operation in Los Angeles, told me, "I like to see the big picture of what an artist can become and who an artist wants to be and what their vision is at the finish line. That finish line can continue to move and continue to change, and it should change." Stavros continued to say that managers must "align a vision with the artist, because oftentimes a management relationship that goes sour is one where the manager's goals are very different from the artist's goals. But once you have that vision and once you have the end goal in mind, it's really about strategy" (Stavros, interview, 2020).

Stavros said that decisions that artists need to make about whom to work with, whether to affiliate with a brand or event, should be easy if the musician has a good sense of who they are and their career: "It's about song choices, it's about creative decisions, it's about creative direction, it's about album campaigns and deciding which songs are chosen and when they drop and what are the singles. All of that feeds into my role as a manager." Stavros said that some managers are numbers people, but for him, being a manager is about "maintaining and building those relationships that will help bring in opportunities and grow an artist's career" (interview, 2020).

Possession of this vision is so important, Stavros told me, that it is integral to what he considers to be a great artist: someone who not only knows how to make their music but also holds a vision of themselves as an artist. Someone may have a great song and a great voice, but that doesn't mean they're a great artist: "I think that great artists are artists, and they know what they want things to look like and they know how they want their stories told, and they know how they want their music to look in videos and in packaging and whatnot. I think it's about amplifying all that. It's elevating it and it's shouting it out and making sure that people are engaging with it" (interview, 2020). Recordings play a role in this long-term vision. Katz addressed artists on the need to think of a recording as "the thing that's going to get you on to your next, bigger show, and that show may pay you for it, if it recoups"; musicians need to realize that a recording is a promotional vehicle for their career, not an isolated business venture, he said (Katz, interview, 2014).

Working with a client involves several different tasks at the beginning of the manager-client relationship. Artists may have little sense of how the music business works, and so their manager must educate them. Little said that because musicians entering the business don't always know what they're in for, they fail to realize the extent to which the music business is a business (interview, 2014). Katz said that for many musicians, the music business is some strange creature that is remote from what they do. They think that "there's this monolith of 'the music industry' that has something to do with *Billboard* magazine and Warner Records or something, and they think, 'I just don't know how those things overlap. I sit in my room, making songs on my computer and then somewhere over there, there is this music that you see on *Good Morning America* or whatever'" (Katz, interview, 2020).

Katz views educating his clients about the business and the possibility of earning a living as part of his job, which he says he attempts to do in "bite-sized ways," helping his artists realize that securing a record contract or achieving another sign of career success isn't something that is unattainable.

> That's one of the first hurdles to get over—"There's nothing so special about those people over there that you over here can't do or don't have access to." And you don't need to be a member of the Illuminati or have an old dude in a suit who works with the Eagles associated with you to chip off your little piece of this multibillion-dollar thing, because you don't need to make billions of dollars.
>
> You need to make as much as you want to make to live the life that you want to live and create the music that you want to create. (Interview, 2020)

In our second interview, Little spoke of the process of educating the client: "What does it mean to work with a label? What does it mean to work with the booking agent? What does it mean to have a lawyer?" Artists who become more successful have more business partners and, he said, "each one now is a totally different relationship that needs nurturing" (interview, 2020). Katz said he needs to lead his artists into the business slowly: "The first thing is to take the big question and shrink it down into a little question. I think just earning the first dollar or the first hundred dollars or the first thousand dollars starts to illuminate how this happens." Katz gave an example of a client he started working with at the end of 2018. In March of 2019, they had a record-release show for the first album they had made with Katz. They made several thousand dollars on that show, he said—"not a fortune but more money than they'd ever imagined making from playing music in their lives. And their question to me after the show, standing in the empty room after selling out the hall was, "'What do I do with all of this money?'" Katz said he explained to them:

> "Well, that's the money that you're going to keep investing in growing the project. And if you have money left over, then that's the money you pay yourself to live your life." And you could see in their eyes, the concept dawning on them: "Oh, if I play a show every night and

make, you know, three thousand to four thousand dollars, and I do that fifty nights a year, that's actually a pretty good living that can sustain all the things I like and care about." It had nothing to do with some guy who knows the Eagles or Warner Records or whatever—it had to do with carving out my little niche of a few hundred fans and then motivating them to do something that was based on their love of the music. (Interview, 2020)

Katz views part of his job as moving his artists to that point, where they realize they can possibly make a living at music, benefit from their scalability.

As other things happen, you start to see how it really snowballs into a career, where somebody who wants to put a song in an advertisement, or somebody wants to sign you to a record deal or whatever. It's five thousand dollars here, ten thousand dollars there, five hundred dollars. Then they're at twenty-five thousand dollars. They begin to realize that over the course of a year it makes sense. That's how careers are built, and that's what you do. And you're accountable to yourself to do the work and to the people who love the music to keep providing them with music that they love and building a relationship where they continue to relate to you. (Interview, 2020)

Stabilizing Sound and Image

Once a manager has a client and begins working with them and has educated them about the business they are trying to enter, the manager attempts to do everything they can to make their clients' work scalable. Managers must discern where they can fit their client into the existing field of production of popular music. Katz said, "You start with talent and then you have to figure out how it maps into the industry or where it connects into the industry, or not even necessarily into the industry, maybe more just how they'll make some money" (interview, 2020).

In our first interview, Little and I talked about the beginnings of a relationship between a manager and client: "When you find an artist that you can tell has crazy, raw talent, but hasn't found their voice, that's where the manager or other people who can help pull that out of them, whether that's a songwriter, producers, a stylist—there's different people that you can bring to the mix to help them find that" (interview, 2014). Little said that, in addition to listening to recordings together, he and his clients would "look at magazines, to try to figure out, 'What are we saying?' 'What is it?' And, 'What kind of genre are we? Are we smashing that? Are we just representing Los Angeles 2014, what it's like to live here now? Or are we a piece of the past, are we a piece of the future? What is this entity?'" (interview, 2014). For Little, that was the most exciting part of the entire process.

Katz told me that artists don't always know what their strengths are, so occasionally his job is to tell artists he is trying to sign to his indie label, New Professor, that they have something special that is going to find an audience. Someone who is eighteen or nineteen years old and who has mostly played in their garage doesn't always know how to locate an audience, so Katz tells them that they must work on that themselves; the record label (or anyone else) will not do it for them. He said that it's important for artists to be willing to work, and that he increasingly prefers those that are: "I want bands that want everyone to hear their music and are just like a freight train on a track; they will go out and find an audience for it whether somebody helps them or not. I really like that" (interview, 2014). Katz gave yOya as an example, one of his label's best-selling bands. They tour a great deal and spend a lot of time on social media, which, with their emotionally powerful music, is a compelling combination that is attracting interest from bigger labels.

Reducing the possibility of indeterminacies in projects of scalability involves everything managers do, from stabilizing sound and image to choosing a team. Stabilization limits the nonscalable and facilitates scalability. Part of the process of stabilizing the artist or band concerns their sound. In today's extremely competitive environment, most musicians strive to sound unique in some way to stand out. But much of what managers do is identify what is unique, but not so unique that it can't be positioned in the field of production of popular music, and then stabilize the sound and image. Such efforts make musicians' work comprehensible to listeners in the field of popular music production, since categorization is important in the music business: listeners need to know where to go in a physical or online provider to find what they want. Allen writes in his guidebook for musicians, "As consumers, we want a commercial product that is quickly defined in familiar terms. It is the same in the music business" (2018, 45). Allen says that "key gatekeepers" will ask musicians what kind of music they perform and that musicians need to be ready to describe their music succinctly and in ways that are legible to these gatekeepers, who think of music in terms of radio formats or streaming service playlists. Allen offers both positive and negative examples of how to answer this question: "When a manager, label, or publisher hears an artist describe their music as 'contemporary acoustic alternative blues with hints of jam band influences but not as heavy as Hendrix,' it suggests that the artist is still trying to find a place in the commercial marketplace and that they may not be ready for a management, recording, or publishing contract." But, he writes, when a musician says, "'My music is alternative rock using catchy lyrics and a killer live show that appeals especially to younger audiences,' it shows that the artist has defined his or her music, understands audience types, and knows that appealing to a younger listener is attractive to record labels." For Allen, this indicates that the musician recognizes that the label is looking for a business opportunity that the artist is prepared to deliver (2018, 45).

In the early days of a manager-client relationship, managers say, it's important to try to identify and build on an artist's unique sound and generate a repertoire of original material. Some managers play important musical roles in their clients' careers if they have a musical background and the ability to recognize good songs. Little said that song selection is very important. Listening to recordings with clients helps them find their own sound: "For a new idea, I'd send them links to other artists from the past and from now that they might want to consider a take on, an idea that they could rip off" (interview, 2014). Little told me in our later interview that his listening to records with clients was "a process of picking some songs, having them either write new songs [or] get songwriting help—just bringing them in and working on it together, sharing ideas and getting the songwriting flowing" (interview, 2020). Stavros said this early conversation with artists can be about them finding their unique sound or positioning them in a genre, but ideally it's about them finding their own sound and image, since audiences can easily detect phonies. Stavros said that part of his job is to try to make his artists authentic (interview, 2020).

Managing a musician's image seems to be nearly as important as refining their sound. Baskerville and Baskerville describe the early stage of the artist-manager relationship in terms of refining the artist's act, once the artist and manager have come to an agreement: "One of the first tasks they face is polishing the act—creating the presentation of the artist to the public. Many artists owe a big part of their success to how attractively they are presented" (2018, 159). Early in the relationship, they say, assessments must be made about the artist and their audience (2018, 160). According to Peter Thall, it is at the beginnings of their careers that musicians solidify their image, so that they look like what they are trying to communicate (2016, 234); Thall's book says that this is the moment to show others that you are new and special through your look. "But," he says, "a statement must be made or you will be forgotten and melt into the fungible band category and disappear. 'Nothing jumped out at me,' the professionals will say" (2016, 235). Another guidebook for musicians emphasizes the importance of image, saying that artists need to realize that aside from the music, image is the most important element that fans identify with. The stronger the image, the wider the appeal; the wider the appeal, the better the chances of success (Davison 1997, 40). Marc Davison says that a group's image derives from the members' "ability to highlight marketable traits within their personality," characteristics that make them stand out and attract listeners (1997, 40). Davison says that "image is so important that at times image may supersede the music and can launch a band's career faster than a band with better music but no image," and he gives as an example the grunge scene of Seattle in the 1990s (1997, 40).

Little said he would advise artists about clothing if necessary. Some artists have their own fashion sense, he said, but others need work. "That's a subtle thing, and you want them to embrace it. I'm not like a guy that put together boy bands and tells them they have to all wear red shirts. But I would tell somebody if I thought it was inconsistent with their sound: 'You're saying you like this, and then when I look at you, I'm feeling this'" (interview, 2014).

This concern for visual appearance goes beyond artists' clothes to include artwork and other visual representations. Little said, "If something stands out to me, I think it's going to stand out to a fan, too, when they're standing in the audience, and you see the people that find their look and their vibe, and in time their audience takes on that vibe" (interview, 2014).

Managers are agreed that an image that seems to be inauthentic will be noticed by fans. Davison warns readers that their image cannot be phony; if you wear cool clothes that aren't you, the clothes will be cool but not you. Little told me that "there's a line where it feels genuine, it feels consistent, but they can see it on your face if it's not genuine" (interview, 2014). Stavros made much the same point, emphasizing that social media have made it easier for fans to sniff out what they think is a fake. He said that he thinks that inauthenticity "runs rampant in the music industry," but because "as time goes on and we have access to artists' lives through social media, it's becoming more and more apparent how easy it is to smell a fake" (interview, 2020).

Building a Team

Once an artist has successfully entered the business, decided on sound and image, the next phase in their development, as described by Thall, is "marketing," a period when perhaps the artist is opening for a bigger acts, has a assembled a professional team, and manager and artist "have to consolidate—and reconcile—[their] musical and professional (read 'financial') goals," which involves many decisions about with whom to perform, whether to do charity work, hire a full-time publicist, and more (2016, 235–36). It also means engaging more and more people—lawyer, publicist, and others. More people on one's team increases the probability of destabilizing and destandardizing what Tsing calls "project inputs," which are necessary to scalability. Little says that each new member of the team "may have an agenda that maybe fits part of what you're doing, but maybe not the overall picture. And it can get really crazy, just managing the different agendas and getting the artist to see that 'it's necessary for us to have these people and we appreciate and respect their input'" (interview, 2020).

Stavros described the process of coming into agreement in order to realize one's career goals as a process of

> aligning yourself with the right people to get you there, from our producers, to the sound of the record, how the record is mixed, who photographs the artists, finding the right agent who gets the kind of audience that the artist wants to be playing in front of and who they think the entry point is for growing that audience, deciding and routing the right shows to play and the right clubs to play in the right rooms. To align with all of that is part of the bigger picture. (Interview, 2020)

Little spoke of how to choose a compatible agent, part of the process of "honing the image and the vision, finding the right partners and building a team." Locating an agent and other members of the team, he said, begins with thinking about the band's sound, finding out which musicians they admire, who has a career they would like to emulate, and then "reverse engineering," finding the agents and other members of the team—business manager, tour manager, lawyer, booking agent, publicist, and more—who would work best with a particular artist (interview, 2014). This is essentially a process of stabilizing the elements of the project, making the nonscalable as productive of scalable work as possible.

Managers must work diligently to make what Tsing calls the "indeterminacies of encounter" support the characteristics of the artist-brand that managers and artists have worked out and agreed on and not derail those plans. This is usually discussed in terms of "alignment," the word music managers employ to describe the meshing of their clients' interests with theirs to avoid the sorts of transformations that Tsing writes about, which can upset the stability of the project. Managers must ensure a relationship in which a transformation doesn't occur, either in the relationship of the manager to artist or in the relationships to everyone else that the manager brings in to be on the artist's team. Tsing says that scalability is only possible "if project elements do not form transformative relationships that might change the project as elements are added" (2012, 507). According to Tsing, "scalability projects banish meaningful diversity, which is to say, diversity that might change things" (2012, 507). There are many examples of a new musician or influence on a group of musicians that have upset or even derailed a band's career, with Yoko Ono's influence on the Beatles perhaps the most (in)famous. There is also the converse case from the late 1990s in which Ripper Owens, who had been the lead singer for a Judas Priest tribute band, replaced Rob Halford, the lead singer of Judas Priest, after his departure (see Oakes 2005). This is not to say that musicians cannot change; they can alter their sound or image slowly over time without alienating fans (though the history of popular music is replete with stories of how an artist changed something in a way that enraged their fans—as did, in perhaps the most notorious example, Bob Dylan's move toward the electric guitar in the mid-1960s). And there are artists for whom a changing and chameleonic nature is essential to their brand (Madonna is a good example, given by Evans [interview, 2020]). Scalability in cultural production—at least among musicians—means fine-tuning the sound and image—the brand—of the musician to make it stand out and be recognizable in a market flooded with other musicians, but then also stabilizing it.

Given the importance of finding the right people to work with a particular artist, social capital matters, because managers need to have a broad network from which to draw to find those who align with their clients. Stavros said that the music industry is a social industry, where people are "constantly convening" (except during the COVID-19 pandemic, when we spoke). The ability to forge relationships with everyone—promoters, agents, attorneys, label workers, A&R (artists and repertoire) people, publicists, writers, editors, and more—is "the most valuable currency in management," Stavros said. When he takes on a new client, part of his work involves simply plugging them into his network of relationships in his role of overseeing every aspect of that client's career (interview, 2020).

Little said that this process of alignment early in an artist's career can be stressful for musicians, who can get pulled in different directions by the various members of their team. He said that artists can wonder, "'If we just go around and change every time somebody tells us we need to change, what's the trade-off, how long is it going to be until we don't even recognize ourselves?'" Little said that it's a complicated issue, teaching an artist "how close they should get to their A&R guy or to their label. What do you tell them? What do you not tell them? And this goes across the board, everyone you work with, even the publicist" (interview, 2020).

Managers of musicians with established careers—the next stage in Thall's progression—face more difficult decisions, including about whether their "musical style and material need to be modified or whether doing so might end up destroying a formula that works (from a business point of view)." This sort of alteration of what has been standardized can also raise problems. Thall admits that people's styles can evolve without necessarily being driven by financial considerations, but, he says, "many artists have messed up their careers at this point by making decisions that, on their face, sounded right but that resulted in their losing the very audiences that supported them in the first place" (2016, 237–38). (Thall posits two more stages, "stardom" and "the legacy," which don't need to be considered here.)

Some managers think that artists need to evolve constantly. Evans referred to Madonna's various "album cycles"—like a virgin, material girl, and after. He said there were nine cycles that she went through, each lasting about three years. Evans described these as a process of Madonna reinventing her brand, but she would always return to her "core brand principle," which he characterized as "radical for the young at heart." If an artist releases an album that's just like the previous one, their fans "are going to slowly dwindle away." It's therefore important, he says, to work with extremely talented people who are going to push you. Producers can impel artists to do the best, can take them out of their comfort zone (interview, 2020). Nonetheless, most artists keep fairly close to their established brand to minimize the diversity that might change things too much and negatively affect the potential scalability of their output.

Scalability of Consumption and Fan Loyalty

Now let me turn to the question of what potentially can be scaled—the number of listeners and their loyalty. Today, the scalability of consumption is based on two aims of musicians and those around them, such as managers: employing social media to build a fan base and exploiting it to maintain the loyalty of their most devoted fans (I won't be discussing Spotify and other services' strategies for increasing streams; that will have to wait for another time; though see Hodgson 2021).

Australian music manager John Watson says that in the old days, there were business gatekeepers who had to be impressed by a band before the musicians would be allowed to pass through the gate and cultivate an audience. Now it's the opposite, he says: he and his clients must demonstrate to a room full of people that the band or artist already has attracted many Facebook likes, a lot of views on YouTube, many searches on Shazam. So now, he said, the first step is to show the "reactivity" of the public, which is what attracts the business. This gives musicians more power to resist whatever the label might want them to alter, since they can claim that they already have a fan base. Today, artists and managers must absorb more responsibility themselves to cultivate an audience, the labels don't do as much promotion as they once did (Graham 2019).

Building a Fan Base

In the broadest sense, the advent of digital technologies and social media have not diminished the importance for artists of gaining recognition, building a fan base, and scaling up the audience; this is just attempted differently. I asked Stavros about taking a local artist and promoting them, and he said it's really about amplification.

> The whole development game is about telling their story and figuring out how to amplify their story. You find the right publicist, and you find the right person to write their bio. And you have that angle, and you start banging on doors and getting people to write about your

artists, getting radio to play your artists, getting Spotify to playlist your artists, Apple Music to playlist your artists. It's all about finding every single entry point you can for someone to discover. And then once that discovery process starts, it's about connecting the dots to bring it all together. (Interview, 2020)

Note that "playlist" has become a verb.

The role now played by social media in musicians' careers is significant, for social media have made it possible for musicians to interact with their fans more directly at greater scale than in the past, which in turn has meant that musicians now must spend a good deal of time building and maintaining their fan base in the hope of keeping it loyal, while at the same time trying to expand it. According to Watson, in this situation, the only businesses that will exist are those that can add value not only to the artist but also to the fan in particular, since fans are paying up front. Record labels, merchandise manufacturers, retailers, and managers need to learn to "add value on the way through" (Graham 2019, 74). "Value" here isn't necessarily economic, it's whatever fans want—the stories, the connections, the "moments" (to be discussed below).

Releasing music isn't enough to attract fans. Today, Evans said, "You've got to have a connection to a fan, but you've got to build a connection to a fan base that is based on something outside of the music and where the music will expand on it." Evans said that "the ability for you to discover and build your own fan base is one of the biggest keys right now." He wondered if Amy Winehouse, whom he holds in very high regard, would have survived in such a system. Today's musicians who break through have followers on social media: "They're building it, they're building an audience and making it push." Evans told me that his advice to people trying to succeed in today's business is that they need to be a good musician with something to say, and that they need to find an audience, find something to say to them, and say it, though he laments this situation, believing that there are brilliant musicians who might not be noticed because they aren't adept at building a digital following (interview, 2020).

Social media can make it easier to build a following because the artist can create it themselves through various platforms. Evans thinks the main platforms for musicians are Instagram, TikTok, and Twitter (now X), but no longer Facebook. And there are many firms that analyze data about performers, according to Evans (he didn't go into this in much detail; I think he thought it was a dirty secret). He said that it is possible to build a fan base that matters on any one of these platforms, though he thinks that managers must start with great music and begin to build fan engagement from there: "If you're an artist and you can't get anyone interested in what you have to say, then you shouldn't be an artist." Managers must ask themselves, "What are the best ways to build? What are the best practices toward that following? Where are the places you need to be? Who do you have to hook up with?" Evans thinks that musicians today need more than a good song, or many of them. Musicians, he said, need to do more than make music: "They've got to be their own content creators; they need to make long- and short-form videos. They've got to have a conversation with their fans and followers. They've got to continue that conversation on Instagram, TikTok, and Twitter or whatever platform they're using. The artists need to tease new music and be willing to share and be vulnerable with the fans. They need to be having a conversation about something that matters" (interview, 2020). Evans said that just doing the promotion work is a full-time job on top of being the artist.

I asked Evans if a manager helped people develop a social media personality. They do, he said, but artists must learn to cultivate their own personalities; fans, as I have noted, can discern a fake. Evans said that artists develop their social media personalities in different ways, but it must be done: "Maybe it's humor, maybe it's messaging—like an empowerment message—whatever it may be, whatever they're talking about, but they have to be willing and able to build that" (interview, 2020).

Artists have adjusted to the new reality of dominance by Spotify. Stavros said that albums still matter and that artists should try to make great records, but the advent of streaming services has meant that "now it's really all about moments": "We can create those moments in any way you want, whether it's an album or a single or whether it's other ways to be continually pointing and raising your hand and making sure people are paying attention to what you're doing as an audience—not just paying attention—ideally consuming and enjoying it and reacting and connecting to it" (interview, 2020). Until fairly recently, Stavros said, the business was all about making a record and "working that record." But now, he said, there are artists who release a recording "and a week later, put out a new single and a week later [are] doing a job in collaboration, and it's all pointing back to the record. It's all promoting you as an artist." Stavros says that there is value in such activities, and it has allowed artists to be more creative and diversify how they engage with their audience (interview, 2020).

Almost as important as a social media following is the appearance of it. Watson has specific advice about what he calls inertia, making sure the band has momentum, especially early in its career. This can involve some subterfuge.

> So your job in the early days is to do whatever you can make it look like this roll is happening. Don't play too many shows so that they're not selling out, do only the ones that sell out, then it looks like you can sell out more shows. . . . Do whatever you can to strike a chord with the public and to make it look like you're striking a chord with the public. The whole game is about that, about generating a perception of momentum. (Graham 2019, 66)

The appearance of an artist's success, of momentum, is just as important as success and momentum. Watson says that the business is about exceeding expectations all the time, and it's therefore the job of the manager to increase them,

> to present anything you do in a way that makes it look like a win, make it look like you're the artist that's got momentum: "Have a look at our YouTube views, don't mention our Facebook likes." Do things that generate more Facebook likes so it looks like you're happening. If you build it, they will come, but you actually have to look like it works, like it's already working, and then everyone wants to get involved. It's a real paradox—it has to look like it's already working, then it will work. (Graham 2019, 66)

If it doesn't look like it's working, he says, no one will be interested in it. Watson says that whatever level the artist has reached, it's his job to make it look higher, through what he calls bullshit, which will eventually be found out. But people still do it, "goosing their YouTube views," "goosing their number of Facebook likes" (Graham 2019, 82).

If all of these efforts pay off, musicians might be able to scale up the consumption of their music enough to make a living. Katz said, "Building up an artists' career is really finding that core first few fans and making them the kind of nucleus of excitement around the artists and the artists' business." He gave what he characterized as an example he often employs for clients:

"You need 5,000 fans who pay you $50 a year for what you do, right? If you can monetize them all to the tune of $50, then you are going to make a quarter million dollars a year," which is a living if there are one or two or three or four people involved, but obviously less than a living the more people you get involved. I think that's one of the ways to make the challenge seems simpler to an artist: "We've got to find this core group of 5,000 people who cares about you enough that you're worth $50 a year to them. It's not so much money and it's not so many people, but if you're going to find those 5,000 people, you're going to have to hit around a hundred thousand people to locate that 5 percent who really resonate with what you do." (Interview, 2020)

In a way, this is rather like the subscription model that many content and software providers have adopted. A robust and reliable income stream is preferable to the occasional purchase or stream.

Today, building and expanding a fan base depends greatly on getting an artist's music on a playlist of a streaming service. Previously, Stavros said, a fan base would be built by the label attempting to place recordings in record stores. The streaming services employ editors who decide what goes on the playlist, so one of his jobs is to pitch to the right people and hope that they love what his artists have to offer. "Now," he said, "you're trying to talk to twenty-five different editors to get featured on a playlist. Then people who are throwing on a playlist are going to stream your song and hopefully come back to it." Stavros said it's a strange expectation—that an artist is going to be found on a playlist that fans subscribe to not because of a particular artist on it but because of "a sound that you play into." Stavros finds this situation terrifying because of what he perceives as its capriciousness; an artist could become irrelevant overnight, if fans are attracted to the playlist category more than to the artists themselves (interview, 2020).

The problem with the streaming services, according to the managers I spoke to, is that they, like most cultural businesses, strive for the lowest common denominator—the music that's least likely to offend the most people. Stavros doesn't like this trend, saying that he doesn't work with artists who make background music, and that the greatest artists in history weren't making music for listeners to use as background. He thinks that the artists who try to get themselves onto a playlist may be doing well now, and he commends them for that, but he doesn't think they'll last very long.

Some managers I spoke to think that the advent of streaming is less of a shift than it is often represented to be. Katz thinks that since building the fan base is what matters the most, the rise of Spotify and other streaming services represents less of a change than is frequently assumed. He thinks that people in the business do indeed employ a kind of lowest-common-denominator mentality, but he thinks that that is a poor strategy if an artist is trying to build a fan base, which involves attempting to sound unique. Katz says there are plenty of artists who don't follow the expectations of the business and who are nonetheless successful, but this doesn't cause the people in the business to rethink what they want (interview, 2020).

Maintaining Fan Loyalty

To build, maintain, and scale up their fan base today, musicians need to post frequently to various social media platforms, to the extent that a band member may have to assume the role of social media administrator. But many artists who view themselves as artists don't want to do that, they simply want to deliver the music in person, like the Sermon on the Mount, as Little put it (interview, 2020). Today, however, musicians are asked to be marketers who devise new morsels for social media daily, or even hourly.

In the old days, Little told me, there was a mystique around musicians: "When we were growing up, with some bands, the mystery was everything. Musicians would come through once a year just so you could see them, and you'd just go to the show. And you could open a music video or something so you could see them, but you had these small doses or windows of seeing them. And it was so important that mythology was able to be built." But now, with social media affording opportunities for endless self-reportage and -promotion, the situation is completely different: "You know what they have for breakfast, you know what their dog looks like. And in some cases, that's really great, but in others, you think, 'There's your dog again.'" Little finds this to be a challenging environment (interview, 2020).

Audiences' demand for information about their favorite artists seems to have risen; Stavros described the environment as "wild," and contrasted it with the grunge era of the 1990s:

> Could you imagine, at the height of Nirvana, Kurt Cobain was on Instagram, and we saw what was going on in his life? Would it be less

cool? I'm sure it would. Or would it be more tragic? Maybe, but I have no idea. But that curtain being pulled back all the time, I resist it constantly, quite frankly. I think that some artists do really well with that access, but I tend to work with artists where there's the mystique—the stage, the curtain only being pulled half back—that bodes well for what they do. (Interview, 2020)

Evans said that for established artists it's still important to connect with fans on social media. But if they're reasonably big, they already have a team working for them that is "responsible for understanding [their] voice," and they are also responsible for the artist's social media, which means they're having meetings about what to say and when to post; posts are usually approved by the artist.

I asked Evans about his client Andra Day, whom he describes as having "one of the finest voices on the planet," and he remarked on her honesty, in terms both of her true character and her public persona. His description exemplifies the kind of image making that managers strive to create with their artists. He said,

> She calls everything like she sees it. She stands for truth and transparency and motivation and love and care. Several things happened and her honesty surfaced—it was very good. Andra wrote one of her first songs, "Mistakes," a story about how she had ruined a relationship by cheating on somebody. And when the marketing people heard her explain the song, their attitude was, "Well, maybe we should find a different angle because we don't want you to go out there and say, 'Hey, I cheated on people.'"

Evans said that they heard out the media people, but Day

> went out and had her first interview and she talked about the song in pure, honest form, and talked about her mistakes as a human and blowing an important relationship and how she wasn't going to make that mistake again. And this was very vulnerable about it—the complete opposite of what the press and marketing people told her she should be. And that's what endeared people to her. How many people have made that same mistake? A ton, they all related to it. (Interview, 2020)

Day then wrote her famous song "Rise Up," which Evans says has become an anthem expressing many things that afflict people. Evans said, "Whenever anyone needed the song, she was there to perform it and talk to people and be a part of it." Evans's language helps us understand the complex ways that artists are "built," their images crafted, their brands fashioned: "There are a million other things, but those are kind of the cornerstones of what we did to build her and to stick with what her brand is and who she is, no matter what all of those marketing and consulting people were telling us to do. We just believed that people would gravitate to her for who she is and what she has to say. And we were right" (interview, 2020). This is as clear a statement on how managers attempt to "build" and scale their artists and audiences as I have seen.

Conclusions

Anna Tsing's writings on scalability and nonscalability are useful in attempting to work out just what music managers mean when they speak of "building" an artist, an activity that, in its current form at least, dates to the beginning of rock-and-roll music. My main concern here has been a question of how the labor of musicians—which cannot be scaled, cannot be turned into abstract labor—is molded into productive labor through the various processes of "building" musicians into artists whose consumers can be sold to at scale, turning musicians' products into surplus-value generating commodities. Managers are essentially agents of the capitalist music business, attempting to usher musicians who are outside the business into it. Tsing's astute argument about the necessity of attending to nonscalability to understand scalability helps us understand the many means by which music managers attempt to negotiate the nonscalable and the scalable.

While it would be simple to see fans' near-constant interest in their favorite musicians as having been caused by social media, I think that would be a technologically determinist view. Social media, like any technology, make it easier or faster or more convenient for people to do what they have always done. I would say instead that social media play an important role in musicians' efforts to brand themselves, an activity that has been increasingly common in this era of neoliberal capitalism (see Taylor 2016b), and it has made scalability easier than in the past. The problems of making the practically nonscalable—musicians' labor—as scalable as possible, and scaling up the audience, haven't changed much over the years, but social media have introduced changes in how musicians and their managers try to make the products of musicians' labor as scalable as possible. And social media have brought with them the productively laborious tasks of image and fan management, activities that have increasingly devolved to musicians themselves.

3

Trendspotters

Agents and Inspectors
of Consumer Capitalism

In his classic essay "Class, Status, Party," Max Weber contrasts class groups —which are economically determined by their members' life chances, but which are not communities, because of their internal heterogeneity—with status groups, for which the term *status situation* designates "every typical component of the life fate of men that is determined by a specific, positive or negative, social estimation of *honor*. This honor may be connected with any quality shared by a plurality, and, of course, it can be knit to a class situation: class distinctions are linked in the most varied ways with status distinctions" (M. Weber 1946, 186–87).[1] Weber clarifies that status honor is not necessarily linked to a particular class positionality: "On the contrary," he writes, "it normally stands in sharp opposition to the pretensions of sheer property. . . . In content, status honor is normally expressed by the fact that above all else a specific *style of life* can be expected from all those who wish to belong to the circle" (1946, 187; emphasis in original).

Pierre Bourdieu similarly sought to theorize how social hierarchies were established and maintained beyond economic positionality. In "Symbolic Capital and Social Classes," he writes of both an objective, material side to classifications and a symbolic side. People have bodies and live in material realities, but those are represented and symbolized by agents and have their own objectivity. He credits Weber with bringing together the more objectivist conception of social class, as theorized by some Marxists, with the idea of status to theorize the "twofold root of social divisions." But Bourdieu critiques Weber for characterizing the two perspectives as distinguishing two groups, rather than two "modes of existence" of any group (2013, 294).

Bourdieu, like Weber, theorizes lifestyles, how they symbolize people's social positionality and seem to justify people's location in a social hierarchy:

> Symbolic capital, together with the profit and power it warrants, exists only in the relationship between distinct and distinctive properties, such as the body proper, language, clothing, interior furnishings (each of which receives its value from its position in the system of corresponding properties, this system itself being objectively referred to the system of position in distributions), and the individuals or groups endowed with schemata of perception and appreciation that predispose them to *recognize* (in the twofold meaning of the term) these properties, that is, to constitute them into expressive styles, transformed and unrecognizable forms of positions in relations of force. (2013, 297; emphasis in original)

Cultural capital, expressed as symbolic capital, legitimates domination, he writes, and "the very *art of living* of the power holders contributes to the power which makes them possible insofar as its true conditions of possibility remain ignored and as it is perceived, not only as the legitimate manifestation of power, but as the foundation of its legitimacy" (2013, 300; emphasis in original).

In this chapter, I'm interested in these lifestyles, these arts of living, which I would characterize as socially recognizable and recognized bundles of ideologies and practices, expressed in symbolic form through consumer choice of all sorts of commodities, including music (though music is less central in this chapter). I'm particularly interested in how consumer tastes can be harvested, codified, and reinforced or reshaped. In his consideration of neoliberal capitalism, globalization, and social consciousness, Terence

Turner observes that "general categories, symbols, and representations" can be abstracted from the schemas that circulate in social consciousnesses and "become reified as elements of cultural systems" (2003b, 39). This dynamic process is perhaps better understood in a practice theory framework in which social actors' meanings and values both shape and are shaped by structures. Turner's point about the contradictions in social production of persons gestures at how such reifications occur, as part of the dynamic of the empowerment of the middle class to (re)produce itself through consumption while simultaneously being disempowered "through the consolidation of control by capital over conditions of work, commodity production, and marketing" (2003b, 63). It is this last category I am concerned with in this chapter: the examination of the forces—not just marketing but also advertising and branding—that attempt to stabilize, concretize, formalize, and officialize meanings by taking the always-in-motion practices and values of people and attempting to fix them as signs in the dominant culture. These sorts of endeavors are part of what Devon Powers has called the "subcultural market doctrine," which she characterizes as "an increasingly widespread set of assumptions that viewed subcultural groups as trendsetters and thus market leaders" (2019, 65). This doctrine emerged from both industrial interests in trends and academic theorizations of subcultures.[2]

As I have explained elsewhere in this book, I do not assume that capitalism is total—commodifying everything, devouring all meanings produced by consumers. In spaces that are more conditioned by capitalism and awash in commodities, values can spring up that are something other than capitalist. As is clear from the other chapters in this volume, I have been inspired by recent writings, especially Anna Tsing's, that posit spaces where noncapitalist sorts of value exist or can be produced, though these forms of value can be—"can be," not "always are"—appropriated through processes of what Tsing calls "translation," thus converted from noncapitalist value into capitalist value in an inventory (2015). Occasionally, these values and meanings are prompted by advertisers or marketers, but consumers frequently find or make values and meanings that weren't pre-authored for them, values and meanings that are created by and circulate in particular social groups. I'm not arguing that consumers' meanings are "outside" of capitalism, simply that they are not all manufactured by capitalists, and so in that restricted sense are "outside." But they are still meanings and values that consumers devise to attach to capitalist goods, meanings and values that can be discovered by capitalist industries to generate or complement or enhance advertising and marketing efforts, improve products, learn about markets, and more.

But who does this work? Reading many writings on capitalism, recent and not so recent, one might assume that capitalism is an agent, that something like "commodification" or "financialization" are processes that happen on their own. But real people in real times and places make decisions that extend capitalism into places it hasn't gone before, or, seemingly less frequently, pull capitalism back from where it has been. Some of these real people are trendspotters, the subject of this chapter.

That people make their own meanings is very much a Birmingham School sort of claim, of course. What interests me in this chapter is the way that the meanings and values that consumers are constantly in the process of working out—and defending or contesting—are studied and harvested by trendspotters. They employ vast amounts of quantitative and qualitative data about what people are thinking about goods and how they use them, in the attempt both to market those goods more efficiently and widely and to improve them. Trendspotters must do this because all meanings and values of goods aren't fabricated by advertisers; some—many—are authored by consumers, which can then be captured by trendspotters and amplified and generalized by advertisers.

While consumer research has been with us for nearly a century, in the last few decades it has changed dramatically, in two opposite directions: big data and ethnography (the latter of which had been maligned for years in the business, according to Powers [2019]). More and more big data are employed to target consumers ever more accurately, and there are also more and more qualitative data, much of which are gathered in person, a method described by these workers as ethnographic. Those who compile this qualitative data are the subjects of this chapter. They were usually difficult to reach; one told me that since they usually pay their interviewees, the fact that I wasn't offering to pay might have been an impediment. And perhaps some thought I was going to write some sort of exposé, not understanding the nature of academic ethnographic work. Nonetheless, I was able to speak to five people, which, combined with trade and other publications, afforded me insights into what they do.

These workers in various consumer research fields, sometimes referred to as "coolhunters," do not just seek trends; their work, which is very qualitative, is a kind of commercial value orientations project (Kluckhohn 1956, 1961, 1962; see Graeber 2001): they enter into people's homes, go shopping with their subjects, accompany them to concerts and other events, and generally attempt to find out what their interlocutors' values are, sometimes concerning particular commodities.

Before proceeding, it's necessary to dispense with the idea is that there is such a thing as coolhunting; consumer researchers don't think of themselves this way. Baysie Wightman, who was profiled in a 1997 article by Malcolm Gladwell called "The Coolhunt," said that she thought that he invented that term (Wightman, interview, 2016; Gladwell 1997). She said that she didn't like the label and that she and the other person profiled in his article, DeeDee Gordon (her colleague at Converse, the sneaker manufacturer), told Gladwell, "Don't call us that! That's not what we do, we make sneakers. We just do it to make sure the sneakers are going to be cool and that they're going to sell," adding, "It was never a profession" (interview, 2016). Powers's interlocutors felt the same way (2019, 76). What these consumer researchers do is attempt to discern what a particular segment of a society is interested in and how that relates to particular consumer goods.

A Very Brief History of Consumer Research

First, let me offer a brief overview of consumer research before considering today's workers. The United States has been a consumer culture for over a century, though the ways that consumers have been hailed, or interpellated, as consumers has altered greatly in this period. Mainly, it is a narrative of increase: more advertising (which seems ever more ubiquitous), more advocating for consumption (which has also risen), more consumer research in the form of polling, focus groups, and other modes of inquiry, including, more recently, big data and ethnography (both also increasing, especially the former). At the same time, there is growing knowledge on the part of consumers that they are the targets of this consumer research. There has thus not only been an increase in market research and advertising, but such practices have become more refined, aimed at ever more precisely defined groups of consumers, who themselves have become more sophisticated and knowledgeable as subjects in consumer culture, not just objects. Some have even become marketing entrepreneurs as "influencers."

Polls and studies of radio audiences took off quickly in the late 1920s and early 1930s, as the business model of radio broadcasting shifted from a process of devising a program and then seeking a sponsor to pay for it to a strategy of locating a sponsor and developing a program based on the sponsor's consumers, real and desired. This change necessitated high-quality data about audiences (see Stamps 1979; Taylor 2012).

In the late 1930s, what was known as "motivation research" became extremely influential. It was an approach popularized by University of Vienna–trained psychotherapist Ernest Dichter (1907–91), who used Freudian ideas to ascertain what consumers—studied in focus groups, an innovation—wanted and to sell to them based not on rational sales techniques but by evoking particular feelings (see Dichter 1947, 1949, 1956).[3] Dichter's approach was popularized by Pierre Martineau (1957), director of research and marketing for the *Chicago Tribune*, and famously critiqued by Vance Packard in a best-selling book, *The Hidden Persuaders* (1957).

In the 1960s, the advertising and marketing industries discovered the potential consumer power of baby boom youth, which reoriented the business toward a focus on the youth demographic, which has been assiduously studied ever since. It was in this period that coolness began to be sought after (see Frank 1997), both among baby boomers, but also among subsequent generations of young people, aggregated demographically: first, the baby boomers, born 1946–1964; then Generation X, 1965–1980; millennials, 1981–1996; and Generation Z, 1997–2012 (Dimock 2019). Everyone has things they value, but in an ageist and youth-oriented culture, it is young people's values that are thought to be cool. Coolness, as I've written elsewhere, is an articulation of antistructural positions (Taylor 2001), antimainstream attitudes that we call "cool" because young people evince them—it is they who are socially and culturally permitted to be the authors of coolness, especially young people of color.

Today, coolness is cool (see Taylor 2016a). It is much written about, much theorized (Frank 1997; see also Dinerstein 2017; Haselstein et al. 2013). And there is a vast trade literature as well as marketing literature devoted to the subject.[4] Coolness is the subject of a good deal of labor in the advertising, marketing, and branding industries, as brands attempt to make their products cooler or discover why they aren't. These practices have been critiqued; much of the existing literature tends to characterize trendspotting in terms of "identity burglary" (Barile 2017; see also N. Klein 2000), but this presumes that capitalists are striding into unspoiled territory and co-opting pristine values and meanings. But that territory isn't pristine, it has already been shaped by capitalism: trendspotters go where commodities and their consumption are already established; what trendspotters study is the relationship between people and commodities. Commodities can be used, of course, to make identities, to identify oneself in a social scene, but they are still commodities in capitalist cultures.

The studies performed or funded by advertisers, marketers, and content providers of various sorts today have sought ever more ways to understand and better target audiences, by dividing them into demographic groups, socioeconomic groups, "psychographic" groups (socioeconomic cohorts with common psychological characteristics)—groups that are characterized in increasingly granular fashion (see Tedlow 1996; Tedlow and Jones 1993). These workers seek to know what is cool not just among younger groups, but in every group.

The Rise of Account Planning:
Identifying "the Voice of the Consumer"

Let me now discuss what today's consumer research workers do, since not much is known outside of this world except through a few exposés (e.g., Gladwell 1997) and critiques (e.g., N. Klein 2000).[5] Consumer research workers perform several functions. Brands hire consumer researchers (and subscribe to their pricey reports) to discover what a segment of the market desires in a product, in order to develop a product or improve an existing one (and thus, they hope, increase sales). Consumer researchers also work to identify market segments; to reposition brands in different market segments; and to educate their clients about their particular market segment. And these workers are frequently called upon to make big, quantitative data more qualitative.

Much of the work of consumer researchers is conducted face-to-face with consumers in their own environments; their goal is to capture consumers' meanings and values. This approach, several people told me, grew out of a British innovation of the 1990s called account planning (or brand planning or strategy), intended to complement the account management group and the creative workers in advertising agencies. Baysie Wightman, one of the earliest of these workers in the United States, described account management as relationship management focused on clients, and account planning as fulfilling "a need for somebody to ground the insight [into consumer behavior] and tell them what was real" (interview, 2016). Advertising agencies in the United States began to open planning departments; Yvette

Quiazon of WHY-Q? INC., a consumer research firm, characterized the planning department as offering "the voice of the consumer," and described its roles this way: "The account team interfaces with the clients, talks about budgets; the creative team involves everyone from coming up with the actual ideas and copy, the script for the commercial, or TikTok commercial or whatever, and producing the work; and then there's this group, strategy, which is supposed to represent the consumer in the whole process" (Quiazon, interview, 2020).

Outside of advertising agencies, independent consumer research firms like Quiazon's began to open, to provide data for these account planning workers. These firms gather qualitative data on consumers, though not always through ethnographic encounters. Irma Zandl, who in 1993 founded the first trendspotting firm, called the Zandl Group, said that when she first started, her ethnographic work was conducted only in malls, in combination with online questionnaires.[6] Her company subcontracted the ethnographic work to other companies, which solicited people in malls to fill out the questionnaires. Zandl told me her company read every questionnaire to be sure that people were taking them seriously, since it was her client who was footing the bill. She said it was very labor-intensive, but the data were high quality. Her clients would verify the results with their own children, she told me (Zandl, interview, 2016).

This period saw the rise of ethnography as a market research method. For market researchers, "ethnography" (a term that entered their lexicon in the 1990s) refers to face-to-face encounters with customers or potential customers; an article in *Advertising Age* from 2007 (by an author identified as having a BA in social anthropology from Harvard and an MA in social anthropology from Princeton) characterizes ethnography as "the study of culture. Not individuals (psychology) or populations (demography) or nations (politics/history) or trends (coolhunting)." Why bother with culture?, author Alison Demos asks; she then answers, "Think of it as the basic software we all need to navigate the world—the operating systems that we carry around in our heads and use without really being aware that we're doing any such thing." There follows a reassurance that "it isn't necessary to bury our noses in Claude Levi-Strauss [*sic*]" in order to understand participant observation, which Demos then discusses, taking her fellow market researchers to task for failing to attend to the first part of the method, participation, and failing to go beneath the surface. What ethnography should be about, she writes, is revealing "competing value systems, a collection of behaviors and rewards that create tension with those values—in fact, a complex web of cultural values and meaning—that will never come to light if all we do is listen to people's explicit statements" (Demos 2007, 27). Most market research "ethnographies" don't really live up to the recognizably academic standards outlined by Demos, though certainly some of the people I interviewed reported doing more than speaking with their subjects—like hanging out with them, going shopping, going to concerts, and other shared activities.

Quiazon, who once worked at a major advertising agency, described her dissatisfaction with the use of focus groups in which participants would sit in a room with a one-way mirror, observed by the advertising agency workers and the clients. Quiazon described this as a "very sterile environment" and uncomfortable for the participants. And some of the same focus group subjects would appear several times a week, as though they were on the payroll (focus group participants are paid). Quiazon said that she thought there must be a better way to find out what consumers care about, reasoning, "If we want to learn about video games, let's sit and watch the kids play video games and have them show me their games and show me how the games work and show me what the most exciting part of it is, and not just tell me about it" (interview, 2020). Quiazon cofounded her firm in 1999 to pursue this more qualitative sort of consumer research in friendlier spaces.

Kristin Jones of Trendera, another consumer research firm, told me that this shift away from focus groups to more qualitative, ethnographic modes of study has been a major change in the consumer research field; her clients want to know how their customers act in their own environments. She said, "We've done stuff from sleepover ethnographies to shopalongs," she told me. And if the client does want a focus group, "we try to shy away from an actual facility and maybe we'll plan a fun dinner party; we did a cocktail party [for young people], where of course we couldn't really serve alcohol, but we had fun little mixology drinks and got people mingling and interacting in new ways and getting people to talk to us." Jones says that this sort of research yields better results: "We find that the research is much better that way because people are comfortable; they're going to tell you what they think; it doesn't feel stuffy or like you could have a wrong answer." Jones says that clients have shown a good deal of interest in Trendera's "nontraditional" and ethnographic research, rather than "the cold, hard focus groups" (Jones, interview, 2016). Nonetheless, focus groups are still common, to the frustration of consumer research workers.

Locating Subjects

Some of these consumer research companies pursue specific projects for specific clients, seeking information on markets, on how people use particular products, and other such data that can only be gathered through meeting consumers face-to-face; Jones, of Trendera, called the resulting documents "proprietary reports." But most of these firms conduct more general research with many subjects. Jones told me that Trendera searches for micro- and macrotrends by surveying over a thousand people. She said that throughout the year, the firm travels the country attending cool events and visiting cool neighborhoods. Their data aren't just quantitative, she told me; they rely on a "huge panel" of influencers. She said that her company will do product demos and app trials, such as locating subjects for Apple to test a new phone. And she gave a hypothetical example of a representative of an entertainment studio approaching her company and saying, "Hey, we have this new show, we want to appeal to this demographic, what are the themes that we really need to flesh out in our marketing campaigns? We really want to pivot our brand to appeal to this type of person, what are some things that we need to go back and rework in our brand identity to make that evolution?" (interview, 2016). Jones said that Trendera has done everything from facilitating partnerships to recruiting participants for marketing campaigns, and much more.

Taylor Clark, who worked for a company called Cassandra when I first interviewed her in 2016 but now has her own firm, called Irregular Labs, told me that at Cassandra she had access to a group of five thousand subjects, a group collectively called Cassandra Speaks, with whom her company regularly kept in touch. Clark said they would conduct two rounds of follow-up research for each data point, "to make sure why is this trend happening and getting their feedback, and then going back in, doing quant again, back to qual. So, doing a lot of research all the time on young people to make four reports per year." Cassandra Speaks, she said, is geographically and ethnically diverse, "a community of hand-picked people," whom they once met in person but now connect mainly by FaceTime (before the COVID-19 pandemic). Clark said, "We go through an interview, essentially, making sure that they can analyze themselves in an eloquent manner." Cassandra also makes sure that their trendsetters actually are trendsetters, so their friends are asked to take a survey as well. Clark said, "We look at our data on a much broader scale, there's a lot more people in our quantitative research, and then in our qualitative research we try to just home in on why that data is occurring" (Clark, interview, 2016).

Clark said that Cassandra possessed twenty years of research on fourteen- to thirty-four-year-olds, mainly in the United States, and that they have a very good understanding of Generation X, millennials, and Generation Z. Clark said they keep an eye on mainstream trends as well as trendsetters. The mainstream group shows "a more typical consumption pattern . . . , and then we have trendsetters. So, we look at how the data over time is progressing among trendsetters or if there's a huge discrepancy among the mainstream" (interview, 2016). Clark said that they record all the interviews they conduct with their subjects, and then choose from many hours of videos to include in their reports, which are then made available to subscribers as part of Cassandra's web-based reports.

If a focus group is used, the client's budget determines its size. Jones of Trendera said that a typical focus group would be capped at around ten people, while the cocktail parties they host might have a couple of dozen people, "but then we'll have a few different moderators, and arrange the furniture in a certain way so that people naturally cluster, so that there is a way to break off into slightly smaller but not too-intimate conversation settings." I asked Jones for an example, and she provided one of an unnamed entertainment brand that was pursuing young viewers between the ages of eight and fourteen and was seeking ways to reach them and in general wanting to know what this group's values were. Trendera used traditional focus groups in one of the phases of their study, speaking with a variety of kids all over the country, learning that "entertainment consumption among this audience is drastically different from even millennial or older teens." After that, Jones said, they did some "supplementary cultural analysis," and put together a comprehensive report which said, in Jones's paraphrase, "These are the primary values of this audience, these are the platforms they're on, this is how much time they're spending where, and here are the titles you're looking to market to them, here's a few different recommendations or approaches that you might want to take in developing your strategy" (interview, 2016).

For proprietary studies, Trendera recruits its subjects in various ways. Jones told me that sometimes they simply ask people in their network of consumers for referrals, and she gave an example of a women's beauty brand: "They wanted to talk to a specific type of influencer on social media, almost fashion blogger but not quite, but aspiring to be, and we just went straight to Instagram and reached out to them via direct message, saying something like, 'Hey, we're working on this really cool brand on a project, and we'd love to get your thoughts,' and they were just honored that we would even reach out to them" (interview, 2016).

Some consumer research firms locate and provide subjects for clients to interview. Wightman told me that she can find people to talk to herself, but sometimes she relies on "a special recruiter who is good and recruiting cool people"—who happens to be Quiazon's partner at WHY-Q?, Teddy Liouliakis. Wightman relates the process: "[I tell him,] 'Get me ten of these people,' and they get me exactly what I'm looking for. If you have the right people, they know what's up and they know how to do it." These subjects are paid. Wightman says it's important to use a firm like WHY-Q?, or else you could end up getting "slumped"—interviewing people who appear in focus groups for a living, such as those Quiazon encountered in her days working for an advertising agency. Wightman said she can learn what she needs to know from about six people but thinks ten is better. She is usually accompanied by a note-taker, and sometimes a videographer as well (interview, 2016).

Finding Influencers

Coolness and hipness have become so cool and hip and diffused throughout the culture that they are more difficult to spot than they were when trend-spotting began to take off, and what is thought to be cool doesn't necessarily occur only among youth demographics. Jones of Trendera spoke of when its founder, Jane Buckingham, entered the business a couple of decades prior to our interview in 2016: "It was really easy to spot who was trendy, because back then you could easily identify them by the way they dressed, or the places they frequented, but now that being hip and being a hipster is horrendously mainstream, you can't really tell who's an influencer based on the way they look now, or necessarily on where they're going."[7] Now, Jones told me, "The sphere of influence has really fragmented, and certain people can be really influential in very specific areas, and [in] their lifestyle, but you don't have an all-encompassing influencer like you might once have had" (interview, 2016).

The aspect of consumer research that interests me here is the practice of seeking out influencers in different demographic groups, an effort that has only been active as a business in the last couple of decades (to be an influencer today can be a vocation; see "How Influencing as a Career Has

Impacted Today's Economy" 2019). By the time of my interview with Trendera's Kristin Jones in 2016, the term *influencer* was entering common parlance outside of the world of consumer research; the use of the word began to skyrocket starting around the end of the first decade of this century. Jones told me that she thought the term was overused and defined it as "a person and culture that is doing things differently." She said that another term in use was "popularizer," someone who takes a new idea and shares it with others and helps it grow" (interview, 2016). Jones also said that "influencer" is extremely relative and that there is a spectrum: "If we're talking about an influencer on people who are shaping culture, that's a very different type of influencer than one who just happens to be the leader among their friends and who has the most social currency in that resource that her friends look to for new ideas and products." So, for Trendera's work, Jones said, it is important to "nail down what kind of influence you're looking tap into" (interview, 2016).

Jones said that influencers or popularizers exist in all groups and that young demographics tend to influence the adjacent younger one: "Teens dictate the trends for the tweens, and millennials dictate trends and hand them to older generations, but it's always relative to the group you're talking about." Today, she said, demographics matter less than they once did; generation, gender, and income are not as significant as before. Jones told me that her firm has begun to study cohorts "by mindset, shared values, because as things get more digital and our culture gets more global, it's democratizing access to a lot of culture, so you can have a teen and a sixty-year-old that are into the same show or the same people." Because of this, she said, the "avenues of influence" are increasing. Jones nonetheless thinks that hipness and coolness remain youth-oriented, because young people are driving a lot of change in consumer tastes. "And that's where we focus our research efforts," she said. "You're going to have tastemakers and leaders and movers and shakers at all areas of the spectrum, but I think that focusing on youth is still the way to go" (interview, 2016).

Brands are increasingly using influencers to help reach and expand their markets. American Eagle, the apparel company, created a young consumer council called AexME, described by Trendera as a group of nine influencers in their teens and early twenties "who are 'living out their values'"; it includes a cofounder of March for Our Lives, Delaney Tarr, the founder of the mental-health organization Buddy Project, Gabby Frost, and the creator of the political group Bridge the Divide, Joseph Touma. The group meets regularly, Trendera says, "to help make important decisions on behalf of the company as well as to receive mentorship from leaders within American Eagle." This council's recommendations "have resulted in an in-store program that planted 155,000 trees in forests impacted by the California wildfires as well as a denim recycling program that has collected over 11,000 pairs of jeans" (Trendera n.d., 8). Since some influencers are becoming celebrities just for being influencers and have significant followings on social media, brands can hope to derive some additional value from forming such panels.

The Work of Trendspotting

Since the rise of account planning in the 1990s, independent firms have sprung up that perform many functions, from improving the product to humanizing big data, all as part of their work in learning about consumers' meanings and values. Mainly, though, they attempt to learn about the market segment they're studying, sometimes, I would say, even creating that market segment, especially around demographic categories such as generations; I'll examine their construction of Generation Z as an example. (These workers also educate their clients about their markets, though I won't discuss that here.)

Improving the Product

On the subject of the production of commodities, Marx writes in volume 1 of *Capital* that "the work of directing, superintending and adjusting becomes one of the functions of capital" (1990, 449), and it has become no less necessary in the realm of consumption. Trendspotters study people's relationships to commodities, learning what meanings they have created for them and trying to figure out how to improve them, based on users' usages and input. Product improvement is about making a product to suit, or better suit, a particular market, but it is only an indirect way of increasing a market and it might not work. Product improvement is really a kind of inspection: trendspotters play the role of inspector, especially when they think a particular demographic is on the front lines. Clark said that the members of Generation Z are "the product-testers of culture"; they are quick to pick up on innovations and can influence their siblings and parents (interview, 2020).

Trendspotting started with firms like Irma Zandl's and was a way of attempting to discover what young people actually wanted from products, what characteristics they wanted them to possess, and how to improve a product and increase sales. Malcolm Gladwell's 1997 article about trendspotting followed Wightman, who at the time was working for Converse, and would frequently visit young African American men in Brooklyn to learn what they liked and didn't like about Converse's shoes and prototypes. Wightman's job then, as somebody working in account planning, was known as "cultural strategist" or "consumer insight" person. Wightman described her work for Converse to me this way: "I had to create products that would be cutting-edge to a certain niche subculture, and the way to do that was to take prototypes to key spots where a lot of the trends were bubbling out of and to get the prototypes in front of the right people. We could figure out where those people tended to be." For Wightman, trendspotting "really just means to go find the best influencers for the sneaker, people who could just look at a sneaker and say, 'It's going to go, it's going to be something I'm going to want and people like me are going to want'" (interview, 2016). Wightman's view is that she was showing potential consumers her company's product.

Wightman told me that whatever product she might be trying to market, she will try to find where innovations are being made and learn about them. "I like to go to the root of where things are changing and try to figure out where it is going," she said, and she finds these roots by attending to particular subcultures that tend to be ahead of the mainstream in finding trends. She offered the examples of snowboarders and skateboarders, who "tend to not want to be like anybody else—they want to have their own identity. So, you would go to places where snowboarding or skateboarding was the most thriving or the most cutting-edge" (interview, 2016).

Wightman told me that she and her associates don't go out as much as they once did but that "we still do ethnography—if we're going to be selling kitchen appliances and we want to meet the new mom, the new dad-mom, we'll go out and meet those people." Her whole approach, she said, is to identify the target market, since she knows it is rarely her. "I learned that premise when I was assigned to snowboards and I had to study those freestyle snowboarders and I'm thinking, 'I'm not them, so I'd better hang out, I'd better understand'" (interview, 2016).

Humanizing Big Data

Everyone I spoke to in this field said that quantitative data are followed up with the qualitative studies that they provide for. Zandl thinks that the rise of big data has meant that there will be more and more information coming in. She said her early work in the late 1980s and early 1990s was all hand-written, and then input by hand into websites. She had about five hundred people to survey, but today, she said, there could be fifty thousand people surveyed, which makes for more accurate data. But, she said, "the question is going to be, how do you use it and how do you decipher exactly what it says?" (interview, 2016).

Wightman said that the biggest change she has seen in the sort of consumer research she does is reflected in not only the sheer amount of data but also the overreliance on it. People don't want to get out of their chairs, she said, and "It's a rarer and rarer thing that clients will spring for the ethnographic study—it's unfortunate." Gathering online data is very cheap, but the sort of data that can be collected inexpensively online doesn't explain why real people like what they like, choose what they choose; Wightman mentioned a firm that makes entire segmentation studies (studies of market segments) without meeting a customer. Her clients, she says, will spend hundreds of thousands—or more than a million—dollars on a segmentation study, but she doesn't think they are necessary. What frequently happens, she said, is that a client will say, "'We have a segmentation, can you go out and find people and make a little video for me, so I know who they are?'" (interview, 2016).

Clark used the example from Cassandra's 2016 *Love* report, which asked its many subjects about that topic. Their research revealed that over 50 percent of people globally thought that they would entertain the idea of an open marriage, a finding that "was an unexpected stat. So, our job was to go in and see why that is happening and getting quotes that support the general consensus in a way that makes it easily digestible for our readers."

Clark says that, in Cassandra's reports, "our macro trends are laid out with our summary of what they are, and then quotes supporting the data along with marketplace examples of either campaigns advertising new companies [or] new apps that have come up that are popular among this generation and explaining why they're on trend this year." Clark also offered an example of a trend they discovered from Cassandra's *Love* report: millennials use apps to find other people but don't want to admit it; they want to be able to tell people that they met someone by chance. She gave an example of a marketing campaign in which Starbucks partnered with Tinder to allow people to meet in person (interview, 2016).[8]

Wightman said that today, conducting digital research is all about a user's online cookies (small data files),

> so you don't really know them, you just know a little bit about them, where they've been and where they're likely to go on the internet. That's the quantifiable stuff that people can hand to a media company and say, "I'm farming these people, I'm sending messages to them, and the only thing I know about anybody is that she visited all these sites and she's been back three times, so I think she might want to buy a car." And that's how the world works these days.

But Wightman thinks that qualitative data still matter: "I think if you want to create a message that's going to resonate with somebody, you really need the other sort of data, because you have to get the insight. Behavior is one thing—what they do and where they go online—but to know how to speak to them is something else." Wightman said that her work involves writing a creative brief that might inspire a copywriter, but to do that, she has "to go into the homes. We really crack the case when we go into their homes, and we see these funny little insights." Wightman says the usual process is to gather the quantitative data, then attempt to locate interview subjects to recruit (interview, 2016).

Clark described what she and her colleagues do as "adding character to the data," which means "giving people the why behind what's happening and understanding [of] their target consumer." Clark said that companies rarely take the time to learn about the demographic for which they are producing a good. And the high-level executives are usually far removed from their customers, tending to be less tech-savvy and not on the same platforms as their targeted market. Clark said that "the world has changed so quickly, so much, social norms have changed, and the way that you communicate with someone is very different, and so rapid, that is very hard for companies to keep up" (interview, 2016).

Big data do not reveal what is driving trends, and it is the identification of new trends that Jones believes her business to be. A national survey will reveal what a hot brand is, but not the next big thing. Those who employ more quantitative approaches, she said, "don't know how to anticipate what brands are next and what's bubbling up, what's under the surface that's not showing up in their data yet that we know about because we know the right people and we're studying the right brands and cracking what's coming." Jones said that everyone loves big data, and that there is a lot of security in being able to refer to numbers, but if you are in a predictive business, qualitative data—and the art of using them—still matter (interview, 2016). Clark also thinks that big data are useful, but she thinks it's also important to study niches, which can shed light on the results provided by big data and obviate broad assumptions (interview, 2020).

There is also a move toward hyper-nichification, which is partly driven by big data, and which makes examining trends—and living one's life—even more difficult. Zandl told me, "Hyper-nichification is going to make peoples' lives just more and more complicated. When you go in to buy tomatoes, for example, you used to buy maybe three different types, now, there seem to be around 160 types, and it's the same thing with every other fruit and vegetable. Milk is also like that" (interview, 2016). Hyper-nichification may also be driven by the increasing specialization of these trendspotting firms. Clark told me that at Cassandra, they focused on people from the ages of fourteen to thirty-four; she now runs her own firm that focuses on Generation Z.

Learning about/Creating Market Segments

Consumer research workers also conduct what is recognizably ethnographic research to learn more about their clients' customers in order to create advertising and marketing campaigns that will resonate with them. At the time of our interview, Wightman was employed at an advertising agency, and she described for me the process of working with a client. Most likely, she said, they would have commissioned a segmentation study (everyone likes to spend a lot of money on them, she says) to identify the particular segment that a client believes that their product will appeal to. Wightman said that such a study is a combination of psychological and behavioral traits of the people in the target segment, and she gave what she initially presented as a hypothetical example, but later in our conversation proved to be an actual case. "If you are selling kitchen appliances and you are not an American brand—you happen to be a brand from Korea—you want to make sure that you find a target that is not going to just go for a traditional American brand. So, we came up with this idea of the new mom, that not everything has to be perfect: She's real, and she's not an alpha mom at all." But the only way to understand these new moms (or anyone), Wightman said, is to enter people's homes and hang out with them, view the order or disorder of their homes, parents' interactions with their children. "And then," she said, "you really get it. There is no quantitative study in the world that is going to give you the insights that spending an hour-and-a-half with a really strapped, stay-at-home mom" (interview, 2016).

Wightman then elaborated on the hypothetical example, which, as our conversation progressed, turned out to be the Korean company LG. The women whose homes she visited were "drinking wine down in their laundry rooms; it was like their washing machine was their coconspirator, as if, 'Honey, what are you doing?'—'I'm doing laundry, don't bother me!' It was just a great insight, learning that the appliance was not only on your team but your coconspirator." In particular, she said, there was one woman "who invited us down to her—we called it the mom cave—where she had her laundry, and she had her wine, and she would watch *Breaking Bad* on her iPad because she couldn't do that around her kids" (interview, 2016).

This insight generated Wightman and her agency's strategy for advertising these appliances to such mothers: "The typical appliance positioning is 'Hi, I'm part of mom's team,' but we thought, 'No, you're part of the momtourage, you're her coconspirator,' and out of that came a campaign that was called 'Mom's Inner Voice.' We did this whole campaign about mom's inner thoughts and what she's really thinking when stuff's going on around her, and they're slightly subversive thoughts." Wightman said that they also created a social media initiative on Tumblr (which later relocated to Twitter) called "Mom Confessions," where mothers could confess to things that "aren't exactly good mom things" (interview, 2016; see Greenberg 2014).[9]

Wightman thinks that her ethnography helped move beyond the normal representations of moms on American television, which she thinks are vastly oversimplified. "The way moms are portrayed on TV, they're either alpha moms or they're saints or whatever, and the new mom is thinking, 'Are you kidding me?' Moms today are thinking, 'I'm not doing that. I'm looking for shortcuts.' And to the client's credit, they gave us this segment that said she prefers shortcuts. She's not a perfectionist, which is good" (interview, 2016).

After a discussion of the importance of finding or creating the right environment in which to talk to her subjects, Quiazon said that about 80 percent of her work (before the COVID-19 pandemic struck in early 2020) was visiting people's homes; she would also go shopping with them. Quiazon told me that it's important to speak with people and observe them, since they may say one thing and do another. She said she can spend four to five hours with each of her subjects. If they're young people, she will also interview the parents. If a WHY-Q? client was a sneaker manufacturer, she said, she might ask someone in their home, "Hey, how would you wear these? Why do you wear these? What's your favorite thing? Show me these outfits" (interview, 2020). Quiazon also said she asks people about what she sees in their homes: "Plenty of times, I'll say something like, 'Oh, I see you have a picture of XYZ you put on your bedroom walls, tell me more about this.' Or, 'I see you have these sneakers front and center but this other one way in the back under stuff in your closet. What makes this one get shoved into the back and these in the front?'" Quiazon thus also wants to learn why people are no longer interested in particular brands (interview, 2020).

Quiazon described a music project her firm conducted for a brand that was trying to decide how to embrace music. They interviewed people in their homes, viewed their music collections, attended live music events with them, asking why their subjects wanted to take them to particular concerts and what it means to them. They also asked their subjects how they wanted to see brands embrace music and discussed initiatives such as Rubber Tracks, a program by Converse, the sneaker company, that records bands gratis (interview, 2020; see Taylor 2016b, and chapter 5 in this volume).

This sort of qualitative research is expensive. Consumer research firms talk to members of Generation Z (and others) all over the world. Irregular Labs' *Fluidity* report surveyed over two thousand Gen Zers in the United States, United Kingdom, Germany, India, China, Brazil, and South Africa, for example (Irregular Labs n.d., 12). In an informational PowerPoint presentation that WHY-Q? shows to clients, the firm says that it conducts its ethnographic research globally, "in any part of the world, . . . whether it be Beijing, Milan, Berlin, Seoul, Paris, Shanghai, Rio de Janeiro, Sydney, Tokyo, or wherever our clients' strategic needs take us" (WHY-Q? INC. n.d.). The results from this research are packaged in snazzy reports, either proprietary or more general, the latter of which can obtained individually for a hefty fee or purchased through an even larger subscription (Cassandra charged $45,000 annually for access to its online reports in 2016). These general reports are usually on particular themes, such as Cassandra's report on love.

Companies once produced more general reports on particular demographic groups, but Zandl said this sort of research became too costly. The

Table 3.1 Excerpt from Zandl Group's "Young Adult Hot Sheet," February 2007 (bracketed passages in original)

Males 21–24	Males 25–29	Females 21–24	Females 25–29
FAVORITE MUSIC			
Rock	Rock	Rock	Rock
Rap/hip hop	Rap/hip hop	Alt	Country
Alt	Pop	Rap/hip hop	Pop
[Also: country/ R&B/techno/ acoustic/ indie/punk/ '90s/jazz/ grunge/ reggae/oldies]	[Also: country/ alt/classic rock/ top 40/metal/ hardcore/'80s/ '90s/soft rock/ drum & bass/ blues/jazz]	[Also: pop/ country/punk/ classical/emo/ industrial/ goth/'80s/dark wave/R&B]	[Also: rap/ indie/alt/ R&B/'80s/'90s/ trance/hip hop/ reggae/drum 'n' bass/soul/ Celtic/dance/ techno]
FAVORITE MUSIC PERFORMER			
Jay-Z	Eminem	Incubus	Justin Timberlake
Justin Timberlake	Mariah Carey	Sarah McLachlan	Willie Nelson
Metallica	Deftones	Mary J. Blige	Beyoncé
[Also: Snoop Dogg/U2/Dave Matthews/ Beck/Fall Out Boy/ Radiohead/ Keith Urban/ Nickelback/ Ludacris/Death Cab for Cutie/ Keane]	[Also: Céline Dion/Jack Johnson/Johnny Cash/Coldplay/ Gnarls Barkley/ David Bowie/ Death Cab for Cutie/Panic! at the Disco/Rush]	[Also: Green Day/Nirvana/ Tim McGraw/ Gretchen Wilson/ Ladytron/ Fiona Apple/ Coldplay/The Killers/Alice in Chains/Chris Brown]	[Also: Madonna/ Jojo/Jessica Simpson/ Gwen Stefani/ Toby Keith/ Bob Dylan/ Coldplay/Black Eyed Peas/Snow Patrol/ The Fray/Jay-Z]

NEWEST MUSIC YOU'RE LISTENING TO/HEARING ABOUT			
The Killers (e.g., new album)	Jay-Z (e.g., *Kingdom Come*)	Indie (e.g., local LA)	Punk cabaret (e.g., Dresden Dolls)
Beck (e.g., new album)	Lily Allen	Beirut	Neko Case
Lily Allen	TV on the Radio	Joanna Newsom	Girl Talk
[Also: podcasts/Tom Waits/Justin Timberlake/ Weakerthans/ Hello Goodbye]	[Also: Beirut/ Arcade Fire/ Bloc Party/ Badly Drawn Boy/Voxtrot/ Cold War Kids/ Cool Calm Pete]	[Also: alt/ Evan's Blue/I Love You but I've Chosen Darkness/ Tortoise]	[Also: metal/ TV on the Radio/Justin Timberlake/ Snow Patrol/ hip hop/ Ghostface Killah]

Zandl Group formerly published something called the *Hot Sheet*, which broke down consumer taste by age cohorts and gender. Zandl said the *Hot Sheet* began with the requests of clients who knew she had cultivated a network of cool kids and their parents. She was asked, she said, "You have all these kids, all these parents, why don't you put together this thing for us?" She was told, "'I want it by ages, and here are some questions I'd like to be asked.'" Zandl said that her clients liked the way she displayed the data and that none of her competitors presented it that way, but she said it was prohibitively expensive, because all the questions they asked were open-ended, so inputting all that data was time-consuming. It was financially possible in the past, she said, but since she, like everyone I interviewed in this field, operates on a subscription model, mergers and acquisitions cut the number of subscribers. Zandl gave the example of Disney, which bought ESPN and then ABC and still other companies; all these firms once paid for individual subscriptions from the Zandl Group, but the number greatly decreased, so she couldn't maintain this level of consumer research. Zandl said she produced the *Hot Sheet* for ten to fifteen years. Table 3.1 shows the sorts of generational and gender breakdown with respect to music preferences.

Today, however, as noted, reports are more thematic. Clark's Irregular Labs, which specializes in Generation Z, has produced reports on "influence," "fluidity," "regeneration," and "failed authenticity," with more in the offing. These reports contain not only discussions of the theme but also snippets of interviews with the consumer research team's subjects (video if the report is online) and case studies about particular individuals or particular brands, all connected by extensive discussions that describe the particular culture and values that are the focus of the report. Clark told me,

> We try to understand based on, first, where they're directing us in terms of what's currently trending . . . . And then we focus our studies onto something that is particularly important in that time, and we continue conducting studies, we continue to grow the number of interests we look at, but we don't try to do everything. We try to do it in a way so that we don't just randomly put together a group based on an interest that we don't see. But people's interests tend to be something that ultimately dictates so much of not only consumer behavior and trend forecasting, but a lot of the movements that we're seeing. (Interview, 2020)

Clark describes her subjects as having "interests," but it's clear that, since these interests drive more than consumer behavior, we are in the realm not just of interests and consumer preferences but also of values and meanings. Clark's observation resonates with a comment by Kluckhohn in a late work when he is introducing his concept of values: "In the broadest sense, behavioral scientists may usefully think of values as abstract and perduring standards, which are held by an individual and/or a specified group to transcend the impulses of the moment and ephemeral situations" (1961, 17). Kluckhohn proposes to focus on "cultural values" of the "highest level of generality" (1961, 18). But something as seemingly mundane as a consumer choice can reveal deeper convictions and beliefs, these "cultural values."

Generation Z

Let me now tackle a case study in greater depth. Much of the work of market research, including trendspotting, is concerned with identifying generations, cohorts of like-minded consumers united by their demography—a focus that dates back to the business's discovery of the baby-boom generation (see Taylor 2012). Labeling of generations extrapolates from demography to impute shared meanings and values to that generation; the demographic data gives such assumptions an aura of scientific accuracy, but these generations are as much constructed by market research and other processes as they are demographic phenomena (see Ortner 2006).

So, let's start with the demographics. Generation Z is an observable demographic phenomenon, a cohort born between the mid- to late 1990s and the early 2000s, the first generation to grow up surrounded by digital technologies, so much so that these youth are frequently called "digital natives." The many ethnographic and other sorts of studies of Generation Z attempt to understand what its members care about. One such concern is for what market researchers call "authenticity," manifested, for example, by a preference for old photos with people with closed eyes, not edited or retouched photos, as Quiazon told me (interview, 2020). Clark thinks that Generation Z has high moral and ethical standards (interview, 2020).

Clark labels a Generation Z ideology "fluidity," which, her firm says, exists on several vectors:

No binaries or rules/
Creativity and imagination/
Fragmentation and decentralization/
Impermanence and ephemerality/
Inclusivity and activism/
Multiplicity and hybridity. (Irregular Labs n.d., 22)[10]

Fluidity is evident in Generation Z's musical tastes. According to Clark, its members "have such diverse musical interests, and they are so genreless—what we currently call "genreless" because there's no name for it—a genreless generation. And so, in looking into that and their interests around music, we realized the nuances of their interests needed to be dug into more deeply." Clark gave example: "What they love about an artist like Billie Eilish and people like that has been that there's that fluidity of genre where you can't define the person or the artist" (interview, 2020).

These beliefs, inclinations, proclivities, ideologies, preferences, are values in the raw, which market researchers codify and officialize as the values of the particular generation in order to market to it more efficiently. The reports that they produce show how celebrity members of a particular generation market themselves and how marketers can learn from them. Irregular Labs presents in its fluidity report what they call a case study of the musician Kelela (b. 1983, thus approximately Generation X), whose 2018 release *TAKE ME A_ PART: The Remixes*, they say, is "a study in fluidity." Kelela took her album *Take Me Apart* from 2017 and gave it to a team of re-mixers, "predominately black, queer collaborators," according to Irregular Labs, with whom "she produced re-imagined revisions of her own work." In essence, they say, she "channeled that Meme Dynamic and fan-fictioned her-self." "Rather than complying with the industry-approved formula of covers and re-recordings ('copies' of 'originals')," they write, "*TAKE ME A_ PART* produced 'originals' of 'originals'—a wholly autonomous and unique body of work." Kelela's (second) recording was an "'open container' within which artists from a variety of genres were set free to reinterpret songs, putting their individual stamp on them." This is characterized as 100 percent Gen Z–style collaboration, "the We accommodating the Me" (Irregular Labs n.d., 192).

Trendspotters also have learned that Generation Z is interested in social justice more than the previous generation, the millennials. Clark told me that Generation Z is far more socially aware, possessing more of a sense of a personal responsibility to fight injustice, perhaps, she thought, because millennials were daunted by the magnitude of problems (interview, 2020).

These kinds of observations are purveyed to trendspotting firms' clients, who, if they decide to act on them, modify their marketing strategies and perhaps their products. A Spotify online publication, *For the Record*, profiled Generation Z in 2019 and noted their political commitments, facili-tated by technology, which, Spotify said, makes them more engaged than any previous generation. Spotify said that podcasts that mix lifestyle and politics top their charts. And, speaking to the promotional industries, they write, "A solid 66% of respondents said they expect brands to be part of the debate, to promote progressive values, and to play a more meaningful role in society. 'Our eyes have been opened to the lack of leadership by those in positions of power,' says Canadian pop star Alessia Cara [b. 1996], 'and in turn, so many of us have had to step up in their place'" (Spotify 2019).[11] Through studies such as these, workers outside of the branding, market-ing, and consumer research fields contribute to the hardening of consumer preferences into meanings and values that they attribute to particular co-horts, even entire generations.

Conclusions

This chapter has detailed the myriad ways that trendspotters attempt to elucidate preferences that consumers hold for the products they use or critique, preferences that can be harvested and codified, regularized, and turned into values of a particular group. Trendspotters can collect and amplify these meanings and values so that they become, in Turner's words, part of a "cultural system," part of "structure," signifiers and signifieds in a system of objects. They can also be used to improve products.

And while it may seem as though trendspotters are speeding up the conveyor belt in consumer capitalism, where everything moves faster than in the past—including, and perhaps especially, consumer trends—Zandl thinks that it's actually a slow process. Looking back at the *Hot Sheet*s, she told me she is struck by the amount of time taken by trends to move. "It takes twenty years for something to really become mainstream and really get big. When you really look at some fad like skinny jeans, how long have we been wearing them now, ten or twelve years at least? So, it's really an interesting thing, because things in the press seem to get a lot more traction than sometimes they're getting in real life" (interview, 2016).

Perhaps the process is slow because some people resist, not wanting to be pigeonholed or targeted by marketers, seeking out artists such as Billie Eilish who, as cultural producers, also resist categorization. Examining the resistance to advertising and marketing is a project for another day, though here I would note that such resistance that exists can certainly gum up the works, making the work of trendspotters more complicated, but also more easily justified to those who pay for it.

The complex dynamics between the production of a good, its consumption, the bubbling up of consumer preferences and desires, their capture by trendspotters, their codification by market researchers, the transformation of products and their marketing, and the resistance to marketing and advertising may not have speeded up from Zandl's perspective. But these processes are increasingly common, even if at the same time, they are selective: it takes a good deal of money to undertake studies such as these I have discussed, and a good deal more to implement their recommendations, just as it takes a good deal of money to launch an advertising campaign or brand a product. But selectivity doesn't imply rarity—ours is increasingly a commercial culture in which no one is untouched.

4

4

Taking the Gift Out and Putting It Back In

From Cultural Goods to Commodities

This chapter is about how the economic value of cultural commodities in the capitalist marketplace is created or increased. I am interested in the ways that cultural goods are transformed into commodities through processes of translation and purification, which appear to strip away the noncapitalist social relations and noneconomic forms of value that went into the production of a particular cultural good, and I am interested in the processes of consecration and promotion that reanimate cultural commodities with values that are designed to emulate noneconomic forms of value, in effect seemingly—but only seemingly—defetishizing them. The many processes of consecration and promotion are designed to make the newly minted cultural commodity appear to be something other than what it is, a commodity, the product of alienated labor. In essence, I am arguing that capitalism takes the gift out of the commodity (as Tsing [2013] theorizes the process usually called commodification) by alienating labor and masking social relations and then, through processes of consecration and/or promotion, creates a simulacrum of a gift through representations of unalienated labor and intact social relations.

To distinguish between economic and noneconomic forms of value (or commodities and gifts) is something of a heuristic; I do not conceptualize "the economic" as an autonomous realm; rather, people are engaged in practices all the time that make capitalism appear to be autonomous (see Bear et al. 2015). Here, I am concerned with how goods circulate and move through different regimes of value. Goods circulate, possessing social lives or cultural biographies (Appadurai 1986b; Kopytoff 1986). I can spend money to buy a musical instrument, but that doesn't capture or quantify the pleasure I derive from playing it and, at least in my mind, bears little or no relationship to the occasional income I derive from playing in Irish bars. But capitalism is the dominant economic system in the West and, increasingly, everywhere else, even if as I will discuss, it depends on other modes of the production of value. So, I align myself here with anthropologist Anna Tsing's (2015) view of things—that is, with an acknowledgment of the prevalence of capitalism, but while recognizing just how much it relies on other modes of production, other forms of value. The dominance of capitalism, alongside the continuing existence of noneconomic regimes of value, constitutes the reason that I still believe it useful to focus on capitalism while employing the heuristic of sorting out economic and noneconomic forms of value.

What interests me in this chapter is a specific set of processes by which a musical good is transformed into a commodity—a good with an economic form of value—and how some forms of noneconomic value are (sometimes) created for it after it has become a commodity. What is usually reduced to "commodification" is actually a set of processes in which noneconomic forms of value seem to be systematically removed. I write "seem to be" because commodities remain full of the social relations of their production, and new social relations are created in their circulation and consumption: Commodities remain social goods (see Maurer 2006). But the processes of commodification seem to strip away these social meanings. The purpose of consecration and promotion is to execute a kind of sleight of hand, the creation of an illusion of a good that represents noneconomic forms of value that may precede economic forms and is superior to them. The history of consecration and promotion—and not just of cultural commodities—is a history of attempting to build ever-stronger connections between commodities and consumers as supply chains grow longer—both in number of workers and discrete nodes and geographically—and more complex. In other words, the more alienated a commodity becomes through its traversal of ever more nodes in a supply chain, the more that strategies of consecration and promotion are required to present to consumers the appearance of a unique good. Such processes aren't always employed, however, since decisions always need to be made about what to promote, with what expenditure of resources, and so on.

In making these arguments, I will be examining the production of music as part of a supply chain in what Tsing has called "supply-chain capitalism"; economic value, she argues, is created at every stage of a supply chain (Tsing 2009, 2013, 2015). For her, supply-chain capitalism is a way of amassing wealth without much factory work and without rationalizing labor and raw materials. Supply-chain capitalism relies on what she calls "translation" from one social or political space to another, from one regime of value to another (2015, 62).

I will also be drawing on other anthropological theories of value and updated treatments of a classic sociological theory to understand how processes of consecration and promotion can create or add value to cultural commodities. Examining these two ways of creating or adding to the economic value of cultural goods—supply chains and myriad strategies of promotion and consecration—is a useful means for understanding how the value of cultural commodities is created and amplified. Tsing seems to view the workings of supply-chain capitalism as fairly distinct processes, commenting that the athletic shoe giant Nike chose advertising and branding as ways to generate economic value rather than "making value through trade as translation" (2015, 118). The point of this chapter, however, is that promotion isn't simply another way to create value but is a way of producing or generating value necessitated by supply-chain capitalism. Processes of promotion only seem to be incidental because people need to decide what to advertise, market, or brand, as well as how and with what resources. Not necessarily all goods in an inventory are promoted, and if they are, not all to the same degree or in the same way. Nonetheless, I argue that industrially produced inventory necessitates, at the very least, decisions about advertising, marketing, and branding to make one firm's inventory appear to be different from, and more desirable to consumers, than another's.

Tsing's insightful discussion of the importance of assessment—sorting—in the collecting and sale of matsutake mushrooms gathered in nature (2013, 2015) might seem to be far from the world of the production of cultural commodities. But she makes important points about the workings of supply-chain capitalism and the integral role played by distinct groups of social actors in these processes. While supply-chain capitalism of mass-produced goods is indeed far from Tsing's study, the capitalist music business is not that different, with its own supply chains, whether of published music, recorded music in physical formats or digital formats, or music produced for film, television, streaming, or gaming.

Tsing makes powerful observations about the nature of today's capitalism—that it is not a totality and that it continues to rely, as it always has, on noncapitalist modes of production, whether the gathering of mushrooms by volunteers harvesting them from public lands or, to move to the realm of musical goods, all the labor performed by fans, disciples, colleagues, and many others in discovering this or that musician and championing that musician over another, defending that musician against critics, and more. The practices of assessment carried out in the sorting of mushrooms—much of which is logically unnecessary, as mushrooms are sorted multiple times—is, Tsing argues, how they are converted from gift status to commodity status, purified as commodities. And this is also, I argue, how cultural goods such as music become cultural commodities as well.

I will continue to employ Tsing's arguments in what follows, but at this point I need to lay the groundwork for the discussion of the other main way that economic forms of value of commodities are created or enhanced, through processes of consecration and promotion. I use the latter term to encompass not just advertising but also marketing and, later, branding. In part, of course, Tsing's ideas still obtain, since all of the mechanisms of promotion constitute more nodes in the supply chain. But in what follows, I will mainly be relying on some nineteenth-century social theorists: Werner Sombart, whose work I have found to be useful in considering questions about this sort of value, especially as taken up by Chandra Mukerji (1983) and Arjun Appadurai (1986a).

Appadurai proposes to place luxury goods—which, in his formulation, correspond nicely to artworks—in a special "register" of consumption: they are not the opposite of, or bereft of, use-value; their principal use, he says, is rhetorical and social. They are "incarnated signs," and "the necessity to which *they* respond is fundamentally political" (1986a, 38; emphasis in original). I would construe "political," however, as "cultural" more broadly—certain goods take on seemingly nonutilitarian values in certain social groups in certain places and times.

Sombart's (1967) theory of the origin of capitalism is founded on an analysis of the consumption of luxury goods in the French court beginning in the thirteenth and fourteenth centuries, viewing luxury goods as nonutilitarian. Appadurai wisely does not follow Sombart and dwell on the lack of utility of luxury goods. At least with respect to the arts, I would argue that the utility (or lack thereof) of a cultural good can only be understood ethnographically and historically. Appadurai also makes a point about luxury goods that carries over equally well to artworks: "From the consumption point of view, aspects of this luxury register can accrue to any and all commodities to some extent, but some commodities in certain contexts, come to exemplify the luxury register" (1986a, 38). Some artworks come to be considered important, timeless, and indispensable, while others do not. But this can change over time. Appadurai argues that this definition of luxury goods means that they can be found in all cultures, as can, of course, practices and cultural goods that could be considered artistic.

Appadurai provides a useful list of the characteristics of luxury goods in this special register of consumption: they are restricted, by price or law, to social elites; there is complexity in their acquisition, which may or may not be related to actual scarcity; there is semiotic virtuosity in their social signifying and interpretation; specialized knowledge is required for their consumption in ways that are thought to be appropriate (such as behavioral norms at concerts); and there is a close connection between the consumption of such goods and the consumer's body, person, or personality (Appadurai 1986a, 38). If we view cultural goods as luxury goods, we can then begin to understand why consumers might decide to invest time in seeking them, collecting them, and consuming them and why they might desire to spend disproportionately more money for artworks than other goods produced by the same amount of labor time (see Taylor 2017).

The Advent of Sound Recording and Advertising

Now let me briefly consider Tsing's discussion of assessment—sorting, judging. She calls forms of assessment that are intended to block gift-like social relations "alienation assessment" (2013, 23)—this is how the gift is taken out of the commodity in her thinking. Alienation is also achieved through other strategies, which, she believes, are designed into all commodity chains, "from design through marketing." "Thinking through assessment," she writes, "allows us to consider how the commodity form can be made without industrial labor though a process of translation" (2013, 23). "Alienation assessment," she writes, "privatizes and commodifies by interposing a process that is self-consciously blind to constitutive social relations." And Tsing points out the importance of assessment in supply-chain capitalism, in which the rationalization of inventory takes precedence over the disciplining of labor and natural resources (2013, 24).

The advent of sound recording in the late nineteenth century introduced a new form of the music commodity—music as sound, not as a concert ticket and experience or as sheet music—and also incorporated new nodes in the music supply chain and new workers, such as recording engineers and everyone involved in reproduction, promotion, distribution, and sales of the recorded music. Assessment is present at every stage—of who to record, the quality of the result, what to release, and which recordings to distribute, advertise, and stock. And inventory becomes more important. One way that player piano roll manufacturers peddled their wares was by claiming that people could purchase more player piano music than they could ever learn to play themselves (see Taylor 2017), and both these manufacturers and the record labels touted a better roster of artists than their competitors; this is part of supply-chain capitalism, in which, as Tsing writes, "discipline is directed toward inventory" (2013, 25). Industrialized promotion thus begins to emerge as a powerful way of creating value for inventory, though in this instance it is closely tied to the consecration of record labels or label lines by drawing on the cultural prestige of classical music, as I will discuss.

At first, sound recordings could not be mass-produced—musicians had to make them one or perhaps a few at a time by singing or playing into the recording horn. Each phonograph recording was therefore in some sense an original, unique, or one of just a few, closer to being a gift than a commodity, its value determined by the labor time of the musicians and others in the supply chain. This was part of a nineteenth-century ethos in which many goods were still not mass-produced and people were accustomed to purchasing unique goods, whether or not bespoke. Thomas Edison's famous 1878 article on the uses of the phonograph makes it clear that he is thinking of the phonograph as an instrument mainly for individuals to create sound recordings for themselves and others, as gifts (reprinted in Taylor, Katz, and Grajeda 2012). One could make one's own recordings using Edison's machine—that's what he thought it was for. Recordings of prerecorded music were thus not the alienated commodities they would become.

The focus in the recording business in this period was therefore more on the machine than the recording: The machines provided a way of continuing an earlier set of social relations by recording oneself and sharing with others one knew—making gifts of unique objects. Commercial recordings of music were sold in this period, but there were few stars; most recordings were sold by genre or instrument or vocal group. Phonograph manufacturing companies advertised recordings in the most basic fashion, simply listing what was in their catalogs, and not always including names of performers.

In 1900, processes of mass reproduction were introduced. Performers were already somewhat alienated from their audiences (stories abound of the difficulties performers had performing for recording horns or, later, for radio microphones rather than live audiences; see Taylor, Katz, and Grajeda 2012) and from their recordings. But the advent of mass reproduction added a node in the supply chain—factories for the mass reproduction of sound recordings. To generate inventory, major record labels in the United States and Europe immediately sent recording engineers to record music in East and South Asia and other places to generate more inventory; hundreds and hundreds of such recordings were made (see Gaisberg 1942; Gronow 1981; A. Jones 2001; Lubinski and Steen 2017). With this emphasis on inventory, the modern sound-recording business was born. The main commodity ceased to be the playback machine and became instead the sound recording, which was increasingly commodified through the processes of supply-chain capitalism and became the main means of creating economic value. Individual recordings were no longer unique possessions, the gift having been taken out by this new reproduction technology, a development reminiscent of the absence of aura famously declared by Walter Benjamin (though not in relation to music) (Benjamin 1968; see Taylor 2001 for a consideration of Benjamin's argument with respect to music).

The introduction of mass duplication technologies meant, of course, that recordings could no longer be sold as unique items. Consumers had to be convinced that these new mass-produced recordings were more desirable than the originals they were accustomed to purchasing, and the recording business adopted much the same strategy as the player piano business had, by emphasizing the quality of performances and touting especially highbrow releases—and by advertising heavily (see Samples 2011). Prices of prerecorded music fell, from one to two dollars each to fifty to seventy-five cents each, as recordings began to flood the market. Demand for playback machines and recordings skyrocketed early in the twentieth century (Millard 2005, 49).

The rise not so much of recording technology as such but of the music recording business more generally after the introduction of mass reproduction in 1900 is a quite striking transitional moment, particularly if one is interested in questions of value. Before mass reproduction, some people conceptualized recordings as commodities, but the vast majority of proselytizing and advertising in this period was for playback devices, not recordings. Not until the rise of mass reproduction did the business shift from a focus on playback technologies to an increasing emphasis on prerecorded music. And with this shift we find an explosion of promotional strategies surrounding music recordings, invoking every conceivable discourse of noneconomic value in attempts to consecrate these commodities: from the sociopolitical (access to the world's greatest music has been democratized) to value in terms of preservation (the world's greatest musicians are now recorded for posterity), convenience (one can listen to the world's greatest music in the comfort of one's home), quantity (one can own more recordings of music than one could ever learn to perform oneself), and still more (see Taylor, Katz, and Grajeda 2012).

With the mass reproduction of recordings of music and the shift of emphasis toward them, more detailed advertisements for labels and their wares appeared, sometimes focusing on particular segments of manufacturers' catalogs in ways that were intended to create perceptions of value. Here we see the beginning of the necessity for creating value through advertising and marketing as a way of not only promoting a particular firm's own inventory but also competing with other firms and theirs.

One strategy was to originate specialty lines for certain kinds of music. The creation of value was frequently attempted around high-prestige music, for it was thought that it would be easier to justify charging higher prices for recordings if they were of music considered to be highbrow, about which there was a fair amount of discussion in this era (see Levine 1988; Taylor, Katz, and Grajeda 2012). The creation of specialty lines like Red Seal at the Victor label consecrated those lines by valorizing certain musicians, perhaps especially the Italian tenor Enrico Caruso (1873–1921). Before the Red Seal line, introduced in 1902, all of Victor's recordings had been issued on discs with black labels, but the company conceived this upscale line for its classical artists, such as the celebrated tenor. Victor used different packaging, placed the Red Seal releases in a different catalog, and charged more for these recordings than those with black labels. Victor attempted to leverage the fame of its musicians not only to create the new Red Seal line but also to justify charging more (see Suisman 2009): two dollars, when most recordings cost between thirty-five cents and one dollar (historical inflation calculators don't go back to 1903 dollars, but two dollars in 1913, the earliest year for which calculations are available, would be worth over forty-eight dollars today, a shocking number).

Victor was quite naked in its strategy of both producing and profiting from the fame of its artists. "The reputation and popularity of Victor artists is a large factor in the merchandising of their Records," declared the company to its dealers in 1924. "Their fame is really one of the things you deal in, and yet one that costs you nothing. Therefore, it is to your advantage when that fame is widespread" (quoted in Suisman 2009, 130). With respect to Caruso, Victor exhorted its dealers in 1910: "Push Caruso—push his great big name (the biggest in the musical firmament) and his wonderful records for all their worth. . . . He is *the* one artist who stands alone" (quoted in Suisman 2009, 130; ellipsis in Suisman, emphasis in original).

Victor's Red Seal recordings were peddled with lavish, full-page advertisements, sometimes in color, in national magazines; a 1904 advertisement read: "Just think of it, to hear in your own home the soul-stirring arias and concerted numbers that have immortalized the names of Verdi, Gounod, Donizetti, Mozart, Wagner, Puccini, Leoncavallo and all the other great composers . . . to hear the masterpieces of music that before the days of the Victor were almost always hidden mysteries, which few indeed could ever know or hope to understand" (quoted in Suisman 2009, 109–10; ellipsis in Suisman). This lofty, even hyperbolic, rhetoric and extravagant advertising persisted for decades (see fig. 4.1).

David Suisman writes that between 1901 and 1929, Victor spent $52.7 million on advertising, making the company one of the most extravagant advertisers in the world (2009, 114). Frank Presbrey's history of advertising in the United States reported that the center-spread advertisement for the Victor Talking Machine Company made up one-fifth of all the advertising of the thirty-eight pages of the April 25, 1903, issue of the *Saturday Evening Post*, one of the most popular magazines in America in the period (1929, 440). In 1903 alone, the company spent $1.5 million on advertising (if this were 1913 dollars, it would be over $46 million today).

Advertisements did not simply push these goods but attempted, as I have been arguing, to create an illusion of a unique good, a good that was

4.1   Victor advertisement featuring Enrico Caruso, from *National Geographic Magazine*, 1921.

not a commodity fetish, not produced by alienated labor. Recorded musicians would be pictured listening to recordings (see fig. 4.2), or sometimes, as Suisman (2009) writes, they were shown touring factories, as if to lessen the distance in the supply chain from artist to factory and, by implication, from factory to listener.

Victor wasn't simply borrowing the prestige of classical music; it was building on discourses of prestige that already existed, discourses that created a form of noneconomic value for this music. These discourses weren't that old at the time of Victor's employment of them to consecrate its prod-

Caruso and other noted artists hearing their own rendition of the great Masked Ball Quintet

Caruso, Hempel, Duchène, de Segurola, Rothier, and Setti (Director of the Metropolitan Opera Chorus) listening to their Masked Ball Quintet (Victor Record 89076).

When you hear the famous concerted numbers of opera on the Victrola, it is just as though you were hearing them in the Metropolitan Opera House.

They are rendered by the same great artists, and with all the beauty of tone and thrilling power which earn for them the plaudits of enthusiastic opera-goers.

Hearing is believing. Any Victor dealer will gladly play for you this great concerted number or any other music you wish to hear.

Victor Talking Machine Co., Camden, N. J., U. S. A.
Berliner Gramophone Co., Montreal, Canadian Distributors

Victrolas $15 to $200   Victors $10 to $100

New Victor Records demonstrated at all dealers on the 28th of each month

"Mention the Geographic—It identifies you."

4.2   Victor advertisement showing Enrico Caruso and others listening to a recording, from *National Geographic Magazine*, 1914.

ucts. Lawrence W. Levine has written of the campaign waged by the journalist, critic, and editor John Sullivan Dwight, who was a tireless champion of classical music not only for itself but also as something sacred. Dwight was instrumental in the founding, reflecting those ideals, of the Boston Symphony in 1881, aided by a sympathetic financial backer, Henry Lee Higginson (Levine 1988). The point here is that the sacralization of western European classical music that now goes largely unquestioned by most in American university music departments and concertgoers is actually a regime of value with a history—and a fairly recent one, at that. Victor and other record labels drew on this history in the consecration of some of their products. This is the sort of noneconomic form of value created in noncapitalist social relations that capitalism requires not just for its continued hegemony but for its existence. Supply-chain capitalism in the sales and distribution of recordings draws not only on various nodes in the chain to create value; some of those nodes are dedicated to making commodities seem to be gifts again.

Brands and Branding as Modes of Enhancing Forms of Economic Value

Let's move now to branding, which is of course a form of promotion, but also a sort of commercial consecration. What we now call branding began in the late nineteenth to early twentieth centuries, mainly as a form of distinctive packaging, a way for consumers to distinguish easily between different products on store shelves (Moor 2007). The rise of inventory creates the necessity for producing differences, illusory or not, between one firm's inventory and another's. Capitalism requires these sorts of distinctions, and we have seen them already with respect to record labels or lines within labels, such as Victor's Red Seal. But in the 1930s and 1940s, advertisers and their agencies began to realize that it might be possible to produce psychologically closer relationships between consumers and brands (see Taylor 2012). By the 1960s, particularly after the publication of some influential articles (Gardner and Levy 1955; Levy 1964) and changes in market research (see Taylor 2012), brands in some ways became seen by consumers as more important than the products themselves. The process that makes this all happen became known as "branding," which is analyzed and proselytized in a massive number of works in the advertising and marketing trade press and which is beginning to be taken seriously by scholars (some cited previously). It has become, as Jean Baudrillard once observed, the "principal concept of advertising" (Baudrillard 1988). I will reserve the term *branding* to refer to this more recent phenomenon, viewing usages of the term before the 1960s (e.g., Vazsonyi 2010) as anachronistic, referring more accurately to forms of self-promotion and publicity that have a much longer history that continues to the present.

Today, branding is a concerted industrial effort to use the apparatus of advertising and marketing (and polling and the use of focus groups, cool-hunting and trendspotting firms, ethnography, and more) to attempt to create personal connections between consumers and commodities. Commodities are animated, and consumers are encouraged to think of them almost as friends or confidants, part of their social worlds. Branding in effect is a kind of further heightening of the fetishism of the commodity, in which the actual but unperceived social relations that went into its production are not revealed but are replaced with social relations manufactured by advertising agencies and others. Such processes can be used for all commodities, and cultural commodities are no exception. It has become routine to speak of musicians and bands as brands, of their "brand image," and of what is good or not good for their brand (see Taylor 2016b).

There is today a massive apparatus available to be deployed to create noneconomic forms of value for cultural commodities. Some of this is fairly rudimentary marketing and publicity, but some of it could also be considered branding. According to the International Federation of the Phonographic Industry (IFPI), marketing and promotion are the biggest expense in "breaking" (introducing) a new artist to the public, a process that creates a fan base and opportunities for merchandising and touring. It costs roughly $1 million to break an artist. Table 4.1 shows how IFPI details the costs.

Marketing and promotion can be anywhere from about a quarter to a third of this budget, and, as many have argued, music videos—another significant chunk of the budget—are really nothing more than advertisements for recordings and could just as easily be counted in the marketing and promotion budget. In film, the increase in marketing costs is even more dramatic: in 1980, the average cost of marketing a studio film in the United States was about $4.3 million (almost $16 million today). By 2007, that figure was almost $36 million (about $53 million today), a figure that has become standard (McClintock 2014). Another statistic tells a similar story: in 2008, the average cost of producing a film was $106.6 million, $70.8 million of which was for production costs and $35.9 million, or roughly a third, of which was for advertising and marketing (Friedman 2008).

Early efforts to brand musicians were not based on their practices as musicians but were instead endeavors to cobrand them with other commodities, the recording business perhaps being savvy enough to let consumers form their own emotional connections with music and musicians they liked. Probably still the best example is a series of commercials for Pepsi featuring

Table 4.1   Typical investment by a major record company in a newly signed artist

Advance	US$200,000
Recording	US$200,000–$300,000
Two or three videos	US$50,000–$300,000
Tour support	US$100,000
Marketing and promotion	US$200,000–$500,000
TOTAL	**US$750,000–$1.4 million**

Source: IFPI 2012, 11.

Michael Jackson in the 1980s (see Love 2015). In 1997, *Billboard* reported that Sony Music's arm Sony Signature Music (SSM), founded four years earlier, was attempting to cobrand its stars with all sorts of merchandise, "taking recording artists' images, logos, and even their names far beyond concert souvenir stands to shelves in department and specialty stores across the globe" (Kaplan 1997, 59). Dell Furano, CEO of SSM, said, "Our goal is very simple: We have to bring in more value to the artist than simply selling their merchandise at concerts" (Kaplan 1997, 59). Clients of SSM included artists that weren't signed to Sony.

The company licensed music and genres as part of a strategy it called Totally Integrated Music Marketing (TIMM), which combined live events, retail merchandising, radio, sponsorships, and commercial endorsements, all designed to generate nontour revenue (Kaplan 1997, 59). The initial aim was to earn $500,000 annually for artists in royalties from licensing; Furano hoped to reach $3 to $4 million eventually, by developing products sold at major retailers and elsewhere (Kaplan 1997, 59). He wanted to move beyond merchandising of common items such as T-shirts and move into entire lines of clothing and "apparel accessories"—backpacks, bandanas, hats, jewelry, scarves, shoelaces, umbrellas, slippers, wallets, and purses. And then there were housewares—lamps, sheets, blankets, curtains, glassware, shot glasses, towels, and more. According to Furano, "Just think of any accessory in the licensing industry that's been exploited somewhat, some way, with something" (Kaplan 1997, 59).

Sony's SSM subsidiary had three different options they could pursue in linking clients to brands. One was through imagery, employing the artist's logo or signature, such as the Grateful Dead red and blue skull (the Dead were clients). Another approach was to find a manufacturer to create a line of a product, such as Toni Braxton jewelry, and match that product with what were thought to be the performer's qualities—in Braxton's case, "her sassiness, her appeal, her sexiness, her sophistication" (Kaplan 1997, 59). This strategy was not intended to be very overt, but simply an association of a client with a brand. Kristine Ross, SSM's vice president of worldwide licensing and marketing, said, "It becomes more of a branding issue than having the product itself actually say Toni on it" (Kaplan 1997, 60).

Around the same time, a strategy known as "brand extension" was in use—finding an outside partner, to both "enhance their brand and . . . get our product into the hands of the target market at a low price," according to PolyMedia senior vice president John Esposito (Fitzpatrick 1998, 10). Esposito was speaking specifically of a compilation CD aimed at teen girls that PolyMedia was producing with *Teen* magazine. By the end of the last century, licensing and merchandising in the music business were worth about $5.5 billion in royalties, the result of about $110 billion in retail sales of licensed products, according to Charles Riotto, executive director of the International Licensing Industry Merchandisers Association (Traiman 1999, 63).

Today, guides for budding musicians frequently contain advice about how to create and manage one's brand. These guides, both published (e.g., Tortorella 2013) and online (where they are ubiquitous), articulate the gospel according to today's marketing and advertising business: to stand out in today's crowd, it isn't enough just to be good; you have to have a recognizable brand or "branded image," one that "immediately tells your fans who you are and what you do." This is accomplished in part through the creation of a logo, which allows a band "to instantly gain recognition and set a mood" for its audience. "The more your audience sees your branded image," one website advises, "the more likely you are to gain credibility and earn fans . . . paying fans." More than that, "a branded image establishes you as a legitimate musician and makes it easier for your fans—or 'customers'—to identify with you, and it presents upsell opportunities such as apparel, hats and other merchandise." If you don't have a branded image, you have nothing but a band name, but "with a branded image, you have a unique style that sets you apart from all other musicians." In other words, it's not your music that sets you apart from other musicians, but your branded image, which is created by considering both the genre of music of the band and the fans, "their likes and dislikes, their passions, and what they respond to." And it is important to research your competitors and attempt to figure out how you are different ("Musician Marketing: Branding" n.d.)

In processes of branding, cultural producers can lose control of their own self-representations, their own self-authored forms of publicity and self-promotion, surrendering to an business that specializes in such things. Branding today is really an attempt largely by people external to cultural producers themselves—more nodes in the supply chain—to create non-economic forms of value for cultural producers and their image and work to generate greater profits. It is a recognition that the profit derived from the creation of noneconomic forms of value around an artist can be worth more than whatever profit the artist generates through his or her actual cultural production.

Many have written of how human labor was reconceptualized by propo-nents of neoliberal capitalist ideologies and policies as "human capital," and branding is one manifestation of this shift (see Taylor 2016b). Every pro-motional strategy from the past—merchandising, music videos, and much more—has been pulled in and subsumed under the ideology of the brand, and each is yet another way of employing a form of economic value to (it is hoped) convert noneconomic forms of value into greater profits. Today, most major musicians routinely sign what are known in the business as "360 deals," contracts that cover everything—recordings, touring, merchandise, licensing, guest appearances, and more. Such deals make use of all of the modes of creating and amplifying noneconomic forms of value that I have discussed: they give to those who control the deal a cut of all possible reve-nue streams. All this contributes to the branding of the artist, though many resist, since they realize that the record labels are taking money out of their pockets (see Taylor 2016b). Table 4.2, from a 2013 book on the music busi-ness shows just how many strategies are currently available for the industrial use of economic forms of value to brand artists, and so create, disseminate, and translate noneconomic forms of value into economic forms—many nodes in an almost bewilderingly complex series of supply chains.

It need not be said that the workers who perform the operations laid out in table 4.2 are numerous, and they are increasingly decentered—no longer located at record labels, which have left to musicians themselves many promotional functions that they formerly performed. Musicians to-day are expected to spend a good deal of time on social media, but record

Table 4.2 Layering of texts in musical production

Layer 1	Layer 2	Layer 3		Layer 4	Layer 5
		MERCHANDISE	*News*	**WEBSITE**	**GIGS**
		T-shirts		Newsletters	Stage design
		Sweatshirts		Tour	Lighting
		Hoodies		Record news	Instruments
		Hats		News archive	Equipment
				Talk	Sound mix
SONGS					Movement
Music					Setlist
Lyrics	**COVER ART/ SLEEVE NOTES**	**MUSICAL PRODUCT**	*Creative*	Lyrics	Musical performance
Sounds		Vinyl		Music	
		CD		Art	
	Artwork	Concert DVD			
	Text	Music DVD			**PERSONAL APPEARANCE**
	Lyrics		*Partners*	Side projects	Jewelry
VISUAL IMAGES	Logo				Tattoos
Artwork	Photographs	**MARKETING COMMUNICATIONS**	*Community*	Noticeboard	Piercings
Photographs		Interviews		Links	Clothing
		Posters		Contact	
		Flyers			**MERCH BOOTH**
		Advertisements	*Market*	The Shop	Musical product
		Website			Merchandise
		Social media			

Source: O'Reilly, Larsen, and Kubacki 2013, 136.

labels also employ specialty firms that advertise, brand, or publicize their musicians. The supply chain has grown immensely—perhaps we should call it a supply *web*—creating value at each of many nodes, some of which are concerned with consecration or promotion.

We could just as easily speak of value chains, though perhaps a more apt metaphor would be scenes or situations in which value is in constant motion. A Los Angeles–based music publicist who didn't want to be named explained the complex ways that musicians in the indie rock field are related to fans, and how fans in other industries are able to support musicians through brand relationships. The indie rock field, with its dominant noneconomic value of the hip and the cool (see Taylor 2016a), is attractive to many outside the field. This worker's job is to bring brands, musicians, and fans together, commingling noneconomic and economic forms of value, while making noneconomic forms appear to be available outside of the field where they originated. This requires a good deal of effort, part of which is directed at laundering economic value so that it still appears to be authentic and intact as a noneconomic form of value. This publicist told me:

> Indie music in particular is full of creative fans. If you really want to look at the psychographics of someone that listens to a band that's on 4 A.D. [a British indie label], OK, let's look at The National, for instance, one of my favorite bands—seen them a million times. It took The National four records to ever chart. They got a *New York Times* piece about it, for god's sakes. There's a documentary about it. You know the average National ticket is now seventy to eighty dollars, 'cause they're playing these really special things, and they wear rag & bone [designer clothing], the people who go to see them wear rag & bone, the people who go to see them probably have a four-year degree if not more, probably work in the ad or entertainment media space in some capacity, and the ones that probably don't live in metropolitan areas are probably the coolest, most hip people in the area that they live in. And they're drinking twenty-five-dollar bottles of wine, because he's drinking a twenty-five-dollar bottle of wine onstage. And there's a science to that, there's a methodology to that, and there's a longevity that comes from that as well. The people that follow that type of artist are the people that have disposable incomes, so it makes sense for a tech company to want to back them. It makes sense for rag & bone, which makes a two-hundred-dollar T-shirt, to

back them, because at the end of the day, you've really hit on something, because people want to feel cool, they want to feel a part of something. And the psychology behind that is never going to go away. (Anon., interview, 2014)

So, we have an indie band with a lot of credibility—a noneconomic value—that has achieved some degree of success and wears expensive clothes supplied by a hip brand, clothes that are copied by their fans (see Zemler 2013), who also drink wine that is consumed by the band. The National has such a reputation for being independent that it is effectively inoculated against whatever negative impression might arise from being seen as promoting commodities, with the result that The National essentially launders those goods, turning them from commodities with economic value into signs of indie credibility, a noneconomic form of value important in the indie rock world. In a sense, these goods are actively "untranslated" or "retranslated," to refer back to Tsing's framework—transformed from commodities to signifiers of indie insiderness, of hipness, that represent something other than their commodity status, having been reinjected into a world as social values.

Conclusions

I have attempted to show that what is usually called "commodification" is, as Tsing argues, a process of translation, of taking something produced in a system of noneconomic (or noncapitalist) social relations and transforming it into a commodity bearing economic value. This process can occur through the workings of what she calls supply-chain capitalism, and there are many examples in the history of the music business that bear out this argument. There are also many examples of how economic forms of value are created through processes of consecration and promotion. One could argue that the labor theory of value underlies all of these forms of the creation of economic value, but this, I would say, risks reductionism and the distraction of a red herring. Our focus, as Tsing writes, should be on these processes of translation and, I am adding, consecration and promotion, which can perform translation work as well.

While one could conclude that capitalism has become ever more efficient at locating the next big thing from which to profit, I will instead recall Tsing

(2013) one last time, in particular her very useful point that capitalism is not total, even if, I would say, it is increasingly hegemonic. And it relies, as it has always done, on noncapitalist modes of production, as well as the employment of noneconomic forms of value, in fields of cultural production and in other fields. Thanks to Marx and those after him, there has been a tendency to think of modes of production in terms of historical succession ("precapitalist," "capitalist," and so forth). But capitalism's very existence produces—even cultivates—other modes of production that are symbiotic with it (see Gibson-Graham 2006). Today, many noneconomic forms of value are co-opted to be used by capitalism as economic forms, while still retaining their facade as noneconomic forms—if they can even be considered to be distinct forms of value in fields of cultural production. Labor can be expended to convert noneconomic forms to patently economic forms, but it can also be dedicated to make noneconomic forms appear to be more separate from economic forms in order to preserve the value of those economic forms, as the anonymous publicist's story illustrates. Capitalism appropriates, and creates, different forms of value that are constantly in circulation and constantly in processes of translation, untranslation, and retranslation. Through supply-chain capitalism and these forms of translation, capitalism takes the gift out of the commodity, alienates labor, and masks social relations, but through advertising, marketing, and branding, it adds simulacra of the gift, unalienated labor, and social relations, to make the commodity appear to be a gift again.

Maintenance and Destruction of an East-Side Los Angeles Indie Rock Scene

This chapter is based on an ethnographic project in a particular corner of the indie rock scene on the east side of Los Angeles centered in a neighborhood called Echo Park.[1] While the Echo Park scene is diverse in many ways—in terms not just of musical style but also of race, gender, ethnicity, and economics—this chapter focuses on musicians and small, independent label owners (some individuals are both) who are mostly white millennials (born 1981–1996). The musicians and label owners in this subscene all play or promote what is identifiably rock music rather than more marginal kinds of independent music. Most of the labels are tiny, with not many more than a handful of releases, though there are a couple of behemoths in the scene (discussed in Taylor 2020).

What struck me about this part of the scene, apart from questions about social class (also discussed in Taylor 2020), was the relative absence of money in circulation; most people had day jobs, some music-related, some humble. In part because of the lack of music-generated money in circulation, there was a marked casualness toward money; there seems to be little or no need to keep close track of it when there is so little. Bands were generally paid $35–40 for a gig, and, as one person told me, "Sometimes you might get a beer if you're lucky, or you might not get a beer" (S. Brown, interview, 2018). Musicians might make as much as $100 if they could attach themselves to a headliner act. If a band had a record deal with one of the small independent labels, it was a fifty-fifty sort of arrangement, in which the label first recoups its expenditures and then splits profits equally with the band. Musicians usually bore the cost of making their recordings and brought them to the label, so the label's up-front expenses were the actual production of the recording, whether on cassette, vinyl, or CD. It was also striking that the lack of predominance of capitalist economic exchanges meant that other sorts of exchanges were necessary for sustaining this part of the scene (see Ochoa Gautier 2013 on small, local music scenes). I view these other forms of exchange as producing the sorts of value that capitalism relies on, as many have argued, though my focus here is more on these noncapitalist forms of value and exchange and their relationship to capitalism and less on what is actually exchanged.[2] I am also concerned with how these musicians serve, in a way, as the reserve army of labor for the capitalist music business.

In what follows, I conceptualize this part of the scene not so much as a scene (Straw 1991), a subculture (most famously Hebdige 2012; but see also Thornton 1996), a "little culture" (a concept from McCracken 1997 that I have employed in the past), or even a field of cultural production (Bourdieu 1993; for that, see Taylor 2020). Instead, since I am concerned, as I have been for some time, with the workings of capitalism, I have come to conceptualize this scene more generally as a kind of domestic community, in the sense theorized by some French Marxist anthropologists in the 1970s, particularly Claude Meillassoux (1981). That is, if capitalism, especially in the age of imperialism, was an urban-centered phenomenon that drew on colonialized rural villagers for labor power, we can theorize such scenes as Echo Park's as an enclaved community similar to Meillassoux's domestic community, where noncapitalist forms of value and exchange are common and on which capitalism draws. Capitalist and noncapitalist modes of the production of value are caught up in a complex structure in which the former maintains the latter, but this very maintenance actually destroys the essence of the enclaved community by violating its independence from capitalism. This is quite a different way of understanding such scenes. The common "folk" interpretation of the relationship of indie scenes to mainstream ones—or, for that matter, of struggling musicians more generally to successful ones (an interpretation to which I, like most of us, have subscribed for years without much questioning)—is one overly focused on individuals, on the assumption that there are varying degrees of "talent" out there and that while many musicians work hard, it is only through hard work combined with personal connections, perseverance, and luck (in varying amounts) that some people are able to make a living at music, or even become stars.

The overall schematization of this scene that I will argue for in what follows is that this and other small, localized scenes are in many ways akin to the sort of agrarian domestic community theorized by Meillassoux, existing in a structure of capitalism and noncapitalism in which capitalism treats noncapitalist modes of the production of value as a reserve, which it constantly maintains and destroys, since people don't generate enough money to maintain, much less grow, the community. The capitalist music business treats this and similar scenes as sources of primitive accumulation, where what is thought to be talent and cultural production more generally can be "discovered" by a capitalist entrepreneur who has conceived of a way to profit from them; workers are in much the same subordinated and exploited position as the colonialized subjects described by Meillassoux, though with one major difference: as mainly middle-class people, they have made a choice to do what they do.

My main theoretical concern is to explore the capitalist-noncapitalist relationship as a structure by examining the forms of exchange and production of value in the scene that can be exploited by an entrepreneurial capitalist. I agree with J. K. Gibson-Graham (2006), Anna Tsing (2013, 2015), and others that capitalism relies on noncapitalist forms of the production of value. But there are fewer examinations of the structural relationship between capitalist and noncapitalist modes of the production of value in an urban arena of cultural production.[3] That is my focus in this chapter.

Echo Park as an Enclaved Community

Let me first examine the claim that this scene (or almost any indie scene) can be understood as akin to a domestic community not unlike Meillassoux's, though his is predicated on the idea that the workers he studies are agrarian. Otherwise, his characterization is apt for the Echo Park scene, where these workers "produce and consume together" and "are linked together by unequal ties of personal dependence." And, Meillassoux says, "within this community only use-value emerges" (1981, 3). But the differences between Meillassoux's agrarian, rural workers and my middle-class urban workers is great enough that I employ the term "enclaved community" rather than "domestic community," though the similarities are nonetheless striking.

The Community

People involved in this scene speak of the community aspect of it—all of the face-to-face interactions that occur—which is the basis for most forms of exchange and value production. Michael Fiore of the band Criminal Hygiene talked about working as a pizza delivery person in Silver Lake (near Echo Park on the east side) that is very flexible about letting people find a substitute if they need to play a show or go on tour: "Everyone's behind each other, everyone's friends, so if someone has a show, I'll cover him, because then I know when I have a show, he'll cover me" (Fiore, interview, 2014).

It's not just a community of musicians. A music supervisor who didn't want to be named told me:

> We are definitely part of the scene, in that we love the community. I can talk for hours about how I love Echo Park as a whole as a creative space. I've only ever lived in Echo Park, Silver Lake, and Venice, and I love both places just because there is an actual feeling of community there and I think that lends itself well to the incubation of creativity, and creative spaces, and that includes music spaces.
>
> It's just a very close-knit community, and that's one of the best things about it. In the music industry, everybody just knows each other. (Anon., interview, 2014)

This music supervisor says that having lived outside of Echo Park for a time, living there now helps her appreciate the community feeling:

> I lived in LA a little over seven years. The last three years living in Echo Park was the first time I felt like I had a community of friends. And so for me the music thing in Echo Park is just part of the package of EP: the music, the food, the coffee shops—love that—and the

neighborhood feel, it's all so intertwined that I just love it, everybody fosters everybody, there's such a community support, from the venues to the coffee shops to the touring bands to the bookstores and the music venues—everyone collaborates. There's that community support from the venues, all seem to rally around each other. (Interview, 2014)

The sort of mutual support she identifies is part of the way that value is created in the community, and in the music scene.

Money and Social Meanings

In the economy of the enclaved community of the indie rock scene in east Los Angeles, there is very little money in circulation that has been generated by cultural production, which means that it takes on symbolic meaning: money for gas, money for equipment or equipment repair, and more. Money is frequently thought of in terms of the use-values it facilitates. It is not generally conceptualized in abstract terms; it takes on its own meanings in this community.

Recent anthropological studies of money emphasize that ideas about it are as much a part of a given culture as any other ideas (see, for example, Maurer 2006; Zelizer 1994). Bill Maurer draws on Jonathan Parry and Maurice Bloch, who argue, he says, that "existing world views give 'rise to particular ways of representing money'" (Maurer 2006, 19; Parry and Bloch 1989, 19). And Keith Hart, relying on Georg Simmel's position on money (also adopted by Appadurai [1986a]), writes that the meaning of money is what people make of it: "It is a symbol of our relationship, as an individual person, to the community (hitherto more often singular than plural) to which we belong. This relationship may be conceived of as a durable ground on which to stand, anchoring identity in a collective memory whose concrete symbol is money" (2001, 263).

Whatever form money takes is just as much a part of culture as anything else; people in particular cultures find ways of attaching meanings to money that are not abstract, even though money is usually taken to be abstract. Webb Keane, comparing language to money as two systems of arbitrary signifiers, writes: "Both money and language exemplify an apparently self-contained system of value in which manifest tokens are linked to nonmanifest referents by mere social convention. . . . Money, like language, is not just an arbitrary signifier of some prior and abstract signified, and it does not simply exist within a bounded and autonomous structure of homogenous (or at most, dualistic) character" (2008, 30).

Money lives in social universes, and its apparent abstractness is not total; writes Keane, "The abstractness of money is never, and can never be, as radical as is sometimes claimed, because it requires concrete practical semiotic and therefore social mediation" (2008, 30). Everything people do in this east-side Los Angeles indie music scene is against the perceived abstractness of money. It's simply not the case that money "is" or "isn't" abstract in some ontological sense. These musicians and others in the scene are constantly working to make such questions irrelevant; they are working to make money—and all exchanges—unabstract, real, meaningful, even as they strive to make enough to make a living.

CASUALNESS ABOUT MONEY   While many people in this part of the scene talked a good deal about how little money they could make at music, few complained about their personal financial circumstances. Since, judging by the amount of educational capital they possess, all of the musicians and label owners hail from the middle class, I suspect that they receive support from their parents, or know that they can rely on such support if needed (a suspicion that was verified by one of my interlocutors). This, and the paucity of money in the scene, seems to lead to a casualness about money and makes noncapitalist forms of exchange and value production more common and relevant. Small label owners routinely pay for things out of pocket, take a loss, and overpay their musicians. Money is simply a means of getting things done in the scene, it is not for accumulation. Greg Katz, a musician and label owner, relates: "I started a label three years ago called New Professor. I've got fifteen releases and I've got five or six more coming this year. Some stuff pays money, some stuff doesn't pay money, some stuff pays my bills, some stuff sucks a lot of money out of my bank account, so the value it has in my heart has not much relationship to how much I get paid" (Katz, interview, 2014).

Dean Spunt, a successful musician (as a member of the band No Age) and label owner, said, "I'm not really trying to make money, it's not my interest. I lose money on the label and it's perfectly fine" (Spunt, interview, 2012). Because there is so little money in circulation, and because most of these musicians are part of the same community, it is rare for musicians to sign a contract. Said Spunt:

I take on all the expenses, I don't do contracts, I've done contracts a couple times, not to my label, but if I'm putting out a record and we're licensing it to another label in another country, I've done contracts—only two times, and it's a pain in the ass and I don't like doing it. All of the bands that I've put out are friends, and so I don't really feel the need to make contracts. It's a very open, honest thing. If there's any money that's recouped, it's split fifty-fifty, but most of the time it's not really recouped. I'm giving them free copies to go on tour. So, it kind of comes out in a wash.

If one of his label's bands has a track that is licensed for use in advertising, television, or film (an important revenue stream for musicians today), Spunt says they would follow the fifty-fifty model, which he has done. But "sometimes I've just given the band the money, because they need it, or I don't feel that invested. It's kind of case by case. Maybe not the best business model" (interview, 2012).

Other workers in this scene are just as casual about money. One person who works as a booker (booking bands into venues for shows) doesn't always get paid and doesn't seem to mind:

> I would take a flat rate from the bottom, depending on who I worked with, and how much other work I had to do. If I had to print any posters or anything, or go deal with a manager: "I did all this work, fifty bucks." But everything else goes to them, I pretty much always give to bands, because I just work the doors, and that's I think what we're paid for, so 70 percent to the band and 30 percent to the house is generally it. (Anon., interview, 2014)

Money in this community is only for what it can help you do in the scene and can be a part of the generalized reciprocity on which the scene depends, as I will discuss.

SYMBOLIC VALUE OF SPECIFIC MONETARY AMOUNTS   In the part of the Echo Park scene under consideration here, people attach meanings to specific amounts of money (the pay for a gig, money for gas, money for an electronics purchase or repair); this is the sort of earmarking practice studied by Zelizer (1994). Money was never discussed in abstract terms. Money for gas was a running theme. Fiore, in praise of Katz (whose New Professor label released one of Fiore's band's singles), said, "He's the kind of guy that when you go on tour, he'll donate $30 to your Bandcamp page to help with gas money" (interview, 2014), since $35–$40, the usual payment for a gig, is equivalent to a tank of gas for the band's van (though in southern California, filling a tank actually costs significantly more than that). The fee for a better gig, when there's a headliner, is $100—enough to repair an amplifier. Criminal Hygiene band member Fiore told me that if local musicians in this scene hear of a reasonably well-known band coming to a local venue, and if they hustle, they can be the third band in the show and make $100: "If a show is known to sell out because a headliner is going to sell out, you jump on the bill as the third band of three, then they'll usually give you $100. Which is more than you're ever going to get any other time." Later in the interview he said, "Just repairing an amp can cost $100, that's one night of a show" (interview, 2014).

The music supervisor I interviewed told me that she tries to support the scene by placing songs in films, saying that there is very little money in independent film, and music is usually an afterthought, but she still tries to support local bands as much as possible:

> Now, most filmmakers plan on no money for music, or they're saying, "Maybe we can offer them a hundred bucks." Or, I have worked on a couple indie films where they were saying things like, "This person will give us their song for free." And I always say, "Let's say a hundred bucks," with a hundred bucks they can maybe buy, I don't know, new headphones or like a new cable for their home studio. I think about it that way, for at least a little money, they can do something with that. (Interview, 2014)

Every middle-class person I spoke to in the scene said that they didn't want to make a lot of money, they just wanted to be able to make a living from music (Taylor 2020). I would characterize this professed desire in terms of the symbolic value of money—musicians don't want so much money that it becomes a hoard, an abstract amount. For them, money is for specific things, and, ultimately, for making a living at music. Money is only for the use-values it makes possible.

Value Production and Forms of Exchange

Value is produced in this scene through the myriad forms of noneconomic (or minimally economic) exchange that occur because of the limited amount of money produced by music. Exchanges are largely face-to-face in what is thought of by most participants as a fairly cohesive and supportive community (though record labels ship recordings, of course, and make them available for downloading, so people from around the world can listen to these musicians). But most musicians live, work, and play on the east side of Los Angeles, and while many bands tour, their main locus of activity is fairly restricted, which makes possible a variety of forms of face-to-face exchange. These musicians operate in an informal economy (selling recordings and merchandise at concerts), a system of what Marshall Sahlins (1972) has called generalized reciprocity (by helping touring musicians and hoping for reciprocity), as well as various forms of patronage, whether from major corporations (that want to be seen as cool for supporting indie musicians) or small labels—all in an effort (at least for some musicians) to catapult themselves into the notice of capitalist record labels. All of these forms of exchange are the means by which people in this scene make value for themselves and others in, and sometimes beyond, the scene, and they are the modes of the production of value that are locked in a subordinate structural relationship to capitalism, which, as Meillassoux argues, depends on them. In this section, I'll parse the various forms of exchange and reciprocity upon which this scene relies.

Generalized Reciprocity

Because of the community aspect of this scene, which is connected to other such scenes (see Hesmondhalgh and Meier 2015) through a common ideology of adherence to a do-it-yourself (DIY) ethic and what is usually characterized as a "fuck-the-man" position, many musicians and label owners speak in terms that exemplify Sahlins's concept of generalized reciprocity, a term that refers to exchanges that are thought to be altruistic, aid given and aid returned, if possible (1972, 193–94). This sort of system of exchange is fairly casual. There may not be any overt reckoning of debts, and an obligation to reciprocate is vague in time, quantity, and quality, and may even never be incurred. Failure to reciprocate doesn't mean that the original giver will stop giving in the future (Sahlins 1972, 194).

But reciprocity is broader than face-to-face interactions within the scene, for these musicians rely heavily on musicians outside of the scene while touring, for gigs and places to crash, which they reciprocate when musicians visit Los Angeles. Fiore of Criminal Hygiene told me how this worked in a tour that occurred not long before our interview:

> The tour started with an invitation to play a festival in Toronto, and then we figured, "OK, what do we have between LA and Toronto?," and then we picked the cities we wanted to hit and then we called up friends if we know any in those cities or just cold-called bookers, promoters, or the venues, and said, "Hey, can we hop on this show? Here's a review, here's what we do, here's what we've done before kind of thing." It's a pain in the ass—it took two months total of constant emailing and calling—but it ended up paying off. (Interview, 2014)

Bands also rely on face-to-face meetings once on the road. Fiore told me, "Usually, wherever we're playing, we'll meet someone, or they'll invite us over; if we're playing with a band we know from that area we'll just crash with them, or sometimes we'll just crash in the van" (interview, 2014). Katz told me,

> I throw a lot shows for out-of-town bands on tour, stuff like that, especially because sometimes I'm on the other end of it, so I know when somebody's emailing you it's a mixture of hope and desperation. It's like, "Hi, I'm from Asheville, North Carolina, and I'm really looking for a gig in LA." I know I can do it, I don't know who else they are going to reach out to and whether or not that person can do it, so I try to help out as much as I can. Some of it's just in karmic hope that it comes back to me out of sheer compassion. (Interview, 2014)

As a label owner, Katz says that he feels a heightened responsibility: "I'm differently positioned personally because I have a label, I work in the industry, and I play in a band, so it's kind of like any good thing I can do for anyone that could come back around to me at some point is good, so I'm really not picky about who I'll help out" (interview, 2014). And, he said, "I have no problems pushing people who I think are amazing. I do that because I love the music but also because I might reap some benefit from it down the line" (interview, 2014).

Reciprocity such as this is of the sort theorized by Claude Lévi-Strauss in *The Elementary Structures of Kinship* (1969) as generalized exchange, in which exchanges can occur on a broad scale as no one necessarily gives back to the person from whom they received, but rather everyone is part of a larger system in which one person gives to X, and X gives to Y, and Y gives to Z, and then perhaps Z gives to X. Generalized exchange depends on the existence of a community in which people who don't necessarily know each other nonetheless participate in exchanges and reciprocations.

Informal Economy

There is also an informal economy at work in the scene. There are no contracts for gigs, and there aren't always contracts for recordings, as I have discussed, so a good deal of money in the scene changes hands informally. Musicians might receive free food and perhaps a beer when they play a gig.

Additionally, musicians sell their recording and other merchandise ("merch"), such as T-shirts, at shows, and their concerts on tours are generally one-offs, so do not achieve the sort of scale necessary to consider them as capitalist enterprises. These sorts of supportive purchases grow out of the community aspect of the scene. Even on tour, when visiting musicians might not know the local musicians, the principle of generalized exchange obtains—local bands will show up to hear visiting bands and will purchase recordings and merch.

Forms of Patronage

Several forms of patronage exist in the scene, some of which grow in part from the support that community members want to show each other.

LABEL PATRONAGE   What struck me about my interviews with label owners is that most of them also profess a casualness about money—they were willing to spend their own, up to a point, and be generous to their musicians—but also that labels would help their musicians move to the next level in the business by signing with a bigger label, getting a manager, a publicist, or attaining some other marker of continuing professionalization and success. This chapter has discussed casualness with money in the scene generally, but it is no different with labels. Label owners might be careful with money because they don't have much of it, but at the same time, they are willing to help out their musicians.

Label owners will sometimes put up their own money, as Katz of New Professor said above. Kat Bee of the label Summer Bummer, who had a day job, said the same thing: "I'm kind of allowing myself the option of being really choosey, which a lot of labels don't, and that's just to keep myself safe because I also don't have a huge financial backing, I'm just paying for this out of my own pocket, which some labels don't, and that's awesome. I wish I had someone backing me, but I don't, so I have to be really picky about who I work with" (Bee, interview, 2014).

Katz said, "It's really hard for a small indie label to sell records, but ultimately, with New Professor, it's about providing a platform for artists with a vision, to reach a little larger audience and, more altruistically as a patron, helping them find the funding and the people, the team to put a record out and have a bigger, longer career." He told me,

> The label has a special place with its artists to act kind of like a manager or older brother—just to do things that you couldn't do yourself, to connect you with people that you couldn't connect with yourself. And so that's really what I bring to it. The record is a keepsake of the help I was able to give, and if one of the records breaks and the bands and I get rich, then great. Sometimes I'll do a publishing deal with one of the bands on the label and they'll get thousands of dollars in advances and I'll get zero dollars, but that's just like a good thing that I can bring to them that they can't bring to themselves. (Interview, 2014)

The recording is a token of the value of this exchange relationship.

For Katz, New Professor "plugs the gaps"—if the band needs a producer, he can do that or find someone who will and cover the cost (interview, 2014). Beyond a producer, there are a number of other professionals that artists might not have, so Katz will hire them—a publicist, a publisher—and help to produce a demo, press the vinyl, launch a press campaign, help the band book a tour. Katz gave an example of how he was able to help a band move to the next level: Fiore's band Criminal Hygiene didn't have a manager or publicist or anybody working for them. So, Katz, said, "We did a seven-inch [single] and got particularly good placement in advertisements and web series and stuff like that and were able to make the band a couple bucks. They found a great manager after that, did some tours, and did some really cool shows. That's kind of the dream for the label, to find smaller bands and give them some opportunities" (Katz 2016 [lecture]).

Most of these labels operate on a fifty-fifty model. Summer Bummer works this way, and this is one area where Bee says she is not casual about money, in part because she wants her musicians to get what her label owes them, and because she views it as an opportunity to motivate the band, perhaps encouraging them to be more professional: "Every sale I have to keep track of because I want it to be transparent for the bands, too, because I want them to get paid, I want them to see how on track we are, because they have to hustle, too, that's part of the deal. If I'm going to put up all the money and all this back-end work into it, then the bands have to help me hustle when the record's actually out, they have to help me sell stuff" (interview, 2014). This sort of hustling is one way that label owners (and managers and publicists) help bands professionalize in the hopes of moving up to the next level—a bigger label, more lucrative tours, placements in film, television, or advertising (see Taylor 2020 for more on professionalization).

RETAIL PATRONAGE   Integral to the east-side Los Angeles scene and community when I studied it was a record store called Origami Vinyl, located in the heart of Echo Park. This shop helped musicians in the community not only by stocking their recordings but also by hosting in-store events for bands. Neil Schield, owner of Origami, which was founded in 2007, told me:

> The shop, to be quite honest, is a break-even venture. I work for free, which is fine—it's my dream, and I'm fine with that. All the money goes back into buying new records every week, or paying our employees—there's really no profit. I think last year we even ran at a slight loss. So, that's not what it's about. We built an online store a year ago to help with that, because we're limited by what our square footage is, we can only make so much money off of the racks here, so you have to increase somehow, and I've no interest in blowing out this wall and moving into a bigger space or anything like that. I think it would destroy what we do. (Schield, interview, 2014).

Schield, who had a day job working at a recording studio, told me that he doesn't only purchase local bands' recordings to sell, he also hosts them at live events in the store to help promote recent releases:

Local bands, there's always room for them, and if they've gotten to a point where they're bigger than bringing their own records in for consignment, then I will generally look for that. If they've put something out, I will always order a copy or two to have in the shop, just to keep supporting our neighborhood and the music that's coming out, since generally if they're from here, people come looking for it here. We have a band called White Arrows coming in here tomorrow, they're a local band that's shot up a little bit, recent times, and they're going to come in and hang out and have pizza and listen to the record and presell the record, and it's kind of a cool thing to do around their new record to support it. (Interview, 2014)

A couple of years after this interview the shop closed, because it wasn't sustainable economically (see A. Brown 2016).

CORPORATE PATRONAGE Forms of corporate patronage might seem to be more remote from this intensely local community, but there are many people who are happy to affiliate themselves with corporate entities since there is so little money circulating in the scene.

An increasing number of corporations want to affiliate themselves with youth thought to be hip or cool, not just as a way of selling more goods but in order to make their brands seem hip and cool and thus increase their value (see Carah 2010; Foster 2013; Taylor 2016a), and so they offer ways for bands to record their music gratis. Converse (the sneaker company), Lagunitas Brewing Company, Mountain Dew, Red Bull, and other corporations have launched various programs to record and foster musicians. In an era when the advertising, marketing, and branding industries understand that millennials don't like being targeted, this is a way to employ, as an article in *Billboard* about this trend put it, an "anti-branding music branding strategy" (Hampp 2011).

Converse began a program called Rubber Tracks in 2011 by opening a recording studio in Brooklyn, and in 2015 it expanded in and outside of the United States by opening more studios and forging agreements with existing studios ("Converse Goes Global" 2015). Musicians can apply to be selected to record or edit a few tracks in the studio, gratis. There is a brief questionnaire on the brand's website to sign up your band, along with FAQs.[4]

Nima Kazerouni of the band So Many Wizards applied to Rubber Tracks, and I discussed the experience with him and two of his bandmates, Martin

Tomemitsu and Eric Felix, after a show at the Converse store on the Third Street Promenade (a major retail site) in Santa Monica.

> **Nima** It's cool, they just let you record in a really awesome studio in downtown LA, and—
>
> **Martin** —and they pay for it.
>
> **Nima** They pay for it, it's a great studio, great engineers.
>
> **Erik** I didn't bring any drums, they had an amazing drum set, amazing cymbals. It was perfect.
>
> **Nima** And then you get the file at the end, and you can do what you want with it.

I asked if Converse wanted anything in return, and Martin said that they can use the track for promotional purposes. Nima told me that after they finished their recording sessions, the Rubber Tracks people asked them if they wanted to be part of a recording shared with another band (a split seven-inch), which they agreed to do, adding, "They've been generous. This, actually, believe it or not, pays—it's great." This seems to have helped the band earn favor with Rubber Tracks, which, according to Martin, "has put the word out for us since that happened." "Fostering some stuff for us," Nima added. The band retains the copyrights to their songs, and if Converse wants to use a track for promotional purposes, it pays the band. Nima said, "They just have it in their library, and they like to be able to say, 'Oh, this band is a Converse Rubber Tracks alum, we know these guys.'" And it's cool. We like them, because we wear Converse, we get free Converse." "Yeah," Erik said, "I'll wear free shoes." The musicians sported the shoes they were given before their show started (So Many Wizards, interview, 2014).[5]

All of these forms of value production and exchange occur in the community and contribute to its functioning. They create value by allowing the musicians to practice their art, perfect their craft, gain exposure, build audiences, become accustomed to live performances, and gain experience in the recording studio, in the process trying to build their potential economic value to a point where it might attract the attention of someone in the capitalist music business.

The Relationship between Capitalist and
Noncapitalist Modes of the Production of Value

All of these forms of value production and exchange exist not just alongside capitalism but in a structural relationship with it. Capitalists conceptualize musicians as possessing varying amounts of a natural resource—talent—which is there for them to extract and mold into a capitalist product: a popular song, a branded band. The people who work in the Echo Park and similar scenes make so little money that it costs the capitalist music business virtually nothing to maintain this reserve army, an endless supply of young people struggling to make a living at music. These musicians are exploited by capitalism even as they are outside of it, trying to get in by trying to make a living at music. In making these points this way, I am again allying myself with Meillassoux.

Meillassoux, who is mainly focused on the colonial and imperial era, argues that the system of capitalist centers and margins he theorizes no longer exists, though newer forms of exploitation and dependency derived from it remain. He writes that the domestic economy's production and reproduction of itself and its refusal to prey on forms of social organization subordinate to it has rendered it vulnerable to exploitation, to the extent that all other economic systems have been built on the domestic economy, from feudalism to capitalism, including slavery. "But," he writes, "crushed, oppressed, divided, counted, taxed, recruited, the *domestic community* totters but still resists, for domestic relations of production have not disappeared completely. They still support millions of productive units integrated to a greater or lesser degree in the capitalist economy, disgorging goods and energy under the crushing weight of imperialism" (Meillassoux 1981, 87; emphasis in original).

This imperialist system described by Meillassoux totters along and continues for workers in urban cultural fields of production in today's neoliberal capitalism. Conversations with musicians in Echo Park make it clear that they are in contact with other indie musicians around the United States, since bands frequently tour, relying on each other to hear about venues, gigs, and places to crash. There is a constant flow of musicians in and out of Los Angeles, and Los Angeles–based musicians themselves tour frequently. They disgorge energy and musical goods, most of which are ignored by the capitalist music business. But this industry profits from scenes such as this by keeping musicians largely unremunerated and impoverished while they hone their craft, build audiences, gain experience performing live and making recordings, creating value that a capitalist might try to exploit.

Primitive Accumulation

Let me explore the question of primitive accumulation, for it is the source of value that is extracted by capitalists in the mainstream music business. Meillassoux says that for Marx, primitive accumulation is an "initial historical phenomenon, the point at which, through the dissolution of feudalism, capitalism takes off" (1981, 105). But after that, primitive accumulation is no longer considered; the capitalist economy grows for internal reasons. Meillassoux says this model doesn't take into account colonialism and imperialism:

> History shows that the free transfer of values of pre-capitalist societies to imperialist powers is a permanent, and until now an accelerating phenomenon, which has continued to feed the capitalist economy from its outset. It is thus not enough to assert that primitive accumulation is a transitory and initiatory phenomenon; it is *inherent* in the process of the development of the capitalist mode of production. (1981, 105; emphasis in original)

In other words, as we know also from Tsing (2013, 2015) and others, capitalism depends—as it always has—on noncapitalist modes of production of value. The primitive accumulation that boosted the rise of capitalism did not end, and neither did it end with the demise of colonialism and imperialism. Meillassoux argues that the relationship of capitalism to noncapitalist modes of the production of value is a continuous process.

Meillassoux also argues that according to Marx it was possible for value to move from one mode of production to another though simple primitive accumulation, "when the transfer is achieved through the destruction of one mode of production by another" (1981, 96). But, he says, there was at the time of Marx's writing no theory to account for how value could be continuously extracted without destroying the mode(s) of production that produced the appropriated forms of value. Meillassoux thus wonders: "In such a case, does the organic whole represent a new mode of production, or must we admit that the previous modes of production survive—and if so, to what extent?" (1981, 96).

Maintenance and Destruction

Here, like Meillassoux, I am interested in how different modes of production interrelate—specifically, how one keeps the other intact but subordinated in order to continuously extract value, a structure that, as he says, had not been theorized (1981, 96). Meillassoux writes that when a domestic mode of production is first put into contact with capitalism, the two are obviously different and separate modes of production, though the dominant one begins to change the other. If domestic relations of production continue, then rural communities remain "qualitatively different from the capitalist mode of production" (1981, 97). But over time, capitalism begins to prevail over social reproduction as a whole: "By this process, contradictory in essence, the domestic mode is simultaneously maintained and destroyed—maintained as a means of social organization which produces value from which imperialism benefits, and destroyed because it is deprived in the end of its means of reproduction, under the impact of exploitation. Under the circumstances the domestic mode of production both exists and does not exist" (1981, 97). Read as a description of how the mainstream, neoliberal capitalist music business coexists with this (or almost any) indie scene, this passage could hardly be improved upon. The (neoliberal, not imperialist) capitalist music business needs the seemingly independent music scenes to make itself seem less commercial and crassly profit-seeking than it actually is, while at the same time infiltrating (as in the Converse case; see also Taylor 2020)—even co-opting—these scenes even as it keeps them impoverished. Simultaneously, people in such scenes go about their business producing music and value desired by the capitalist music business while declaring themselves adherents of the DIY indie values and exhibiting "fuck the man" attitude, all while struggling to reproduce scenes in which little money circulates.

People in this scene work really hard, especially those further away from making a kind of music that might generate commercial interest.[6] Shelina Brown, who is also part of the Echo Park collection of scenes, though not the one under consideration here, spoke of the immense amount of work involved, and her comments are just as relevant to the musicians I have studied here:

> Everyone's always just trying to shift and maneuver and navigate and also diversify a lot through social media to always be present. The more photographs you have of yourself, the more you post on

Instagram every day—it's just promote, promote, promote, so that you increase your chances of making or getting opportunities that will hopefully lead to, like, a career making money. Everyone is just trying to stay relevant and visible as much as possible.

Continuing, she told me,

It's a lot of work. It's a *lot* of work. I mean, you have to adjust, and it's all just DIY, because nobody has any money to pay for photo shoots or videos or anything. So, you just have to find your friends and do it yourself and just keep doing it and doing it. It's a lot of time, a lot of work, and a lot of stuff—it's all the extramusical things that go into a band that is so much work when you're doing it yourself. It's a lot. (Interview, 2018)[7]

While Meillassoux views the domestic system as having largely disappeared, much of what he characterizes as an effect of imperialism seems today more of an effect of capitalism itself, and thus persistent. This relationship, in which dominant capitalism both maintains and destroys noncapitalist modes of the production of value, originated with colonialism, which serves as a kind of prototype for how neoliberal capitalism works in noncolonial situations such as the one described here.

Conclusions

Capitalism relies on its reserve army of laborers when it needs workers, but it also relies on laborers who produce the sorts of noncapitalist value that capitalists also need. These east-side Los Angeles musicians labor not just by making music but by building a following, cultivating relationships in the music business, struggling to make enough money (or showing enough promise) to hire a manager, a publicist, or other professional and secure more lucrative gigs in Los Angeles and on tour.

But capitalists profit. They may rarely profit directly from the music in this scene, but in it they have a reserve army of musicians, and, as in the example of Converse, a reserve of recordings that they are free to use—produced by musicians who are unable to participate in their own reproduction.[8] The scene is maintained in order to sustain the capitalist music business, but it is simultaneously destroyed, since musicians cannot make enough money from music to live on and reproduce their system of the production of value and exchange. Many give up. A very few succeed and, in doing so, leave the scene for the capitalist music business. If we know one thing about popular music scenes, it is this: they don't last.

6

World Music, Value, and Memory

There is a common narrative among many of us who study musics from other cultures or the history of Western music: With the advent or hegemony of capitalism, music became a commodity. And with commodification came the creation of a new form of value, what Marx famously called "exchange-value." But what about before music becomes a commodity, or isn't a commodity any longer? How can we conceptualize its value? Rather than ignoring the value(s) that musical practices were invested with before they entered the capitalist system, or viewing their values as uncomplicated until they are commodities, or viewing their values as uncomplicated because they are commodities, it is much more useful to think in terms of regimes of value (Appadurai 1986a; Myers 2001, 2002). Cultural goods, whether or not they are commodities, circulate in multiple regimes of value, sometimes simultaneously. The movement between regimes, writes anthropologist Fred R. Myers, "is a movement between contexts, reorganizing the values of each" (2002, 360).

The creation of the "world music" "genre" category was, for example, a way of bringing many disparate and unrelated musics into the main regime of value of the Western music business, an economic regime. "Commodification" is what we usually call the complex set of processes by which different regimes of value are subordinated to economic regimes or made commensurate with them. But the strategies, forms, and histories of these value transformations vary considerably from one music to the next; commodification is not a single, or simple, phenomenon. Even after a traditional music has been brought into the realm of "world music"—placed in an economic regime of value—that music can exist in other regimes, and not just its former ones. Any music produced as a commodity can still exist in different regimes of value.

We need to conceptualize better the sorts of values that can be given to music when it is not the result of productive labor in Marx's sense—producing surplus value for capitalists; surely music and other cultural goods that are not the result of productive labor nonetheless possess value (see Lambek 2013). Thus, instead of viewing capitalism as a historical social form that enters the scene and eclipses everything that had gone before, we can begin to understand it as a system of economic value production that competes with existing systems, usually becoming hegemonic, but coexisting and feeding off of other forms of value in complex and never-ending processes.

In anthropology, there have historically been two major ways of comprehending value: as a property of a commodity with use-value and exchange-value, drawing of course on Marx and post-Marxian writings; and as a form of value that accrues from gifts in complex rituals of gift exchange, a conception that goes back to the influential work of Marcel Mauss in the 1920s (Mauss 2016). Briefly recapitulated, Marx posited two forms of the value of commodities: use-value, the utility of a good (whether or not it was a commodity and whether or not it was produced by human labor); and exchange-value, which is a form of value that enters with the rise of capitalism, as goods become commodities produced for the purpose of exchange in a large market. Use-value is heterogeneous, since there are many different uses for many different goods; exchange value is homogenous, measured by the amount of commodities that can be exchanged for another commodity. It is not possible to know or understand use-value through exchange-value, or vice-versa; commodities have a dual character, according to Marx. Additionally for Marx, there was unmarked "value," defined by socially necessary labor time—the labor theory of value. Mauss's perspective was quite different; for him, the rituals of gift exchange and reciprocity were a way of holding society together, a classic functionalist perspective.

Since these writings, some anthropologists have usefully attempted to bring Marxian and Maussian thinking on value closer together. I have been particularly drawn to those authors who conceive of value as being produced by action in a larger sense—that is, action defined not only in terms of labor or gift exchange. David Graeber, for example, writes, "Value is the way our actions take on meaning or importance by becoming incorporated into something larger than ourselves." He continues:

> First, value is the way actors represent the importance of their own actions to themselves as part of some larger whole. . . . Second, this importance is always seen in comparative terms. Some forms of value are seen as unique and incommensurable; others are ranked . . . ; for yet others, such as money in market systems, value can be calculated precisely, so that one can know precisely how many of item A are equivalent to one item B. Third, importance is always realized through some kind of material token, and generally is realized somewhere other than the place it is primarily produced. (2005, 451)

Michael Lambek (2013) makes a similar point about the importance of action, a result of doing, rather than making something, such as a commodity. Drawing on Aristotle's distinction between making and doing and Hannah Arendt's discussion of the distinctiveness of action (in Arendt 1998), Lambek argues for a distinction between labor and action, the latter of which can be a source of value. Lambek seeks to distinguish economic forms of value from noneconomic ones, which he calls ethical; ethical values are incommensurable with economic values. Lambek (2013, 142) helpfully employs a musical example: the difference between playing the violin for one's own pleasure and playing it in order to make a living. Both activities have, or produce, value, but not the same sort of value.

These and other anthropological ideas about value can help us understand the workings of value not only in cultures where capitalism is dominant but also in cultures where capitalism is or was emergent. In both cases, however, we need ethnography (and an appreciation of the forces of history) to understand how precisely people conceptualize value and act on their conceptions of it. I am thus, as I have written elsewhere (Taylor 2017), construing these recent anthropological discussions of value as extending Clifford Geertz's (1973) argument that ethnography should be concerned with what is meaningful for social actors. But many studies of music reproduce over and over the same themes about the role played by music in pre- or noncapitalist culture as well as capitalist ones, reliably (and predictably) concluding that music is an expression of identity, or that music creates or reinforces community, or that music produces solidarity, or that music "expresses" culture, and so on. Most such interpretations are functionalist. Many music studies seem to me to be in the place occupied by anthropology once described by Geertz with respect to the study of religion: "in a state of general stagnation," because the field continued to produce "minor variations on classical theoretical themes." Geertz concluded his critique by writing that studies that repeat what is already known "may well finally convince a great many people, both inside the profession and out, that anthropologists are, like theologians, firmly dedicated to proving the indubitable" (1973, 88).

For Geertz, the way beyond this stagnation was to focus on what was meaningful for social actors, which remains a compelling solution. But it needs to be combined not just with Geertzian (and updated Geertzian) conceptions of culture, apprehended ethnographically or historically. Thinking about value helps us attend to questions of meaning. And considering musical activity as a form of action, a kind of medium of value (Graeber 2001) helps direct attention toward the perspective of the social actors involved.

The Irish Traditional Music Session and Sociality

Let me turn now to a "world music" practice that I know quite a bit about, and for which I also possess ethnographic data apart from my own long experience—the Irish traditional music session. "Session" refers to an informal gathering of musicians playing Irish traditional dance music, usually in pubs, but occasionally in people's homes (a "house session"). Sessions are informal; they are not concerts, and they are seen by musicians as different from gigs, which are paid engagements. The development of the session is fairly recent, an effect of the revival of Irish traditional music in the twentieth century (Hamilton 1999). Since then, Irish music has occasionally been commodified, as represented by some of the major bands, such as the Bothy

Band, Altan, Dervish, and others, and, perhaps most visibly, by the River-dance show and the proliferation of recordings of "Celtic" music. But most Irish traditional music, such as sessions, remains largely outside economic regimes of value, though many practitioners hope to be able to make a living from their music, an elusive goal even for some professional-level players.

Virtually all the literature about sessions focuses on questions of how they build or maintain community (e.g., the session is a "ritual of sharing in which the values of the community are enacted" [Reiss 2003, 148]), or how they produce or maintain identity, or how they are exercises in the maintenance of status (e.g., "The musical behaviour in a session is largely controlled by the relative status of the people playing, with the higher status musicians exercising more control over the way the session develops. Status is conferred by such factors as instrument played, ability, reputation, and age" [Hamilton 1999, 346]).[1]

But these are all functionalist interpretations, which are, as I have said, still the norm in many music studies. And they might all be plausible interpretations as far as they go; the means by which ethnicized, racialized, or other marginalized groups can effect a sense of solidarity is not something I would want to minimize. But, following Geertz, we should ask: Why do people do what they do? Why is it meaningful to them? People don't play in sessions to maintain status hierarchies, or to express an ethnic or cultural identity. They do it for reasons that are meaningful to them. Asked most simply, what is it that musicians value in Irish traditional music sessions? In a word, sociality.

Over twenty years ago, I conducted a small ethnographic project on the traditional Irish music scene in Ann Arbor, Michigan, of which I was a part. I never published that paper, but the voices of the people I interviewed remain with me, for they spoke in powerful and very personal ways about what playing this music meant to them—and continues to mean, at least for those with whom I am still in contact. All the musicians I interviewed then, and all of the musicians I have interviewed more recently, discussed sociality and the communal aspect of playing. Many said something along the lines of having been attracted to the music because of the music (no one I interviewed is ethnically Irish, or if they are, only minimally so and not Irish-identified, and no one grew up hearing or playing the music), but then found that it was the sociality of the scene and the session that kept them coming back.

I should admit here that ethnographic interviewing is always a tricky business. Do the following interviews represent the "real" feelings of my consultants? Whether or not they do, it is important to remember that the aim of ethnography is to uncover not necessarily what is true but rather what one's interlocutors find meaningful. Dissembling reveals what one is invested in, just as telling the truth does, whether one employs a discourse of sociality or of something else.

Pam, a fiddler who is not of Irish heritage, told me:

> I play Irish music for the social aspect—to meet other musicians and Irish people whether they're players or not. I really enjoy the Irish community. I've found that the people are really nice. And it's an ongoing thing, I've found, year in and year out—that you're part of them and they'll invite you and that they'll keep in contact over the years.
>
> You go to an Irish establishment, quote unquote, in the United States—I can feel at home. It's a place where I can know and be known, and understand and be understood on personal levels. When I meet people from Ireland or Scotland who live the music I feel such an instant love for them, and they with me. And it's so instantly reciprocal that it's astounding to me. I don't know, maybe it's a vibe I put out or whatever, I mean, I love this community so much that I just walk in with valentines, you know, and they just pick up on that.

She continued,

> I get sentimental, and I never used to. It's like, this is my music, these are my people. I feel like I've grown into it, earned it, lived it. I have a home here. It's a very unique feeling. It's something I didn't grow up with. I can go in to any bar playing the songs I know and the songs I love and feel comforted—real comfort, just real peacefulness. I understand the music, I know the music, and I feel I know the people playing the music even if we've never met. It's family you know, it's just like a family, with some of the headaches. A lot more comfort and a lot less headaches than a real family. (Interview, 1991)[2]

Suzanne, a young tin whistle player told me: "I like very much the community aspect of it. It's so different to just be part of a group that's making music and just playing along, and not to have to be a virtuoso like in the music school. I was really struck, too, by how generous the musicians are, how generous they are in sharing their knowledge" (interview, 1991).

The musicians with whom I currently play in southern California, over two decades later and across the continent, articulate the same ideas.[3] Fiddler Melanie Nolley told me:

> I heard something recently about studies that showed that when people get together and do something in a group—I don't know that it was specifically music that they were talking about—but they said that when people get together and engage in a community social activity their heartbeats line up. And I can only imagine that's only what happens when we're in a session. You know that moment when everybody exhales at exactly the same time? When the set [of tunes] is over? That's the power of playing with other people. It's magical, it's really magic. You really do feel better. I feel better when I'm done. (Nolley, interview, 2013)

Flute and tin whistle player Peri Holguin echoed the importance of the synergy that occurs at sessions, which has become more of a draw than the music itself:

> What I've learned is that this music—even though I guess I will always want to learn these kind of tunes—is that it's not necessarily about the music but it's now ended up being more about the people that I play with. And the idea that you can just come down and you can just sit down and just play, with no [printed] music—it's an amazing thing, and I think that's really what—I think that's what drives a lot of people. It's just more of just coming together and having fun, and getting that synergy going, and playing.

Elaborating, Peri continued,

> There's nothing to me like when we're all playing and there's that groove that just kicks in, and everybody is smiling or their eyes are rolling back in their heads, and everybody knows where everybody is, and maybe it's in tune, maybe it's not, but the flow, I guess, is there. And that's awesome, there's very few things that could match that experience. (Holguin, interview, 2013)

Fiddler Jackie Lang also commented on the social aspect of the scene: "Somehow the music itself is very social, you go to this and you get ideas from other people's playing, and you get tunes from them, and so it's not just that there are people and there is music, but it's that they are very much intertwined" (Lang, interview, 2013).

And tin whistler and concertina player LeeAnn Gorne also spoke about sociality:

> The thing that makes you want to improve, even more than being attracted to the music, is the idea that you're going to be making music with other people. When I was young I was so shy, and I didn't know how to socialize with other people, really. I would just stand around in a bar with a drink in my hand, trying to make conversation with people and it was just excruciating, you know. Now, my chosen social venue makes sense for my personality—you go, and you do what you know how to do. And there's a system to it, there's rules, and kind of an organization to the afternoon, and you can have beautiful music as well, and you get to chat with people, but there's a purpose to it, you know? And that socially makes sense to me. (Gorne, interview, 2013)

Irish traditional music at sessions, like many musics made by amateurs for their own pleasure, can thus be characterized as a form of musicalized sociality, but within the larger sociality, what the Irish call the *craic* (pronounced "crack")—gossip, telling jokes, entertainment, hanging out, fun—of the session.

One of my original interlocutors, a young fiddler named Jim, made an important point about how everyone plays the melody in unison (except a guitarist or other string player who accompanies), which perhaps facilitates the surrender of the self to the group, in what Charles Keil has memorably called "the urge to merge" (Keil and Feld 1994, 98):

> With *céilí* [Irish dance] music, because of the nature of it—everyone playing in unison—there's a certain amount of communication that's going on that's really intense in some ways, you know. And when you're really tuned in with someone else . . . that's the point, that's why we all do it. That's what makes it so great, is the sensation of losing yourself. Well, not even losing yourself, but of participating in this—a real rush—sort of a drug experience. That's probably why we drink so much when we do it. (Interview, 1991)

This temporary loss of a sense of self to the group is one of the most powerful ways that sociality is realized, though it doesn't happen at every session.

Here, one could perhaps make a distinction between what brings people together to play and what they get out of that coming together. But the two are complicatedly intertwined. A typical session involves playing and *craic*. Music is part of this, not separate from it. What might appear to observers to be a poor session because there seemed to be too much talk and not enough music could well have been experienced by the musicians as a good session because of the nature of the talk (see Kaul 2009 for a discussion of *craic* at Irish sessions).[4] Or one could call this, following Durkheim, collective effervescence (Durkheim 1964). The point is, while participating in music might seem to offer something distant from other activities at a session, it is part of the overall activities of the session. It is music that brings people together, but not the only thing that holds them together during a session.

It is perhaps when a stranger visits a session that the communal importance placed on the value of sociality is clearest. A visitor can cause a good deal of instability in a session, particularly at those sessions where strangers are rare. Before continuing with this point, however, let me rehearse Georg Simmel's classic discussion of sociability and the distinction between the "wanderer," "who comes today and goes tomorrow," and the stranger, "who comes today and stays tomorrow" (Simmel 1971b, 143). Wanderers are no threat to long-term sociality of sessions because they are temporary, but strangers can be considered threats to sociality, since they come from outside of the social world of a particular session, and they come to stay, and people know they must adjust.

Wanderers and strangers are thus treated differently in sessions. A wanderer, someone who shows up at a session while visiting a city and who has found a session from thesession.org or another website, is usually treated well, for everyone knows that she will be gone tomorrow. Her musical ability matters, but even a wanderer who is a weak musician would normally be encouraged to play a tune or start a set as a gesture of generosity and welcoming on the part of host session players. This is done in part for diagnostic purposes, to see how good a player the wanderer is, but also as a way of welcoming the wanderer into the scene. Wanderers who are weak players are tolerated because they are transient, they pose no threat to the social or musical worlds of the session they visit. And they are usually asked to play a tune or start a set more than once in a session.

Strangers, however, are treated more cautiously. They are new members of the community and therefore need to be integrated (or not) into the social world of a particular session. This takes time. A stranger might be asked to play a tune or start a set when he first arrives, as a wanderer, but such requests normally taper off, and the stranger musician is left to decide for himself when to start a set. Session members' treatments of wanderers and strangers thus help to show just how much sociality matters, even more than musical skill.

Musical skill is important, though, again, how musical skill is managed at sessions reveals the value of sociality. It is not simply the case that the best musicians always enjoy the highest status, or that high status is only conferred on the best musicians. At a session I used to frequent on the East Coast, a welcomed and fully-fledged member of the session was not one of the top musicians but a celebrated instrument maker, and he was thus treated with as much respect as the best musicians. Similarly, older musicians in sessions are also treated with great respect, regardless of their abilities. Thus, while musical skill clearly matters, musicians frequently award their respect to members of the group who might not play that well.

There is also the issue of musicians who play very well and dominate the session, either through force of personality or through high volume or other musical means. Such musicians can be devalued, despite their skill and even if they possess high status, for such behavior threatens the sociality of the session. In my session, there is a player who attends occasionally who is a virtuoso on several instruments. He usually plays very fast, adds chromaticisms (unusual in this music), and frequently jumps up an octave to play over everyone else. Those musicians' who view this sort of behavior negatively express their disapprobation in musical terms; one of my fellow players, an excellent fiddler, once insisted to me quite emphatically that this virtuoso was *not* a good musician. In many ways, then, the presence or absence of musical skill is a value that is subordinated to sociality.

This musician's behavior is a question of what Simmel, in a different essay, calls tact. Sociability, he writes, has no end other than itself, and thus is dependent on its "personal bearers" and the traits of individuals involved, which determine the "character of purely sociable association." But, he says, individual personalities must not "emphasize themselves too individually," for this might threaten sociability. What keeps individual personalities in check is tact, which "guides the self-regulation of the individual in his personal relations to others where no outer or directly egoistic interests provide regulation" (1971a, 130).

The management of sociality of the Irish session is such that it matters not what one does for a living, how much income one makes, if one has achieved some degree of fame or celebrity, or other such marker of social differentiation. My status as a college professor matters not (though I occasionally act as a kind of clearing house of information for some younger musicians who are thinking about studying music in college or graduate school). Living and playing in Southern California, we encounter the occasional television or film actor who comes to play—one such person is a regular; but none of this matters. Simmel calls sociability, and tact, a "very remarkable sociological structure," for in situations in which sociability is dominant, nothing else matters: "Riches and social position, learning and fame, exceptional capacities and merits of the individual have no role in sociability" (1971a, 130). Sociality and tact are great social equalizers, at least for the duration of the session. The only common differentiating mechanism is musical ability, and even this doesn't much matter if musicians behave tactfully in Simmel's sense.

There might appear to be a fine line between sociality and community in some of these interviews and in my own use of the terms, and so let me explicate the difference as I see it. Community, the functionalist conception, is a more bounded and self-contained entity than what I am concerned with here. Durkheim was quite clear on this point; in his famous definition of religion, he writes that the "unified system of beliefs and practices" people possess unites them "into one single moral community called a Church" (1964, 47). For Durkheim, "society" was *community written large*" (Nisbet 1993, 84; emphasis in original). And what holds a community together is its beliefs, its rituals, its division of labor that produces forms of solidarity (Durkheim 1984). I am conceptualizing community more in Simmelian fashion, such that "community" is viewed as a smaller unit with its own dynamics, some of which can be characterized in broad terms, as we have seen. Simmel insisted that the larger workings of culture and society be apprehended through their specific, local manifestations:

Social life involves the mutual correlation of its elements, which occur in part in instantaneous actions and relations which partly manifest themselves in tangible forms: in public functions and laws, orders and possessions, languages and means of communication. All such social mutual co-relations, however, are caused by distinct interests, ends and impulses. They form, as it were, the matter which realizes itself socially in the "next to each other" and "with each other," the "for each other" and "against each other" of individuals." (Quoted in Nisbet 1993, 100)

I am thinking of an Irish traditional music session as a community in this sense, a small scale, "very remarkable sociological structure" that is governed by the value of sociality and conceptions of tact.

Value and Memory

Value in the Marxist sense is the product of productive labor stored in commodities, in money. But other forms of value are stored as well, as Graeber notes in the quotation above, even when performance is the medium of value (see also Geertz 1973, 127, on the question of storing meaning in symbols). Commodities are not static objects, and neither are other sorts of value-producing acts such as performances: they can be advertised and anticipated before they happen, they might be reviewed afterward, and remembered and discussed after that.

Acts, according to Lambek (2013, 148), do not produce goods, products, but consequences. If productive labor results in objects that can be alienated from their producer in the classic Marxian sense, acts such as musical performances can produce narratives that can circulate, recirculate, and be rewritten. Even after musical groups disband and people die, their work is remembered, curated, passed on. Some concerts are remembered and discussed for years, as obituaries for famous musicians show. I don't think I have ever spoken to a musician who didn't say something like, "Back in the day, this scene was much better than it is today." And as is well known, people's work can be reevaluated after they die, with lesser musicians enjoying greater reputations, or celebrated musicians' reputations waning. In the realm of the visual arts, it is by now something of a cliché that the price of an artist's work will rise after she dies. This is not the sort of value I am concerned with here, but the point is that time and memory play important roles in every regime of value.

The sort of value I am concerned with, value-in/as-action, apart from productive labor, while it can be commodified, is much less likely to be, because of the difficulty in doing so. This sort of value is created from human action and needs to be continually re-created and renewed. Probably the best example for those of us who study music is the vast amount of time and energy spent in academic music departments in the United States on a very small number of composers and works in the western European classical music tradition, even though only a tiny minority of people on the planet listen to that music. All of those acts of teaching and proselytizing are a measure of those people's valuation of that music.

Performances and rituals store value—in tokens, fetishes, and other material forms, but also in ideas, practices, and deities. Lambek writes that certain core rituals. such as the Catholic mass, "regenerate the value congealed in the ultimate sacred postulates, gestures, and objects—and they and other rituals circulate value insofar as they invest new persons, relationships, and circumstances with sanctity and place them under new or renewed descriptions" (2013, 151). This describes no less the ritual nature of a classical music concert (see Small 1987), a rock concert, or an Irish traditional music session. All function as media of value, regimes different from, while sometimes alongside, regimes of value as determined by socially necessary labor time.

At the session where I play in Southern California, value is mainly stored in photographs. There is seldom a week that goes by without a musician or two photographing other musicians and then posting photographs to Facebook; sometimes people post photos to Facebook during the session; videos appear there, too, but not as frequently. I would go so far as to say that taking pictures at sessions has spurred an interest in photography and videography in some musicians, at least at the session with which I am most familiar. From such practices it is clear that sessions are as much about being together, being seen together, and showing that one has been together as they are about music. That is, music is the modality of togetherness, of sociality—the currency of sociality for those involved in Irish traditional music. The rise of social media has allowed Irish traditional musicians to amplify the social aspects of the scene, proclaiming, even advertising, its sociality, realizing value in material form in a place apart from where value is created, as Graeber writes in the quotation above.[5]

Conclusions

I have been employing some recent perspectives on value as articulated by some anthropologists as a way of attempting to move beyond the simple binary oppositions that are frequently employed to discuss the complex processes of the commodification of music, or the global popularization of particular kinds of music, some of which are lumped under the label "world music." I have also taken pains in writings elsewhere to show just how slow and complex the processes of the commodification of musics are (see, for example, Taylor 2007). Even if we don't much use binaries such as "traditional/ modern" anymore, the ghosts of that and other binaries still hover over newer ones, present but not always articulated, such as "uncommodified"/ commodified, preglobalization/globalization, and many more that underlie a good deal of recent scholarship about music and other forms of cultural production.

Theories of value can help us to find more actor-centered ways of understanding why people make the music they make, and why they find meaning in the making and listening. I have found such theories to be, well, valuable. They can help us cut through easy, frequently functionalist, assumptions about music and identity, music and community, and more, and help us sharpen our ethnographic and historical sensibilities, help us make more of what our ethnographies and histories tell us. Otherwise, as Geertz warned, our work will only be a series of attempts at proving what is already known.

Musical Performance
as a Medium of Value

This chapter continues my interest in questions of the value of musical goods, which goes back at least to my work on music as a commodity (collected in Taylor 2017) and on questions of value that appear to be noneconomic (Taylor 2016a, 2017). The essential question concerns how we can develop ways of understanding the value of music that are not determined by conceptions of the economic. As anthropologist Michael Lambek notes in his consideration of value, there is a difference between playing a violin for a living and playing it for its own sake (2013, 142). Both activities produce value, but the former is an overt form of economic form of value and the latter isn't (though it can be brought into an economic regime of value). It is this second form of value of musical performance that interests me here. How can a musical performance be a medium of this other sort of value? In what follows, I will separate economic and noneconomic forms of value in order to make my arguments, but it is important to acknowledge that conceptions of value are constantly shifting and that such a distinction is for heuristic purposes.

In the context of current anthropological theories of value, to which this book is indebted, I was anticipated by Clifford Geertz, since, as I have said elsewhere in these pages, it seems to me that his concern for unearthing what is meaningful to social actors is really a way of thinking about what they value (see Taylor 2017). Geertz's early work bears out this impression, for he sometimes uses *meaning*, *feeling* (or *affect*), and *value* interchangeably (see the earlier essays in Geertz 1973, particularly "Ethos, World View, and the Analysis of Sacred Symbols," originally published in 1957). Value, like meaning, is social—it circulates everywhere, and everywhere it is contested, protected, shifting.

Recent authors of the anthropological literature on value tend not to recognize their debt to Geertz (see Graeber 2001, for example), but their writings have nonetheless deepened my understanding of questions of meaning. According to these authors, value is how we find meaning in what we do and how this meaning or value is understood by a society or culture more generally. Capitalism is therefore only one mode of the creation and exchange of value; goods that are thought to possess value are produced by all forms of social relations, not just capitalist forms (see Graeber 2001; Myers 2001). Value is also not static; a good might not be produced as a commodity but can become one, but if this happens, it is not necessarily a commodity forever; it can become a gift or another sort of good. Goods have careers (see Tsing 2015; Kopytoff 1986), and they exist in what Arjun Appadurai has called "regimes of value," sets of shared standards in which similar degrees of "value coherence" obtain (Appadurai 1986a, 14–15).

This chapter is concerned with understanding musical performance as a medium of value. How can a transient, ephemeral action serve as a medium for the articulation of the values of a particular social group? And how might this work? We currently have many excellent treatments of the question of the value of goods that are commodities, from Marx and later writers, and we have many useful considerations of the value of goods that are considered to be gifts, drawing on Marcel Mauss and later writers. We also possess many illuminating anthropologies and ethnomusicologies of ritual that demonstrate the ways that rituals (re)produce or (re)create social life, or society itself (e.g., Rappaport 1979; Seeger 2004). But aiming at questions of value provides focus: What exactly is being (re)produced or (re)created beyond "society" or "culture"?

Terence Turner's discussion of indigenous people's struggles in the face of colonial or other sorts of contact gives urgency to such issues of the specificities of value. Turner exhorts us to focus on optimizing people's ability to create or manage cultural patterns for their own ends, which, he says, should be the main political criterion (1979, 12). As societies continue to change, whether internally or in response to external forces, questions about the maintenance of what those societies collectively value would seem to be worth our continued attention.

Turner offers a theory of value (which is essentially worked out in greater ethnographic and theoretical detail in Graeber 2001) in which "'action' is conceived . . . as oriented toward socially defined values. Socio-cultural systems are accordingly understood as the means by which peoples define the values that orient their own acts, realize these values in concrete terms through concerted social action and distribute and accumulate the value thus produced among themselves" (1979, 18). Note the employment here of *values* and *value*, which raises an issue to be addressed before I can really get going. This is something that David Graeber (2001) tackles, and there is no need to spend a lot of time on it here. Graeber argues that three areas of thought come together in the term *value*: values in the sociological sense, value in the economic sense, and value in the linguistic sense, the last of which, going back to de Saussure, can be understood as "meaningful difference" (2001, 1–2). Graeber writes that all three usages of the term are essentially versions of the same thing (2001, 2), which he then goes on to attempt to demonstrate. Ultimately, he comes to argue for a capacious conceptualization of value that is concerned with understanding how people imagine what life should be like (2001, 22).

Anthropological theorists of value posit that value needs to be stored in some way, in some sort of concrete token, like money. This is one of the main points Graeber makes (2001, 451–52; see also Geertz 1973, 127). But he also discusses rituals and performances as media of value, and it is an elaboration of this idea that serves as the main goal of this chapter (other theorists also allow that value can be preserved in immaterial ways, though this is not the focus of most theorists of value; see Lambek 2013 for a different take on how acts that create value can be stored in tokens).

The question of value with respect to performed music—instead of music as fixed in a concrete commodity such as a recording—is complex. What kind of medium of value might a musical performance be? Performances, like physical musical goods, can be commodities in the sense that they are events repeated to crowds consisting mostly of strangers—as Marx himself argued (1990, 1044)—but in their ephemerality they are still different than recorded musical sound commodities. And what one considers to be a performance can vary quite a bit: some, of course, are public events, but others can be smaller, more intimate affairs for friends or aficionados; performances can be rituals or parts of rituals; and they can take still other forms.

Discussions of value such as the foregoing have been extremely useful in focusing attention on what is meaningful for social actors while keeping the big picture in mind (see Taylor 2017). As Graeber reminds us, value theory helps understand a particular system of exchange as part of larger systems of meaning (2005, 443).

Performances and Audiences

If musical performance is a medium of value, then it must be seen as such by everyone involved, performers and nonperformers (though this is a distinction I will problematize below). I am thus concerned with the ways that value can (potentially) be transmitted—realized, consummated—through musical performance, and how these transmissions are made, though I will be less concerned here with how these transmissions are received and understood.

If value is something collectively realized, then performance must be something that is public, in the sense that it is not simply for those considered to be performers, when such a distinction exists. Performances require audiences. Performance is socially and culturally recognized as such— socially discernible, in other words like registering the difference between a blink and a wink. What is socially and culturally recognized as performance is set apart from the everyday in many ways—formally, with musicians separated from the audience, wearing special dress, amplified, and so on, or more informally. Steven Feld writes of what he calls the "staging" among the Kaluli in Papua New Guinea of a particular genre of music. Staging, he writes, is the way that the audience is primed to understand musical form and style as a meaningful and intentional representation of sentiments (Feld 2012, 178). Performances (or rituals or other sorts of public events) are seen as something different than the "real" or quotidian, even if they can help us make sense of, find meaning in, the real or quotidian.

Let me make it clear that, while my main concern is attempting to understand musical performances in contemporary capitalist societies, in many societies there is not a clear distinction made between performance and audience—everyone may be a participant. The most canonical example in ethnomusicology is probably Anthony Seeger's brilliant analysis of the mouse ceremony among the Suyá (who now prefer to be called Kisêdjê) of Brazil (2004). But even in contemporary capitalist societies, I would argue, the behavior and activities of the audience must be considered to be part of the performance itself as a social and collective event.

Because performances are socially and culturally understood as performances, they are, by this definition, public—singing in the shower is not a performance, though it certainly may provide something of value to the singer. And it is because performances are public that they can function as tokens of value to particular societies or social groups. Value is public, as meaning is, since both are cultural (Geertz 1973, 12), though such a conception requires that we remember that meanings don't circulate to everyone the same way, and that they never circulate totally.

Everyone who has performed knows that it is a vastly different thing than practicing or rehearsing without an audience; it is not a performance without the audience. Early performers in radio studios and recording studios suffered rough transitions from performing before an audience to performing before a microphone, as many spoke and wrote of at the time (see Taylor, Katz, and Grajeda 2012). The point here is that performances are public, and do not exist without audiences, whether present and seen or present and unseen. Without an audience, there is no performance, no potential medium of value, or of its realization, confirmation, consummation. And if there is no performance without an audience, the audience itself must be understood as part of the performance.

Social Interaction and the Realization of Value

It thus follows that the interactions between people considered to be performers and those considered to be part of the audience (where such a distinction exists) are a crucial part of the performance; value has no chance of being transmitted without the interactions of the people involved in any performance. Different sorts of cultural goods are consumed differently, as we know perhaps most famously from Pierre Bourdieu (1984), though, while reception has been reasonably frequently studied in music, attention to modes of reception and interaction are less common. Every concert scene of which I am aware has proper ways of expressing approbation or admiration for performers, as well as criticisms. Each genre has its expected mode of the demonstration of appreciation, indications of the successful transmission of value. The different sorts of performer-audience interactions reveal the conceptions of value that are on display and being (potentially) transmitted or realized, or, if expectations are not met, diminished, or not realized at all. At classical music performances, for example, audience members are supposed to sit in rapt silence, as in church. No applause is permitted except at the ends of works, no matter how spectacular or pleasing a particular moment in the performance might have been. Classical music concerts are about veneration of composer-gods and their mediums-priests, especially the conductor and soloists (see Small 1987).

This sort of behavior would be disquieting, at the very least, to performers in many other genres. Classical concert behavior is different, however, in opera, where it is permissible to applaud after an aria. Opera aficionados are allowed to show their fandom, rather like the jazz lovers who demonstrate their perspicacity by applauding after a particularly good solo, though this practice has become a matter of politesse and is now routinely offered after every solo. Indian classical music is supported by a robust theory of *rasa*, in which listeners can achieve a kind of transcendental state (see Becker 2004). Other sorts of concerts are different still. Irish traditional music sessions, in which I am a frequent participant, are yet another type, since they aren't really concerts—or viewed by musicians as performances or gigs—but background music to people in pubs. We like it when venues are quiet so that we can hear one another, which usually means an empty or sparsely populated bar, but at the same time we very much appreciate the audience's recognition in the form of applause, compliments, and tips. We whoop and applaud for each other, especially for singers (since songs are fairly rare).

Sometimes different regimes of value are knowingly at play. If a sort of music that is supposed to induce ecstasy or trance fails to do so, the unaffected listener is still lucid enough to note the effectiveness of the musicians' work on others, and, in some cases, offer money to the musicians (see Qureshi 1995). This, I suppose, is a form, over time, of generalized reciprocity, a system in which "transactions that are putatively altruistic, transactions on the line of assistance given and, if possible and necessary, assistance returned" (Sahlins 1972, 193–94): sometimes the musicians get recognized or paid, and sometimes they don't, but either way, they are creating value, which is sometimes recognized in the form of the music's effectiveness and sometimes in the form of money.

Toward Theorizing Performance
as a Medium of Value

Let me begin to flesh out the claim that musical performances (and other sorts of public acts) can serve as media of value. The moment of the performance is the moment when value can be transmitted and can be realized, which needs to be witnessed by the audience. I wrote "can be" in the previous sentence (and "potentially" earlier) because, as everyone knows who has attended any sort of public gathering, there are always plenty of people who are unmoved or not paying attention. Some do not receive the transmission or take issue with its delivery.

While there is an anthropological literature on value, there isn't much that considers performance as a medium of value. This notion comes from Graeber's work on value, which provides a useful rehearsal of the writings of Turner on this issue. Unfortunately, much of what Graeber relies on in making his argument is drawn from unpublished materials by Turner on the rituals of the Kayapo people of Brazil, so I must rely on Graeber's glosses rather than Turner's own writings. Rather than offer a thirdhand account, I will quote directly from Graeber.

Graeber begins to make his case about acts of performance, via Turner, by noting that there are two key values in Kayapo culture, beauty and dominance:

> The Kayapo notion of "beauty" implies "perfection, completion, and finesse"; it is evinced most of all in the harmony of a grand ceremonial that unites an entire Kayapo community, of which the giving of beautiful names is perhaps the exemplary form. In the communal sphere, these two [beauty and dominance] are combined in certain forms of public performance. These are, in ascending order of prestige, a kind of mournful keening performed by elder women at public events, the formal oratory with which senior men harangue the community on matters of collective import, and most all, a form of oratorical chanting, called *ben*, whose use is limited to chiefs. These represent the pinnacles of social value in Kayapo society because they are seen as combining completely uninhibited self-expression (i.e., a complete lack of deference, hence, untrammeled dominance) with the consummate mastery and fullness of style that is the epitome of "beauty."

Graeber argues that value is realized in public, communal spaces in the forms of circulating media of value—ceremonial valuables and social roles—but also in the form of access to what are thought to be the most prestigious types of verbal performance in public: keening, formal oratory, and chiefly chanting (2001, 74).

How can money and something like chiefly chanting both be media of value? Graeber argues that they are measures of value in that they quantify or hierarchize whatever a particular valued quality might be (2001, 75). Such measurement can take any of three possible forms. The first is presence or absence—people possess wealth or they don't. The second possible form is ranking—with respect to Kayapo society, men's oratory is usually seen as superior to women's keening, and chiefly chanting is viewed as superior to both. And third is proportionality, as with money—people possess varying amounts of it. Graeber continues to argue that both money and chanting are media of value since they are the material ways that value is realized. In both cases, value must be realized in some material form, whether tangible or a witnessed performance. Performances either conjure those values in a way that is perceptible to the audience or offer things that can be translated into tokens that bring these values into existence (2001, 75–76).

An important question in this context is the degree to which value can be stored. For economic forms of value, it is obvious that value can be stored as money. According to Graeber, this is one extreme form of value; at the other extreme, social value is stored in things like rituals or performances, for which it is not possible to make a distinction between the spheres of circulation and of realization: media of value such as performances must be circulated and realized together (2001, 78).

Musical Performance as a Medium of Value

The foregoing is pretty much all Graeber has to say on the question of performance as a medium of value. After the discussion outlined above, Graeber then pivots away from considerations of value among the Kayapo to make a generalization about the different spheres, or "units," where value is produced in capitalist societies: workplaces and households, which are mediated by the marketplace. Workplaces produce economic values through commodities; households produce social values. The market, however, acts as a kind of force of social amnesia, of which commodity fetishism is a facet (2001,

79). People in households have no knowledge of the people in the workplace who produce the commodities used in households, while people in the workplace have no knowledge of the social values produced in households.

Graeber then goes on to discuss the production of social values in more traditional societies in which the "units" of workplace and household don't really apply; there is mainly only the latter. But even in these societies, there are other spheres in which values circulate and can be realized. Graeber, however, doesn't consider these other spheres in contemporary complex societies, which is striking, since there is a good deal of literature on the public sphere in several disciplines and a great deal of literature that considers sporting events, festivals, and ceremonies as rituals.

My interest specifically concerns musical performances as media of the potential transmission or consummation of what are thought to be noneconomic forms of value in contemporary capitalist societies. Graeber examines traditional societies' home practices and rituals, but for contemporary societies, he considers only home practices, ignoring public rituals, ceremonies, and performances. In moving from the Kayapo—who have a public space—to contemporary society, Graeber excised all of the ways that value might be realized outside of the workplace or the domestic sphere, in places relatively insulated from the market and the home (he mentions churches and museums in another context). I would also add other sorts of public spaces/events, such as musical performances and sporting events. Value is transmitted there, too. This immensely complicates Graeber's model, of course; it becomes difficult to talk about values in, say, "American society" if we are considering a symphony concert, a football game, a church service. Different sorts of values can be, and are, realized in different sorts of public events.

Public performances can serve to transmit the sorts of values that are produced at home but can't be realized at home. This is one of the things that performances are for—the transmission and hoped-for realization of values taught, inculcated, in the home, but values of the sort that can only be realized collectively, in public. We need to clear more space for the public as a space where values can be realized apart from the workplace and the home. I write "realized" not "created," because my argument is that there are some values that, while they might be created in the domestic "unit" of the home, cannot be realized except in public. You can learn from your parents that it is important to learn how to share with others, but you can't really put that into practice until you get out of the domestic space.

The public must thus be added to Graeber's formulation of the two "units" of capitalist societies, as a kind of proving ground where some of the values learned at home might be realized or enacted in ways that would be difficult or impossible at home, or as a counterpublic space in which general social values might be contested. A quick example that will have to suffice for the time being is the Irish traditional music session, which I also studied as a medium of value, though in a different context (see chapter 6 in this volume). The main value of the session, an informal gathering usually in a bar, is sociality, a kind of musicalized hanging out. The importance of sociality can be learned at home but cannot really be realized without others.

(Meaningful) Action

Performances also require a good deal of activity, what, drawing on Graeber (2001) I have elsewhere called "meaningful action" (Taylor 2017) but will simply refer to here as action. I am in general agreement with Graeber's theory of value as a theory of action—that is, that the actions of social actors reveal what it is they value (Graeber 2001, 2005; see also Taylor 2017). Sometimes these actions can be considered to be labor in Marx's sense— productive labor that produces surplus value for capitalists—but there are many other forms of action that do not generate surplus value but produce other sorts of value. In general, for Graeber, "value is the way our actions take on meaning or importance by becoming incorporated into something larger than ourselves" (2005, 451), and I am in general agreement with this broader position.

With respect to the actions of musicians, we need to recognize, as Graeber and Turner (and many nonmusicians) fail to do, that a good deal of preparation usually goes into musical performances. While they may seem to be impromptu or ephemeral to viewers/listeners, they are in fact the products of individual and collective action over significant amounts of time. Musical performances and other sorts of public events aren't just media of value but the products of practicing and preparation, arguments and compromises—all of which I am calling action. This is obvious to musicians, but most, even all, musicians have often been faced with assumptions that they simply show up and perform effortlessly, without prior effort. Performances, I am arguing, are not simply media of value, public realizations of value, but the culminating public nodes in an array of processes and networks of practicing and rehearsing, as well as instrument and equipment building, buying, maintenance, and repair; costume design and manufacture; and much more, all of which come together in public performances. Through all of these (and other) actions, value is put in escrow, stored, to be transmitted later at the performance. Or sometimes performances take days, as in the case of the Kisêdjê (formerly Suyá) of Brazil as documented by Seeger (2004), in which case all of the teaching, learning and arguing is part of the performance itself, usually coming to some sort of recognized climax or culmination. It might be useful at this point to recall Mauss, writing of northwestern North American potlatches: "There are repeated festivals, continuous and long drawn-out. At a wedding, or at various kinds of ritual or promotions, everything stored up with great industry during the summer and autumn on one of the richest coasts in the world is lavishly expended" (2002, 44). All of these acts, whether of storing (and more) for potlatches, or of practicing and rehearsing (and more) for musical performances, are forms of action that build value, which is then displayed and potentially transmitted at certain key moments that are socially and culturally agreed upon as performances, moments when this transmission might occur.

In this context, while I share Graeber's and Turner's realization of the importance of performance, I am disagreeing with them somewhat: value isn't "stored" in performances/rituals/festivals; it is built up through various actions, usually a good deal of them, that happen offstage, as it were, prior to the performance. Performances are the moment when all of these actions are culturally and socially understood to be realized in public. In a real sense, then, the value of all of these actions is realized in the moment of performance: performance can only serve as a medium of value when it occurs *as* a performance—for, or with, others, in public. Such transmissions of value require not only audiences, but reasonably attentive or appreciative audiences. Nothing is more disappointing to a live performer of any sort—musical, theatrical, or other—than to have an unappreciative audience. Audience approbation is necessary if value has a chance of being realized. Performer-audience interactions are thus more than that; they are moments of exchange—the accumulated actions of the musicians are put on display, and those actions are recognized by the audience. Value is realized in the exchange. This point is rather Marxian: just as we can't know the exchange value of something until there is someone who has a use-value for it and is willing to pay, so the social realization of value in a performance doesn't occur until it is made public and acknowledged. This is not, however, the "consumption" of the performance but the validation of it, the recognition of exchange, the potential realization of value.

Jane Fajans makes a similar argument on the question of exchange by writing that exchange is the moment when the latent value made in production processes and embedded in their products is turned into forms of value that are publicly recognized. Exchange is thus how social actors' investment in production is given recognized social meaning (1993, 8). Fajans sees social life as a quest for value (or meaning, I would say, not forgetting Geertz), and she views exchange as the way that that quest is consummated. For her, exchange and circulation are the contexts in which values stored in actions, goods, or social actors are socially realized, by which she means they are integrated into a web of social relations as they become publicly "recognized, ratified, revealed," or transferred, from one person to the next (1993, 8). In the context of music, value is thus not exhausted with the conclusion of the performance, for musicians continue to act, learning from previous performances, building on them, aiming toward the next one.

Fajans also writes that displays of value can circulate in the public domain without exchange taking place (1993, 7), and it is much the same for passing displays of value such as musical performances. As I have argued elsewhere (chapter 6, above), drawing on Lambek (2013), more ephemeral media of value can continue after their first appearance: people remember such events, discuss them, photograph them, make video or audio recordings of them, thus continuing the circulation of value for which these photographs or recordings or other memorabilia have become tokens.

Symbols of Meaning and Value in/as the World

Before turning to a specific case study, I would like to make a point also about the importance of attending to the specificities of particular tokens of value. According to Turner (1979) and Graeber, we should pay attention to "the nature of the media through which social value is realized" (Graeber 2001, 78). Graeber argues that tokens of value, material or not, come to be seen as ends in themselves: people see the tokens of value not as tools through which value can be realized or measured but as embodiments of value themselves, even as the origins of those values (Graeber 2001, 76, citing Turner 1979, 31–34). That is, media of value aren't just media of value—they possess their own qualities that are worth examining (Graeber 2001, 83).

Geertz actually said much the same thing about religious symbols, making the point not only that meanings need to be stored in symbols but also that symbols take on an importance of their own, apart from what they are thought to represent:

> Such religious symbols, dramatized in rituals or related in myths, are felt somehow to sum up, for those for whom they are resonant, what is known about the way the world is, the quality of the emotional life it supports, and the way one ought to behave while in it. Sacred symbols thus relate an ontology and a cosmology to an aesthetics and a morality: their peculiar power comes from their presumed ability to identify fact with value at the most fundamental level, to give to what is otherwise merely actual, a comprehensive normative import. (Geertz 1973, 127)

For Geertz, meanings or values or feelings are not simply floating about in a culture but are part of broader systems, whether one calls them, as he considered, ethos or worldview. This is the reason that Graeber needed to discuss the idea of the totality. Many a theory has been dismissed as (too) totalizing, but, at the same time, if one thinks ethnographically, people in any culture employ theories that, for them, are viewed as explaining the world as it appears and indeed, for them, truly is. As Graeber explains, "Value . . . can best be seen in this light as the way in which actions become meaningful to the actor by being incorporated in some larger, social totality—even if in many cases the totality in question exists primarily in the actor's imagination" (2001, xii).

Isicathamiya *Competitions and Value*

In one of his few forays into commenting on cultural production, Geertz made it clear that to study cultural production is to study culture itself:

> This realization, that to study an art form is to explore a sensibility, that such a sensibility is essentially a collective formation, and that the foundations of such a formation are as wide as social existence and as deep, leads away not only from the view that aesthetic power is a grandiloquence for the pleasures of craft. It leads away also from the so-called functionalist view that has most often been opposed to

it: that is, that works of art are elaborate mechanisms for defining social relationships, sustaining social rules, and strengthening social values. (1983, 99)

Artworks (broadly understood), "materialize a way of experiencing, bring a particular cast of mind out into the world," where others can apprehend it (1983, 99).

We have some excellent models in ethnomusicology that accomplish this sort of study, books that have served as models and inspirations for many, not just Seeger's *Why Suyá Sing* but also Steven Feld's *Sound and Sentiment* (2012), Louise Meintjes's *Dust of the Zulu* (2017), Christopher Waterman's *Jùjú* (1990), and others. Rather than rehearsing these (or other) excellent books, I will offer a brief case study, one that is pretty much canonical in ethnomusicology, which means that attempting to theorize it might resonate with many readers. This case—*isicathamiya* music from South Africa—today operates in multiple regimes of value, regimes that are local and international, in which *isicathamiya* can be a commodity as an internationally recognized sound, a sound of Africa. (I do not mean to imply that *isicathamiya* wasn't a commodity before Paul Simon came along and before Ladysmith Black Mambazo became famous from Simon's 1986 *Graceland* album; commercial recordings of it had previously existed.) I am primarily interested in *isicathamiya* music as a performed music in competitions.

There are, of course, some excellent studies of *isicathamiya* already, especially those by perhaps its greatest student, Veit Erlmann. What can theoretical focus on questions of value add to them? Let me attempt to talk about *isicathamiya* here from the perspective of the social actors involved. For empirical data, I rely on the excellent secondary literature by Erlmann and others. And some of this literature refers to Zulu conceptions of value (e.g., Akrofi 2001). Erlmann writes of competition itself as a precolonial value that persists with the music's more recent urban practitioners, and he views *isicathamiya* as a complex melding of practices of competition from two different cultures: "Much of the course of *isicathamiya* history was influenced by an uneasy balance between the two models of competitive performance: the urban middle-class concert and the rural stick-fight" (Erlmann 1996, 229).

Competition thus seems to be one Zulu value that carries over into the present. Another that I would argue for and will spend some time on is excellence: *isicathamiya* competitions in the apartheid era aimed to display community-defined conceptions of excellence as an urban Zulu value. *Isicathamiya* competitions were a way of demonstrating that in an environment in which indigenous people lacked access to all legitimate forms of power—political, juridical, economic, and much more—they were still capable of defining for themselves what excellence was, and they aspired to reach the loftiest heights of communally defined excellence in *isicathamiya* performances.

I would not characterize this as resistance, or, perhaps better, not as resistance only. This is the indigenous construction and maintenance of and participation in a regime of value in which white South Africans have no voice, no role—except one, which I will discuss presently. *Isicathamiya* competitions are a world apart from colonialism and apartheid, even as they are caught up in colonialism and apartheid. They are a way for people to define what they believe matters, what is meaningful to them, and to continually enact and refine those beliefs, those meanings, through public competitions.

These public displays of communal values are made with the participation of the audience, the behavior of which is strictly managed. *Isicathamiya* participants make clear distinctions between rehearsals and performances, both of which are public; audience behavior is strictly controlled, as is the movement and placement of musicians vis-à-vis the audience. As one observer wrote: "During the practice, the men wear normal street clothes, and members of the audience are allowed to whistle and clap. During the actual competition, however, the men dress immaculately, in elegant and, more often than not, tailored outfits. And the audience must remain quiet, so as not to influence the judging" (Griffin 1995, 2). As the late Joseph Shabalala told Erlmann, when Ladysmith Black Mambazo went from Durban to Johannesburg in 1973, his group wasn't permitted to participate in the competitions in Johannesburg, for they were already well known and better than the groups in that city:

> We had the largest following. They so much loved us, that after each rendition people would applaud and the rule was that people should not applaud. The first time our performance was cancelled. Then during the second performance it was announced to the audience that they were allowed to applaud all groups entering the stage and also applaud when the group leaves the stage after singing. This, obviously, was an attempt to prevent people to give us the loudest applause. Nevertheless, the audience responded as requested. But when

we entered there was a difference in the applause which was putting us ahead of other groups. (Erlmann 1996, 291)

The competitions, therefore, take on their own meanings in and of themselves, in addition to the value for which they serve as a medium, as argued earlier.

It is also the case that actions or objects can often be fetishized and assumed to be the sources of value rather than the media through which value circulates (Graeber 2001, 81). Drawing on Fajans (1993), Graeber says that both actions and objects can become models or miniature representations of the forms of action that they ultimately represent (2001, 81–82). A particular ceremony or regalia or whatever token is a microcosm of the entire system of production of which it is a part. Such objects encode a theory of creativity that he thinks is implicit in everyday life. Graeber admits that this is a commonplace enough observation, but he wants to emphasize creativity: even the most mundane acts are acts of symbolic production, for they are the main ways that people's most basic definitions of what people are get reproduced (2001, 82).

The belief in the construction of society through *isicathamiya* competitions and the valorization of excellence is made clear in the adjudication of the competitions. It is significant that until fairly recently the only role outsiders were permitted to play in *isicathamiya* competitions was that of judge, usually a white South African, a stranger. A white South African was picked because that person would be known to none of the competitors and was therefore thought to be completely impartial. Carol Muller writes of her experience as a judge in 1984, being seated with her back to the audience so that she and her fellow judge would not be influenced by the various performers' supporters (Muller 2004, 124). Only with this extreme objectivity could true excellence be determined, value be transmitted and potentially realized. (Choosing white judges is no longer the standard practice, and I would say this shift has occurred for complex reasons; see Muller 2004.)

Erlmann, in his comprehensive work on *isicathamiya*, notes how song texts include performers' praise of themselves as part of their efforts to gain prestige and establish their names (Erlmann 1996, 207), and he observes that the most basic form of self-praise occurs in lyrics that mention some sign of excellence and social achievement through the use of personal pronouns (Erlmann 1996, 208–9); common phrases are used to commend excellence in performance. But I am arguing that excellence was even more important than this in the competitions during the apartheid era. It was perhaps the main value that was nurtured and protected and for which *isicathamiya* competitions were both medium and realization.

In some respects, there is little one could add to the voluminous work on *isicathamiya* by Erlmann and others. But I want to pull out of this work the idea of excellence as a value that compelled participation and in part drove the competitions. Following Geertz, as I have throughout this chapter, I would stress that ethnography, and its analysis, privilege what is meaningful and valuable to social actors. The concept of value serves, I have argued here and elsewhere (Taylor 2017), as a useful tool for this endeavor.

If we compare the regime of value of *isicathamiya* competitions to the regime of value of *isicathamiya* as a "world music" following the success of Simon's Grammy-winning *Graceland*, it is easier to see these regimes for what they are—different regimes, in which different conceptions of value obtain. The forms of value visible in *isicathamiya* competitions are wholly different from the forms of value represented by commercial recordings of *isicathamiya* or university concert series performances, even if the music sounds much the same.

One of Lambek's points about ethical value is that they are incommensurable, unlike the values that result from productive labor. The price of goods with economic forms of value makes commensurability a simple matter. But in terms of ethical value, it's not possible to say that a particular performance of, say, violinist Joshua Bell playing Bach is more or less valuable than a performance by Ladysmith Black Mambazo. This does not mean, however, that ethical values cannot be brought into an economic regime of value, as has happened with many musics around the world with the creation of the category of "world music" and the rise of interest in this music in the late 1980s and after. Muller writes of Shabalala's efforts to recast *isicathamiya* as traditional music in the 1990s, which was, I think, a way of attempting to make it more easily commensurable with an economic regime of value, turning *isicathamiya* into "world music," then a newly created niche in the Anglo-American-dominated recording business (Muller 2004, 106; see Erlmann 1996 for a discussion of the commodification of *isicathamiya*). But, of course, such efforts also affect the composition of the audience for the music and the relationship of the audience to the musicians.

Conclusions

Considering questions of value helps us focus on what is meaningful to social actors, which Geertz exhorted us to attend to (see also Taylor 2017). Doing so helps us move beyond the still-common functionalist explanations for how people or social groups make and relate to music. Studying conceptions of value helps us find out what matters to people. As Graeber, drawing on Turner, points out, the ultimate stakes in politics are not about the appropriation of value, but the struggle to establish what value is (2001, 88). Our studies must take such struggles into consideration.

One of the main benefits of employing the perspectives gleaned from the value literature is that it offers ways of developing understandings of forms of value that are not based on economic conceptions of value. This is not going "beyond" Marx or other theories of economic forms of value, but engaging with them, complementing them, so that we can understand how value might be produced in situations that are not overtly economic. Value is stored in material things, such as money or material goods, but is also created and collected in people's actions that are socially understood to culminate in a public display, as some sort of performance, whether musical, ritual, athletic, or something else. Value is produced in the home and the workplace in capitalist societies, as Graeber argues, but sometimes it needs to be displayed or communicated in public spaces, in socially and culturally understood moments of performance. Public performances can transmit values in moments of exchange that resonate with both markets and the workplace and the home, but they can also display forms of value that cannot be realized either in the home or in the marketplace, such as the sociality of the Irish traditional music session (chapter 6). But it is not just the performers who communicate and (potentially) realize value; in order to be realized, value must be transmitted to audiences. The display, realization, and consummation of social values requires a society of performers and audiences, for whom the performed values are, as Geertz said about religious symbols, understood to be expressions of something broader and more fundamental to that society than they might appear to be. As societies around the world change with ever greater rapidity, attending to questions concerning the struggles over value and peoples' attempts to preserve what they value becomes increasingly urgent.

8

Circulation, Value, Exchange, and Music

Circulation sweats money from every pore.

Karl Marx, *Capital*

In the music fields (and beyond), we have for some time been in need of a better way to conceptualize and theorize how cultural goods such as music—whether physical, broadcast, or digital—circulate in an era frequently characterized as global. There hasn't been a time when music hasn't traveled, locally, regionally, or internationally, especially since the rise of publishing, recording technologies such as the phonograph, and broadcasting technologies such as radio. But the digitalization of music (and many other things) necessitates going beyond, or at least refining the concept of flows and various "-scapes" (ethnoscapes, mediascapes, finanscapes, technoscapes, and ideoscapes) as presented in several writings by Arjun Appadurai (collected in Appadurai 1996 and elsewhere), writings that have been quite influential in the music fields (see Feld 2000; Stokes 2004; and my own *Global Pop* [1997], among many other publications).

Appadurai's formulation was useful in giving us a way to theorize how people and things move in what was seen as an increasingly globalizing world, but over time it has proven to be something of a blunt instrument and has largely outlived its usefulness, as many have argued. The idea of "flows" and "-scapes" can imply a kind of uniform movement of money, ideologies, and more, but it is quite clear, of course, that there is nothing uniform about such movements, especially, perhaps, of capital; Anna Tsing (2005) argued some years ago for an understanding of just how messy and unpredictable global capitalism and its movements are. Cultural goods such as music don't circulate equally either, with some musical sounds and styles finding new roots in some places and not in others. In addition, there is the problem of binarizing the global and the local (or the conceptualizing of the "glocal"), as if goods simply flow globally and touch down locally. As Tsing (2000, 338) reminds us, the local is (re)made all over the place, all the time. Other critics have raised the problem of agency: Where do we locate the agency of individual social actors in these flows? (Tsing 2000; Rockefeller 2011).

In many respects, understanding how things circulate is one of the oldest questions in social theory. Early German theorists of diffusionism and dissemination, from Friedrich Ratzel and Leo Frobenius (Hahn 2008) to Franz Boas (e.g., 1891), considered such questions, as have more recent theorists such as Eric Wolf (1997). But the question of circulation has taken on new urgency with the rise of a world more connected than ever. How might we interpret the growing number of ethnographies of globalization and circulation?

Drawing on the anthropological literature on value, I want to move beyond conceptualization of flows to argue that things—whether tangible or intangible—circulate because they have value for people. I am concerned here less with the production or maintenance of value (as I have been in some of the other chapters in this volume, as well as Taylor 2017, 2020) and more with the circulation of things that are thought to be valuable. And where there is circulation and value, there is exchange, not just of money but of time, work, and action. Acts of exchange contribute powerfully to social reproduction, both on broad scales and in small aggregations such as local music scenes. And circulation occurs in the increasingly interconnected public culture in which cosmopolitan cultural forms move (Appadurai and Breckenridge 1988).

Radio

I'll start with a case study, move to a theoretical discussion, then return to theorizing the case study. The case is radio. In today's world of individu-alized digitalized on-demand media, radio may seem a quaint or humble technology, but it is still relevant to musicians. And with radio, we find a fascinating history of attempts to understand the very question of how its messages circulate. When radio first began to be popular in the United States in the 1920s, many people (including academics) speculated about whether radio could communicate directly to individuals, apart from their use of a receiver. Was it a form of telepathy? Such concerns gave rise to the term "mental radio." Researchers at reputable universities devised studies to as-certain if individuals could send thought waves through the ether (Sconce 2000; Taylor, Katz, and Grajeda 2012). Questions about the possibility of individual reception or transmission, occurring in a historical moment that witnessed rapid urbanization and other social shifts, contributed to a grow-ing sense that the United States, as a body of self-determining individual citizens, was becoming an undifferentiated mass. There was thus a tension in this era between hopes for a new technology that seemed to have the power to reach listeners individually while at the same time uniting them into a polity, and fears of the loss of separate selfhood through the creation of an undifferentiated mass.

The advent of the era of mass communications raised complex new ques-tions about the circulation of cultural goods. On the one hand, many em-ployed discourses of democratization of access: everyone would now be able to hear what was thought by urban elites to be the world's greatest music. But at the same time, there were fears that the unwashed masses wouldn't know what to make of this music, and so there arose what in music departments (at least in the United States) came to be known as "music appreciation" — books and classes that teach the masses how to listen to classical music properly (see Taylor, Katz, and Grajeda 2012).[1]

Before radio, at live concerts, audience behavior could be normalized and enforced, and the music could be properly apprehended (or at least, if someone's mind wandered away from the music, this did not interfere with someone else's attention). Exchange and social reproduction in the sense of the terms I will flesh out below are clearly taking place: people pay money for a ticket, they are taking time to listen, and, according to a vast body of aesthetic writings and ideological assumptions of the social groups that attend such concerts, they are hearing music that is uplifting, ennobling, enlightening. They are also justifying and maintaining their high positions in the social hierarchy through such enactments of distinction (Bourdieu 1984). But if one is listening at home to the phonograph or radio, how can it be known that the music is being properly heard? How does exchange happen with mass-mediated cultural goods? Does it happen at all? Or is there a different form of exchange? Can one still be uplifted, ennobled, enlightened? Can one's social position be maintained and justified, normalized? It is in this context that intellectuals such as Walter Benjamin (1968) worried about the loss of the aura of the artwork.

Radio, as Susan J. Douglas (1999, 9) observes, was probably the most important electronic invention of the last century. By the time television came into wide usage after World War II, most Americans were accustomed to mass media. Theories of telepathy had largely dissipated. Nonetheless, the status of radio diminished over time; the medium was seen as secondary to television for decades. It remains, however, an important means for the dissemination of music, even after the advent (and subsequent waning) of MTV in the early 1980s and the rise of licensing of popular music for use in film, television, and advertisements in the 1990s and after (B. Klein 2009; Taylor 2012).

In fact, terrestrial radio is today still the way that most people in the United States hear most new music, whether mainstream or independent (Katz 2016 [lecture]; Cakebread 2017).[2] Radio, a mass communications technology in widespread use for nearly one hundred years, still matters. Extremely specific statistics are kept about radio airplay, with radio charts noting the exact number of spins a particular song receives every week.[3] This needs to be recorded so that musicians (if they are songwriters) can get paid (usually a small amount, except for hits) through their performing rights organizations, such as ASCAP (American Society of Composers, Authors, and Publishers) and BMI (Broadcast Music, Inc.).

Radio airplay, as is well known, represents a kind of advertising for musicians' work and is not usually much of a source of income for them. But it is a measure of popularity that can be easily translated into economic value as represented by sales of recordings or licenses for use in advertising, television, or film. Greg Katz, music business worker by day, and proprietor of a small indie label called New Professor and band member and radio DJ by night, says that "radio stations call out to their listeners and play them samples of songs to see if they dig it, so there's literally a market research aspect as to whether a song becomes a hit." If listeners say they don't like a song, it won't be played very often (2016 [lecture]).

Radio still matters, even in small local scenes such as the indie rock scene in Echo Park (a Los Angeles neighborhood), in which Katz is a figure. In fact, radio in this scene is still crucially important. Despite what one hears—almost daily, it seems—about the dying or the radically transforming record business, for indie musicians, many of the traditional pathways for getting their music out to fans remain important. Katz told me that as a label owner he would like to do everything he can to help raise awareness of his label's bands—securing physical distribution in stores, urging his bands to tour more (ideally in a city where their recordings can be purchased in an independent record store), and trying to get more press. And, he says, "I'd like to expand into doing more radio stuff, because as a DJ I know especially radio is the only unmediated way to encounter new music, so I want to home in on that" (interview, 2014). (Katz is referring to college, public, and community radio stations, which are "unmediated" compared to commercial radio.)

Larry Little, a manager of indie bands in Los Angeles, told me how young bands espousing the indie, do-it-yourself (DIY) aesthetic need to understand that they still must rely on the traditional means of disseminating their music, including radio.

> Radio is a dying thing, but it still is very powerful, and every time I think that it's not powerful I have something happen that reminds me, like a show in Buffalo where 350 people show up unannounced on a Tuesday night, and you've never been to Buffalo before, and you're not getting 300 in San Francisco or the cool cities, and you're pulling 350 in Buffalo. You need to say, "There is some power behind radio," whether you like it or not. So that doing interviews, shaking some hands with some radio guys here and there, it all plays to the fact that it drives more heads to our show, which is more money in your gas tank and more people buying your T-shirt. It's all interrelated, and we're not living in a time where you can be so cool and aloof and give nothing back and expect it all. (Little, interview, 2014)

Clearly, indie rock bands, in and out of Echo Park, still rely heavily on radio airplay to promote themselves. Nima Kazerouni of the band So Many Wizards spoke of a colleague who "told all of her KXLU DJs about the show, and every single one played us. I heard it four times in row" (So Many Wizards, interview, 2014). A college radio station at Loyola Marymount University in Los Angeles, KXLU places its request line telephone number in a large font on its website (https://kxlu.com/contact/) so it is easy for listeners to contact the station. Word of mouth still matters, especially when it is amplified via radio. Value is created in this scene (and not only in this scene) by musicians being heard the radio, which not only might help sales of recordings and attendance at shows but also adds to a band's recognition in the scene. Radio and other forms of exchange (chapter 5, above) play an important role in the social reproduction of this scene.

All this is well known, of course. Perhaps less well known is that radio time can be purchased. Musician Michael Fiore in the band Criminal Hygiene, when talking about publicizing the band in today's market, told me:

> If you have leisure time and you're just living off of whatever, you have all this time to scheme up tours and talk to all these people. If you have money you can make anything happen, you can pay for the best PR, it's easy, just give them $3,000, and they'll do it. Or you can pay for radio. If they like your song or even if they don't like it, you pay a radio promoter, they can send your song to like three other radio stations for a fee and follow up for another fee. That's all stuff that, if you do get to a label, the label will pay for. They'll start paying for your press and for your radio distribution. You'll owe them forever, or probably never make record sales back to pay them. (Fiore, interview, 2014)

Musicians or their representatives can pay for radio time in hopes of creating buzz and increasing attendance at live shows and sales of recordings—not much different from the infamous payola practices of the past. For musicians, there is the obvious and continuing benefit of exposure (which is still so important that there are services they can pay for to obtain or increase it). Listeners can hear the music they like, be in the know, share their enthusiasms with friends, and more.[4] And on it goes, in a never-ending series of cycles of exchanges of time, money, knowledge, and more.

Circulation

Now let me begin to lay out how we can theorize the circulation of music beyond flows. Some recent publications offer ethnographic studies of the global circulation of commodities, musical or not, studies that show in empirical detail just how things move and what people do with them (for just two, see Novak 2013; Sylvanus 2016). I have been especially inspired by anthropologist Purnima Mankekar's *Unsettling India* (2015), which offers deeply ethnographic interpretations of today's globalization and provides subtle and nuanced treatments of what a globalized present and recent past look like. Mankekar's insightful book offers a rich and sophisticated treatment of the movement, or the unsettled stasis, of peoples and the circulation of commodities, media, and affect (and more) in a contemporary diasporic public culture. Mankekar examines how goods and commodities travel and end up in Indian stores in the San Francisco Bay area and how media commodities move. Again and again, Mankekar takes up themes of circulation, emphasizing that the social world is never static.

The idea that money and commodities circulate everywhere was, of course, central for Marx, whose discussions of circulation are built on countless exchanges. His comparison of barter to capitalist exchange is illustrative, a comparison that features a linen weaver who sells twenty yards of linen for two pounds, then spends the two pounds for a Bible:

> The weaver has undoubtedly exchanged his linen for a Bible, his own commodity for someone else's. But this phenomenon is only true for him. The Bible-pusher, who prefers a warming drink to cold sheets [having purchased brandy with his proceeds], had no intention of exchanging linen for his Bible; the weaver did not know that wheat had been exchanged for his linen. B's commodity replaces that of A, but A and B do not mutually exchange their commodities. It may in fact happen that A and B buy from each other, but a particular relationship of this kind is by no means the necessary result of the general conditions of the circulation of commodities. (1990, 207)

Marx then makes a point about how the exchange of commodities takes on a life of its own apart from the participating individuals: "There develops a whole network of social connections of natural origin, entirely beyond the control of the human agents. Only because the farmer has sold his wheat is the weaver able to sell his linen, only because the weaver has sold his linen is our rash and intemperate friend able to sell his Bible, and only because the latter already has the water of everlasting life is the distiller able to sell his *eau-de-vie*. And so it goes on" (1990, 207–8).

For Marx, capitalist circulation, since it involves money, entails its continuing movement. Goods move as well, but more fitfully. "The process of circulation," he writes,

> unlike the direct exchange of products, does not disappear from view once the use-values have changed places and changed hands. The money does not vanish when it finally drops out of the series of metamorphoses undergone by a commodity. It always leaves behind a precipitate at a point in the arena of circulation vacated by the commodities. In the complete metamorphosis of the linen, for example, linen-money-Bible, the linen first falls out of circulation, and money steps into its place. Then the Bible falls out of circulation, and again money takes its place. When one commodity replaces another, the money commodity always sticks to the hands of some third person. Circulation sweats money from every pore. (1990, 208)

Here, I am more concerned with the circulation of commodities than with that of money, but it is clear from Marx that it is money that makes possible the circulation of commodities. But if we understand value to be represented by tokens beyond money—music fandom, for example, represented in playlists and other shareable and movable tokens—Marx's conception is still useful. Things circulate on thoroughfares of commonly understood conceptions of value, whether or not these are made of money, to the extent that, as anthropologists Benjamin Lee and Edward LiPuma (2002, 210) have argued, today's globalized neoliberal capitalism is circulation-based, a new stage in capitalism's history.

Gabriel Tarde on Circulation and Exchange

I have also found the French sociologist and jurist Gabriel Tarde (1843–1904) to be useful in understanding processes of circulation and exchange. Tarde didn't possess a concept of culture, which is normally something with which I would take issue. But the absence of such a concept is a potent contributor to why his ideas are valuable in helping us to think through how ideas and other things spread (and, I would add, gain a foothold or coalesce in particular cultures or social groups in particular places and times): we can't simply attribute the movement of something to cultural causes. Tarde's theories were predicated on the idea that social energy, ideas, affect circulate from one person to the next like a contagion—go viral in a nineteenth-century manner. Re-presenting Tarde's ideas, however, requires a bit of introduction, since he did not subscribe to what is now social-theoretical orthodoxy, and his thinking isn't as well-known as more canonical social theorists.[5]

Drawing on economist Charles Gide (uncle of writer André Gide) to outline what he considers to be the four parts of political economy, Tarde posits production (which he glosses as reproduction), circulation, distribution, and consumption. Circulation for Tarde is only the "imitative repetition of needs, labours, interests and their reciprocal radiation by exchange" (1902, 75).[6] "Imitative repetition," or simply "imitation," formed one of Tarde's main theoretical foundations. "Socially," he writes, "everything is either invention or imitation" (1903, 3). That is, everything is either new or not and, regardless, imitated or not. Ideas, desires, needs move from person to person, radiating out like ripples following a stone tossed into a pond. Society itself consists of those imitating others, or "counter-imitating" them—that is, doing the opposite of others (1903, xvii).

Tarde believed that ideas or practices gained a footing in the world not for social or cultural reasons but because of their transmission, person to person. Opinion and its dissemination mattered. Long before Jürgen Habermas (1991), Benedict Anderson (1991), and others, Tarde considered the importance of the newspaper in spreading and solidifying public opinion: "If the individual members separate to the point of no longer seeing each other or remain so separated beyond a certain short period of time, they cease to be associates. . . . However, not all communications from mind to mind, from soul to soul, are necessarily based on physical proximity. This condition is fulfilled less and less often in our civilized societies when *currents of opinion* take shape" (1969, 278; emphasis in original). These "currents of opinion" can occur through disparate people reading the newspaper:

> The strange thing about it is that these men who are swept along in this way, who persuade each other, or rather who transmit to one another suggestions from above—these men do not come in contact, do not meet or hear each other; they are all sitting in their own

homes scattered over a vast territory, reading the same newspaper. What is then the bond between them? This bond lies in their simultaneous conviction or passion and in their awareness of sharing at the same time an idea or a wish with a great number of other men. It suffices for a man to know this, even without seeing these others, to be influenced by them *en masse* and not just by the journalist, who is the common inspiration of them all and is himself all the more fascinating for being invisible and unknown. (1969, 278)

Newspapers participate in creating currents of opinion by spreading ideas that are transmitted from one person to another. Tarde's aversion to the idea that "society" or "culture" is a whole greater than the sum of its parts necessitated the development of an extensive theory of circulation, both by word of mouth and through publication in what we now call public culture. Marx observed the sorts of endless circulation—of money and commodities—in the capitalist world, but Tarde gives us a way of understanding how immaterial things such as ideas—or radio music or digitalized music—circulate.[7]

Circulation and Value

Thus far, I have mainly shown that circulation entails exchange. In this section, I want to argue that things circulate because they have value for people. This theory of circulation is thus predicated on conceptions of value, a position that is clearly evident in Marx: "The owner of a commodity is prepared to part with it only in return for other commodities whose use value satisfies his own need" (1990, 180). Things produce exchange value in the form of money realized for a seller and use-value for the buyer, though the latter can turn around and realize exchange value herself if she desires. And on and on.

The first part of this argument to flesh out here is that things—including intangible things such as ideas and music—circulate and are exchanged because they have value for people. Koray Çalışkan and Michel Callon make this point in linking circulation, transformation, and valuation. "Nothing moves on its own," they write. Goods are produced because they possess value for those who produce them; goods are distributed because they have value for distributors; and goods are consumed because they have value for consumers. Things circulate because they are valued (Çalışkan and Callon 2009, 389).[8] On the question of value here, these authors, as well as Tarde, are not that different from Marx.

Things of value circulate whether or not they are considered to possess economic value. And here Tarde is useful again, for he recognized that there were other forms of value beyond the economic. Tarde thought that economists had focused too much on wealth as the only measure of value, when it was perfectly clear that conceptions of value existed in other domains (what Appadurai [1986a] has usefully called "regimes of value"), and that in these domains, or regimes, value was quantified as well, with the creation of hierarchies and other sorts of sorting criteria. And Tarde recognized the importance of conversation: "Economists have given the name *market* to the geographical and social domain where the system of market values is circumscribed in solidarity with each other and where there is uniformity of price. What corresponds to the "market" made of moral, scientific or artistic values? Wouldn't it be society in the narrow sense of the word, the "world" where conversation rolls on the same subjects, where one received instruction and a common education?" (1902, 59).[9] Tarde spends a good deal of time fleshing out this idea, even positing the need for a "glorymeter" (*gloriomètre*) to measure the glory of people (1902, 56), which isn't that different from Bourdieu's conception of symbolic capital.

For cultural goods, value outside of market value can be a complex matter, Tarde says: "The *value* of a book is an ambiguous expression, because each of its copies, to the extent that it is tangible, appropriable, exchangeable and consumable, has a market value that expresses *desirability* but that, in itself, is essentially intelligible, inappropriable, unexchangeable, and inconsumable, which does not mean indestructible; it possesses a scientific value, which expresses its degree of *credibility*, without counting its literary value, which signifies its degree of expressive seduction" (2007, 621; emphasis in original, translation edited).

All this may seem rather elusive. Yet it has been axiomatic in the cultural industries for decades, if not centuries, that there is more to value than exchange value as expressed as price, as we know from the creation of canons of great works, the awarding of prizes, grants, and fellowships, and, outside of the academy, the creation of "best of the year" sorts of lists, prizes, awards, and much more. These sorts of values of cultural goods just haven't been theorized as much by those who study them (though see chapter 4 in this volume).

The second point I want to explicate from Tarde is that value is not simply conveyed through circulation—conversation, communication, opinion—from person-to-person or, more broadly, through newspapers. Circulation *creates* value. Anticipating in 1897 an argument forwarded by Georg Simmel in 1900 in *The Philosophy of Money* (1990) (and extended in Appadurai 1986a), Tarde writes:

> As it grows within an individual, the desire for a thing becomes a *special need for that thing*; as it spreads in an outside group, this desire becomes the *value of that thing*. Through the knowledge that this thing is desired or capable of being desired by someone else, or through the judgment on the capacity of this thing to satisfy a desire, there takes place a combination of belief and desire which, quite as much as the communicability of the belief and the desire, is essential to the idea of value. (1969, 227; emphases in original)

I am arguing that value can be created in this same way for cultural goods, since they move through circuits of conversation, opinion, and communication, whether face-to-face, mechanically, or digitally in public culture (see also chapter 7 in this volume).

Rather like Tarde, Lee and LiPuma have also made room for other regimes of value, in the forms of circulation evident today. Circulation as they conceive it possesses "its own forms of abstraction, evaluation, and constraint," depending on the specific sorts of interactions between what circulates and the communities around what circulates. These sorts of specificities lead them to argue for their concept of "cultures of circulation" (2002, 192), which I would say is another way of conceptualizing regimes of value.

I also want to recall Tsing's (2015, 64) extremely useful point, that capitalism coexists with other modes of the production of value, sometimes "translating" them into its own regime, sometimes not; *translation* is the term she uses for the processes by which values produced in varied noncapitalist modes of production are converted into capitalist inventory. In the realm of cultural goods, for example, performed music is converted into inventory in the form of recordings. Paying attention to every step in the capitalist supply chain, every act of translation, can help us understand how today's globalized capitalism works. To put it simply, while the concept of "regimes of value" is useful for understanding consumption of goods and the values they can acquire, we need Tsing's insights to understand that there are not just different regimes of value (really, valuation) but different regimes of the production of value.

Exchange and Social Reproduction

In attempting to move from "flows" to "circulation," I am arguing that we must also consider value. And if things thought to possess value are circulating, then we must consider exchange, both of tangible and of intangible things. Several anthropologists have argued for the importance of circulation and exchange in social reproduction, and in this section I will draw on some of those theories to help refine my conceptions of circulation, value, and exchange.

Anthropologist Jane Fajans critiques theories of exchange, especially those of Mauss and Lévi-Strauss, for focusing too closely on acts of exchange and reciprocity and not understanding the broader role played by exchange in social production and reproduction. Her conception of production includes the production not only of products but also of their values, which are realized once the product is integrated into the wider society.

It is through circulation, Fajans writes, that social values are realized: "Exchange is the point at which the latent value created in production processes and embedded in the products is transformed into publicly recognized forms of value" (1993, 8). I have argued elsewhere, drawing on Clifford Geertz (1973), that the search for value is another way of understanding Geertz's insistence on the centrality of meaning in the lives of social actors (Taylor 2017). Fajans (1993, 8) argues similarly that exchange is normally the context in which the search for meaning is consummated. For her, therefore, exchange is a crucial aspect of social production and reproduction.

Indeed, according to some anthropologists, it is exchange that continually (re)constitutes society. Annette Weiner posits exchange in terms of what she theorizes as *reproduction*: "Any society must reproduce and regenerate certain elements of value in order for the society to continue" (1980, 71). Weiner focuses her argument on Melanesian systems, in which reproduction and regeneration are culturally articulated and elaborated. For her, "exchange interaction is reflective of the kinds of symbolic and material values a society accords its productive and regenerative flow. . . . This flow must be 'fed' or the system (or part of it) begins to collapse. The *mo-*

dus operandi of this 'feeding' is exchange" (1980, 72). The years-long circulation of objects reproduces, nurtures, and regenerates social relations (1980, 79). While Weiner is mainly concerned with Melanesia, I think these insights are useful for understanding complex societies, which is what, in part, my efforts here are about.

But back to Fajans. She makes clear, as I am arguing here, that to understand circulation and exchange, we must be attentive to cultural and historical specificities. She argues that exchange is a common and important medium of circulation (1993, 7), but if we seek the source of exchange values in the act of exchange, we will miss something. Exchange values, as all values and all other social phenomena, she writes, are produced in concrete activities, which are then, through circulation and exchange, integrated into a society's system of social production (1993, 8).

Most theorists of exchange confine themselves to a consideration of the exchange of physical goods, leaving aside those that are intangible. Fajans is rather inconsistent on this point, sometimes stating that exchange, and therefore the realization of value, can only occur in the exchange of objects. But she also says that it is possible that circulation occurs where there is no exchange (1993, 7), mentioning the exchange of knowledge. She discusses at some length the circulation and exchange of values, citing public displays as an example of circulation and exchange occurring simultaneously, without the exchange of physical objects.

Despite this example, Fajans generally assumes that there is no realization of value without exchange of objects. I view circulation as constituted by exchanges, but without a physical object necessarily being exchanged. With concerts, plays, or museums, there is the cost of the ticket, which can represent money exchanged for time, or rather action: one must decide to go to the show or museum, and so what is being exchanged in that action is one's time and attention for whatever one hopes to realize from viewing the painting, seeing the play, hearing the concert. In making this claim, I am building on and extending an argument made elsewhere: that value is stored up through rehearsals and all the things that go into a public performance display. Musical performances are the moments during which stored-up value (through rehearsals, individual practice, instrument manufacture and repair, costume design and manufacture, and much more) is potentially realized (see chapter 7 in this volume).

It was perhaps because of this question of the exchange of intangible objects that Tarde considered the production and circulation of the book and its value, as well as the production of knowledge and its exchange. But exchange, he says, is an economic concept that doesn't transfer to the sort of value represented by books:

> In fact, giving and theft are moral notions, foreign to political economy, but *exchange* is a purely economic concept. It is through metaphor or misnomer that we say of two interlocutors that they "exchange their ideas" and their admiration. Trade, in fact, of beacons and beauties does not mean sacrifice, it means mutual influence by reciprocating the gift, but a gift quite privileged, which has nothing in common with wealth. There, the giver divests himself by giving; in fact, as for truths, as well as beauties, *he gives* and *retains* both. (Tarde 1902; 61, emphases in original)[10]

Tarde also argued, "Unlike wealth, which can only be changed at the cost of someone's sacrifice and which, consequently, requires some measure to regulate the extent of this sacrifice, the exchange of knowledge is an addition on both sides, not a subtraction," except, he says, "when the knowledge is contradictory; but in this case there is no exchange but a duel to the death either in the enclosed field of an individual mind or on the battlefields of sects or parties or religious wars" (1969, 227).

I would continue to argue here that the exchange of ideas and other intangible things is a kind of exchange if we are thinking in terms of regimes of value: people on the giving side may believe themselves to be receiving something in return, and those on the receiving side also believe themselves to be receiving something beyond the ideas themselves. In short, *exchange*, as I am employing the term here, thus encompasses production, circulation, and consumption of tangible or intangible things, all of which, of course, are shot through with conceptions of value. There is precedent for such a conception in Marx's thinking. The term *circulation* might imply a kind of agentless process, or a process (not much different from that of flows) in which agents' desires and intentions—by which I mean the regimes of value into which they place goods—are not taken into consideration, just as *consumption* can too often be taken to refer simply to the act of purchase or the use-value of the goods. By *exchange* I mean to refer to the myriad acts by which social actors acquire and dispose of goods, tangible or intangible, because of the value they are perceived to possess or represent to those social actors. Exchange is more than just the exchange of money and commodities or the giving and receiving of gifts. Most recorded music that circulates, for example, was originally conceived as a commodity, but it exists in that regime of value and other regimes once it begins to move, according to innumerable social actors' acts. The exchanges for music can take the form of the action required to download this rather than that, to listen, to create a playlist, share a playlist, and more (Taylor 2017)—the sort of sharing of ideas theorized by Tarde. This is time exchanged for the labor and actions of those who made the music, recorded it, distributed, advertised, marketed it, and more.

Public Culture

In some of the passages above, Tarde is clearly gesturing toward what we would now call public culture (Appadurai and Breckenridge 1988), the realm of the circulation of representational and mediational forms in which goods increasingly circulate, emanating from outside a country's or region's borders, but also available to diasporic subjects around the world. This constitutes one of the primary loci of analysis for Mankekar (2015) and in a way distinguishes her approach to questions of circulation from that of Tsing (2015), who is concerned with the circulation of a particular good, the matsutake mushroom, gathered in Oregon but ending up in Japan.

Appadurai and Breckenridge (1988, 8) offered a plea to scholars to abandon traditional lenses of analysis such as "popular," "folk," and "traditional" in order to come to grips with the complex way that cosmopolitan cultural goods can circulate. *Public culture* is the term they propose to better understand the countless cultural forms in circulation today, cultural forms that act as media for cultural significance and that can be used in the construction of group identities (1988, 5).

Mankekar (2015, 7), also drawing on Appadurai and Breckenridge's (1988) conception of public culture, views the relatively conglomerated international media companies not as monopolistic but as "rhizomatic and nodal," constructed in specific times and places with particular institutions, such as the state or a particular media business. And she is concerned not with how a new transnational public culture replaces something that has gone before but with how the newer representations, affects, and sensations interact with the older ones and how each remediates the other in what I would call an endless series of exchanges.

The circulation of cultural goods in globalized public cultures also facilitates people finding others like themselves, forming alliances, fashioning identities, as Appadurai and Breckenridge argue and as Mankekar demonstrates ethnographically. Fajans (1993, 8) makes the same point with respect to exchange, writing that exchange is the way that social actors' labor in production is given meaning socially and that actors adopt this value as an aspect of their social identity. What is more, societies (tribes, groups, or other social aggregations) can be formed through the movement of ideas and opinions, as Tarde recognized:

> This transformation of all the normal groups in public is expressed by a growing need for sociability, which necessitates regular communication associated with a continuous stream of information and joint excitations. It is therefore inevitable. And it is important to seek the consequences it has or will have, in all probability, on the intended and transformed groups in terms of their duration, their solidity, their strength, their struggles, or their alliances. (Tarde 1989, 17)[11]

Such an argument predates many theorizations of subcultures, tribes, "little cultures," and more, which have become quite commonplace in analyses of the present and recent past.

Radio, Exchange, and Circulation

Now let me return to radio. This medium, as I said above, remains, perhaps surprisingly, the most important means for the dissemination of new music to most listeners in the United States, and it is scarcely different in the rest of the world, where radio continues to play an important role in presenting music and performs, as well, all sorts of social and cultural work (Fisher 2015), participating in countless exchanges. Radio or any communications medium is predicated on the idea of exchange. People listen or watch or read or view because they believe they are receiving something of value: entertainment in the form of music or something else, information, inspiration to become musicians (see Turino 2000, 79). Those who produce believe themselves to be receiving something in return: people's attention, either to propaganda (Rice 1994) or to what is considered to be useful information, and much more.

If we are to think of the act of listening to radio as part of the countless exchanges that occur in a public culture, then it is useful to revisit the famous argument by the Canadian economist Dallas Smythe (1977) that identifies the audience as the commodity in broadcasting. Smythe's (1994, 259) position is predicated on Marx's theory of commodity exchange, and, indeed, Smythe considered exchange at some length, arguing that communication as a form of exchange is the same as the exchange of money—though what he really means, I think, is that the exchange of money and communication are both social acts. Smythe's understanding of the audience commodity is straightforward: "Because audience power is produced, sold, purchased and consumed, it commands a price and is a commodity" (1981, 26). Advertisers purchase "the services of audiences with predictable specifications which will pay attention in predictable numbers and at particular times to particular means of communication . . . in particular marketed areas" (1981, 27). This involves labor by consumers, who effectively work, unpaid, while watching, and in exchange receive program material and advertisements (1981, 33). Audiences thus labor to market things to themselves (1981, 4).

Smythe's (1977, 16) argument is that Marx's thinking about the nature of production, that production produces consumption, can be used to help us understand the processes of advertising and branding commodities under our more recent capitalism. For Smythe, the relationship of the listener or viewer to broadcasters and advertisers wasn't simply one of receiving proffered ideologies (creating false consciousnesses) or narcotizing messages but one that produced surplus value for capitalists (Fuchs 2012), in what I am characterizing as forms of exchange.

Before proceeding further down the Smythian path, let me acknowledge that there have been plenty of critiques of his arguments. Some critics have raised, for example, the issue of Marx's labor theory of value: is the consumption of broadcasts actually labor if audience members aren't being paid for their time (Arvidsson 2011). I don't think there is a need to try to force the "audience as commodity" argument into a rigid, technical, Marxoid straitjacket. I am more in agreement with Tsing's (2015) argument in various places that capitalism has always relied, as it continues to do, on noncapitalist forms of the production of value; value can be produced in regimes that aren't capitalist or economic. Against the critics of Smythe who find his arguments simplistic or reductionist (e.g., Carraway 2011; Hesmondhalgh 2010; but see Fuchs 2012 for a defense of Smythe), I would say that his main point is that broadcasting and reception (and advertising during broadcasts) are forms of exchange of value(s). Some of these exchanges are capitalist exchanges, and some—perhaps especially in alternative media such as college radio—are less commodity exchanges than other sorts—exchanges of symbolic capital, for example.[12] That is, even in cases of mainstream mass-media broadcasting, where one's case is strongest that the audience could be considered to be a commodity, we still need to pay attention to other forms of value production that might be taking place and how these exchanges of value might work; even if listeners and viewers aren't being paid, that doesn't mean that they do not believe themselves to be receiving something they value. Regimes of value that appear to be remote from economic regimes can coexist alongside economic regimes, and noncapitalist forms of value can be "translated" (Tsing 2015) into capitalist forms.

A final point about radio is that it exists in regimes of value like anything else. That is, certain individuals and certain social groups can value one form of communication over another, with perhaps the best example being young people who prefer text messaging to email. Radio is easily accessible to young people at colleges (hence the important role played by college radio in the United States in disseminating indie rock and other sorts of music), and pirate radio is also easy and cheap to set up (there are many online guides)—two reasons why radio still matters for indie rock musicians. The point here is that certain media can be valued by certain social groups for circulating their music (or whatever), and those media can themselves be placed in regimes of value of particular social groups.

Conclusions

This chapter has sketched out a way of thinking about the circulation of cultural goods, tangible and intangible, that attempts to complicate and add nuance to the useful framework offered by Appadurai a couple of decades ago (though such concerns are part of a longer history of attempting to understand how things circulate). Although this case study is of an old technology that remains relevant, the perspectives presented here should be useful in furthering our understanding of how music moves through various means, whether through broadcast, digitally, or physically. While much has been made about how digital technologies and the internet have changed everything (what I have elsewhere called "technological triumphalism" [Taylor 2016]), people mostly use technologies to do what they have always done, including making music, listening to music, sharing music, sharing ideas about music, recommending artists, songs, genres, recordings, and much more. But with today's digital technologies, such acts can occur faster and travel farther. Regardless of speed or reach, all of the actions involved in making and listening to music and disseminating it reveal and produce what particular social actors value. If something is valued, it will be exchanged, and when something is exchanged, it acquires value.

NOTES

Introduction. Theorizing Value in Practice

1   This is a very brief overview; for a more in-depth treatment of the history
     of value theory in anthropology, see Graeber 2001.

2   Keith Hart, personal communication with the author, March 12, 2006.

3   Kluckhohn quotes George A. Lundberg's "Human Values: A Research Pro-
     gram" from 1950, which argues for what today appears to be a rather Grae-
     berian action theory of value: "It is possible to infer the values of groups
     from the way in which they habitually spend their time, money, and energy.
     This means that values may be inferred from historic records of all times,
     from ancient documents to the latest census of manufactures, scales, and
     expenditures" (Lundberg 1950, 106, quoted by Kluckhohn 1962, 407).
     But Kluckhohn sets aside this inclusion and consideration of money in his
     footnote to Lundberg's text: "Lundberg's basic point is well taken, though
     a caveat must be entered against the culture-bound judgment inherent in
     the emphasis on 'money.' . . . Money is, of course, merely a cover for a very
     large system of needs and values which in our culture become expressed for
     market purposes in money" (Kluckhohn 1962, 407n30). Money, however,
     is more than a "cover," as we know even from McAllester's book and much
     subsequent research) it is a universal equivalent that not only represents
     value but can be a token of value itself.
        Ethel M. Albert, a Kluckhohn associate, in her introduction to a chapter
     about expressive activities by Kluckhohn in *People of Rimrock*, offers a ro-
     bust defense of the importance of focusing on such activities in the overall

Kluckhohnian project of seeking to discover "human universals of which each culture pattern is a distinctive interpretation" (Albert 1966, 265; see Kluckhohn 1966). These universals include recreational and expressive activities that provide insights into cultural values (and, as a Kluckhohnian, she claims that the study of aesthetics and expressive activities can be examined in a "rigorous, quantitively-oriented approach" [1966, 270]). But Albert also notes that the expenditure of resources, in the form of money, time, and energy, in the cultures considered in that volume should convince anyone of the importance of studying the sorts of aesthetic and expressive activities in which people engage: "We cannot figure the costs to the penny, but we know that much time, money, and energy go into rodeos, fiestas, and dances; ceremonials and sings; decisions by shoppers requiring or allowing choice from a variety of available jewelry, clothing, or other objects; funerals and the accompanying concerns with mourning dress, feeding or feasting the funeral party, presenting gifts, and doing services for the bereaved" (1966, 271). Kluckhohn thus seems to have been more inflexible in his exclusion of "the economic" than others even in his intellectual circle.

4   Two other brief reviews appeared, devoting no more than a paragraph or two to *Enemy Way Music*: Nettl 1956a; Streib 1955.

5   Seeger generously credits McAllester and some others.

6   While Graeber largely rejects Bourdieu for being reductionistically economistic, he nonetheless requires some sort of theory of structure and action and introduces one—from Jean Piaget (1970)—that is quite recognizable to students of practice theory. In line with his own orientation toward value, as created or revealed by action, Graeber emphasizes Piaget's focus on action, so that structure, he summarizes, is "the coordination of activity." Graeber writes of Piaget's insistence that the basis of any knowledge system is a set of practices. Structure does not exist prior to action, Graeber says, so that "ultimately, 'structure' is identical with the process of its own construction" (2001, 61). None of this, I would say, is inconsistent with a practice theory approach, though Graeber largely avoids it.

7   It seems to me that Bourdieu has been more thoroughly interrogated and critiqued for his debt to Marx than to Weber. Those who address the question of whether Marxian value is equivalent to Bourdieusian capital tend to overemphasize whatever might be Marxian in Bourdieu's thinking (and accuse him of not being Marxian enough), while de-Weberizing him (see, e.g., Beasley-Murray 2000).

Chapter 1. Supply Chains and the Production of Value of Cultural Goods

1   For more on Herz, see Lott 2003. Thanks are due to Matthew Blackmar for this recommendation.

Chapter 2. Making Musicians into Productive Laborers

1   The few scholarly accounts of music managers include Cloonan 2015; Morrow 2009; and Williamson 2015; but these are focused largely on the British perspective.

2   Though musicians and others have always tried, most recently through technological means (see Taylor 2023) and in the past through the adoption of compositional "systems," such as Joseph Schillinger's and, later, twelve-tone composition (see Taylor n.d.).

3   For stories of some famous managers of the past, see Garfield 1986 and Rogan 1989.

Chapter 3. Trendspotters: Agents and Inspectors of Consumer Capitalism

1   The writing of "Class, Status, and Party," including drafts and revisions, has been dated between 1910 and 1919. Weber died in 1920.

2   I'm indebted to Brent Luvaas for telling me of Devon Powers's book.

3   For more on Dichter, see Bennett 2005; Horowitz 1998; and Taylor 2012. For a critique, see Baudrillard 1996).

4   For just a couple of the sources from the trade press, see Gloor and Cooper 2007; and Kerner and Pressman 2007.

5   Powers (2019) discusses the effect of Gladwell's article on the field.

6   Zandl coauthored a book with a partner from an earlier firm, Xtreme, Inc., Richard Leonard (Zandl and Leonard 1992).

7   For more on Buckingham, see Powers 2019.

8   This is described here: https://cassandra.co/life/2016/02/02/cassandra-report-digest-millennials-seek-brands-help-in-finding-love.

9   The advertising agency, Hill Holliday, describes this campaign at their website, https://www.hhcc.com/work/lg/moms-inner-voice; accessed February 21, 2023.

10   I am relying on Irregular Labs' previews of their reports, since the full reports cost $2,000.

11   There is something of a symbiotic relationship between the marketing, branding, and consumer research industries, so that the findings of each—gathered at great expense and often over long periods of time, as we have seen—find their way into more academic studies, which in turn can influence these industries. More academic studies of Generation Z paint much the same picture as the consumer research firms (see, e.g., Seemiller and Grace 2019).

Chapter 4. Taking the Gift Out and Putting It Back In: From Cultural Goods to Commodities

This chapter was originally published in *The Oxford Handbook of Music and Advertising*, edited by Siu-Lan Tan, James Deaville, and Ronald Rodman (New York: Oxford University Press, 2021), and has been reproduced by permission of Oxford University Press. For permission to reuse this material, please visit http://global.oup.com/academic/rights.

Chapter 5. Maintenance and Destruction of an East-Side Los Angeles Indie Rock Scene

This chapter was originally published in *The Oxford Handbook of Economic Ethnomusicology*, edited by Anna Morcom and Timothy D. Taylor (New York: Oxford University Press, 2020), and has been reproduced by permission of Oxford University Press, https://doi.org/10.1093/oxfordhb /9780190859633.013.27. For permission to reuse this material, please visit http://global.oup.com/academic/rights.

1   For more on this scene, see S. Brown 2018 and Taylor 2020.

2   A few other authors have addressed the production of value (though not necessarily in those terms) in the realm of music, though their treatments oversimplify, in my view, failing to understand the extremely complex relationship between capitalist and other modes of the production of value and how goods can move from regimes of value in their social lives; see Nancy K. Baym (2018), who relies on Hyde 2007. Tim J. Anderson (2014)

offers a nuanced treatment of the production of value in information supply chains, an important way that value can be created in and outside of capitalism (see Tsing 2013, 2015; and chapter 1 in this volume).

3   For recent studies of popular music and its relationship to capitalism in urban settings, see Garland 2019 and Greene 2018.

4   The web page is no longer active: http://www.converse.com/Experiences/RubberTracks/.

5   For more on capitalism capturing coolness, see Frank 1997, McGuigan 2009, and Taylor 2016a.

6   See T. Anderson 2014 on the amount of work involved in trying to make it in today's music business.

7   See Baym 2018 for a discussion of the social-network maintenance and cultivation undertaken by musicians in today's music scenes.

8   Musicians retain the rights to their music, but musicians were told on the company's website that they would "have the option to give Converse limited rights to [their] music, so we can publish it on Converse.com and affiliated Converse sites and our presence on social media sites" (http://www.converse.com/Experiences/RubberTracks/; this link is no longer active). This sounds generous, but there is so little chance that a song will make money that it doesn't matter. Brands such as Converse derive value from the perception that they are hip and cool through fostering new music. With schemes such as Rubber Tracks, they have created a pipeline from the domestic or enclaved economy to capitalism, which simultaneously allows them to be seen as part of the creative economy, not just the purveyors of commodities that they actually are. Similarly, the caffeinated drink company Red Bull, which has been recording musicians since 1998 and owns studios around the world, said on its website: "Red Bull generally has no interest in using any of the music created at the Academy for anything other than Academy matters, and doesn't obtain copyrights for any of your work. Creativity is the only currency here. Music is what we live and stand for" (http:// www.redbullmusicacademy.com/about/faq; this link is no longer active).

Chapter 6. World Music, Value, and Memory

This chapter was originally published in *Speaking in Tongues: Pop Lokal Global*, edited by Dietrich Helms and Thomas Phleps, Beiträge zur Popularmusikforschung 42 (Bielefeld, Germany: Transcript, 2015).

1   For a useful examination and critique of the idea of the Irish music session as a community, see O'Shea 2006–7. Thanks are due to Kevin Levine for telling me of this article.

2   This study was conducted before IRB clearance was required of ethnographic studies. I received oral permission from my subjects to conduct these interviews, but will not reveal their full names here.

3   These recent interviews were approved by UCLA's IRB #11–002035.

4   Thanks are due to Kevin Levine for telling me of this book.

5   One might wonder why the main tokens of value of an Irish music session are mute photographs. It is almost never the case that audio is recorded and posted somewhere or shared on social media—only photographs and, occasionally but rarely, video. Audio doesn't reveal who is present or absent. (Musicians frequently record audio so that they can learn new tunes, but these are private recordings and almost never shared on social media.) In a way, while everyone playing tunes they all know is a form of sociality, another way that sociality is established and reinforced is through the recording of tunes, which is really a kind of gift exchange. Musicians learn new tunes from musicians at other sessions, from teachers, from friends, and from recordings, and they share them with their fellows.

Chapter 7. Musical Performance as a Medium of Value

An earlier version of this chapter was published in *Investigating Musical Performance: Theoretical Models and Intersections*, edited by Gianmario Borio, Giovanni Giuriati, Alessandro Cecchi, and Marco Lutzu (London: Routledge, 2020).

Chapter 8. Circulation, Value, Exchange, and Music

This chapter was originally published in *Ethnomusicology* 64, no. 2 (Summer 2020): 254–73, and is reprinted here with thanks to the Society for Ethnomusicology.

1   See Adorno 1994 for a scathing critique of such endeavors.

2   According to Nielsen Music 360 for 2017, 49 percent of people discover new music from the radio, 40 percent from friends and relatives, 27 percent from online music services, 25 percent from social media, 23 percent

from online radio, and 14 percent from satellite radio (cited in Cakebread 2017).

3   See, for example, the charts published by Mediabase at http://americasmusiccharts.com/.

4   For more on indie and college radio in Los Angeles, see Finkel 2014 and Waits 2008.

5   This introduction is necessarily brief; for a more substantial introduction and overview, see Terry N. Clark's introduction to Tarde 1969 and Latour and Lépinay 2009.

6   "Circulation et répartition des richesses ne sont qu'un effet de la répétition imitative des besoins, des travaux, des intérêts et de leur rayonnement réciproque par l'échange." All translations are mine unless indicated otherwise.

7   Some have found such arguments useful in describing electronic mass communication and the effects of social media today (see E. Katz, Ali, and Kim 2014), though one must still culturalize these approaches through ethnographic or historical research.

8   Thanks are due to Hannah Appel, who recommended this article.

9   "Les économistes ont donné le nom de *marché* au domaine géographique et social où est circonscrit le système des valeurs vénales solidaires les unes des autres et où règne l'uniformité de prix. Qu'est-ce qui correspond au 'marché' en fait de valeurs morales, de valeurs scientifiques ou artistiques? Ne serait-ce pas la société dans le sens étroit du mot, le 'monde' où la conversation roule sur les mêmes sujets, où l'on a reçu une instruction et une éducation communes?"

10   "Et, de fait, la donation et le vol sont des notions morales, étrangères en soi à l'économie politique, mais *l'échange* est une notion proprement économique. C'est par métaphore ou abus de langage qu'on dit de deux interlocuteurs qu'ils 'échangent leurs idées' ou leurs admirations. Échange, en fait de lumières et de beautés, ne veut pas dire sacrifice, il signifie mutuel rayonnement, par réciprocité de don, mais d'un don tout à fait privilégié, qui n'a rien de commun avec celui des richesses. Ici, le donateur se dépouille en donnant; en fait de vérités, et aussi bien de beautés, *il donne* et *retient* à la fois."

11   "Cette transformation de tous les groupes quelconques en publics s'exprime par un besoin croissant de sociabilité qui rend nécessaire la mise en communication régulière des associés par un courant continu d'informations et d'excitations communes. Elle est donc inévitable. Et il importe de rechercher les conséquences qu'elle a ou qu'elle aura, suivant toutes les

vraisemblances, sur les destinés des groupes ainsi transformés, au point de vue de leur durée, de leur solidité, de leur force, de leurs luttes ou de leurs alliances."

12   See Wall 2007 for more on college radio.

REFERENCES

Interviews

Anonymous [booker]. 2014. Interview by author. Echo Park, Los Angeles, November 15.

Anonymous [music publicist]. 2014. Interview by author. West Hollywood, September 18.

Anonymous [music supervisor]. 2014. Interview by author. Culver City, CA, October 16.

Bee, Kat. 2014. Interview by author. Echo Park, Los Angeles, August 24.

Brown, Shelina. 2018. Interview by author. Echo Park, Los Angeles, September 3.

Clark, Taylor 2016. Interview by author. Los Angeles, January 3.

Clark, Taylor. 2020. Zoom interview by author, July 7.

Evans, Jeffrey. 2020. Zoom interview by author, December 1.

Fiore, Michael. 2014. Interview by author. Los Angeles, September 5.

Gorne, LeeAnn. 2013. Telephone interview by author, August 22.

Holguin, Peri. 2013. Interview by author. Long Beach, CA. August 18.

Jim [fiddler]. 1991. Interview by author. Ann Arbor, MI.

Jones, Kristin. 2016. Telephone interview by author, September 9.

Katz, Greg. 2014. Interview by author. Echo Park, Los Angeles, September 1.

Katz, Greg. 2020. Zoom interview by author, November 17.

Lang, Jackie. 2013. Interview by author. Long Beach, CA, August 18.

Little, Larry. 2014. Interview by author. Larchmont, Los Angeles, November 4.

Little, Larry. 2020. Telephone interview by author, November 13.

Nolley, Melanie. 2013. Skype interview by author, August 9.

Pam [fiddler]. 1991. Interview by author. Ann Arbor, MI.

Quiazon, Yvette. 2020. Zoom interview by author, July 21.

Schield, Neil. 2014. Interview by author. Echo Park, Los Angeles, September 12.

So Many Wizards (Nima Kazerouni, Eric Felix, Martin Tomemitsu). 2014. Interview by author. Santa Monica, CA, November 20.

Spunt, Dean. 2012. Interview by author. Los Angeles, November 11.

Stavros, Christian. 2020. Telephone interview by author, November 24.

Suzanne [tin whistle player]. 1991. Interview by author. Ann Arbor, MI.

Wightman, Baysie. 2016. Telephone interview by author, July 29.

Zandl, Irma. 2016. Interview by author. New York, NY, December 13.

Publications and Other Sources

Adorno, Theodor. 1994. "Analytical Study of the NBC 'Music Appreciation Hour.'" *Musical Quarterly* 78, no. 2 (Summer): 325–77. https://doi.org/10.1093/mq/78.2.325.

Akrofi, Eric A. 2001. "Zulu Indigenous Beliefs: To What Extent Do They Influence the Performance Practices of *Isicathamiya* Musicians?" Paper prepared for the African Arts Education Conference, South Africa, 2001.

Albert, Ethel M. 1966. Introduction to Clyde Kluckhohn, "Expressive Activities." In *People of Rimrock: A Study of Values in Five Cultures*, edited by Evon Z. Vogt and Ethel M. Albert, 265–74. Cambridge, MA: Harvard University Press.

Allen, Paul. 2018. *Artist Management for the Music Business*. 4th ed. New York: Routledge.

Anderson, Benedict. 1991. *Imagined Communities: Reflections on the Origin and Spread of Nationalism*. 2nd ed. New York: Verso.

Anderson, Tim J. 2014. *Popular Music in a Digital Music Economy: Problems and Practices for an Emerging Service Industry*. New York: Routledge.

Appadurai, Arjun. 1986a. "Introduction: Commodities and the Politics of Value." In *The Social Life of Things: Commodities in Cultural Perspective*, edited by Arjun Appadurai, 3–63. New York: Cambridge University Press.

Appadurai, Arjun, ed. 1986b. *The Social Life of Things: Commodities in Cultural Perspective*. New York: Cambridge University Press.

Appadurai, Arjun. 1996. *Modernity at Large: Cultural Dimensions of Globalization*. Minneapolis: University of Minnesota Press.

Appadurai, Arjun, and Carol A. Breckenridge. 1988. "Why Public Culture?" *Public Culture Bulletin* 1, no. 1 (Fall): 5–9. https://doi.org/10.1215/08992363-1-1-5.

Appel, Hannah. 2017. "Toward an Ethnography of the National Economy." *Cultural Anthropology* 32, no. 2: 294–322. https://doi.org/10.14506/ca32.2.09.

Arendt, Hannah. 1998. *The Human Condition*. 2nd ed. Chicago: University of Chicago Press.

Arvidsson, Adam. 2011. "Ethics and Value in Customer Co-Production." *Marketing Theory* 11, no. 3: 261–78. https://doi.org/10.1177/1470593111408176.

Barile, Nello. 2017. "Branding, Selfbranding, Making: The Neototalitarian Relation Between Spectacle and Prosumers in the Age of Cognitive Capitalism." In *The Spectacle 2.0: Reading Debord in the Context of Digital Capitalism*, edited by Marco Briziarelli and Emiliana Armano, 151–65. London: University of Westminster Press.

Baskerville, David, and Tim Baskerville. 2018. *Music Business Handbook and Career Guide*. 12th ed. Thousand Oaks, CA: Sage.

Battersby, Christine. 1989. *Gender and Genius: Towards a Feminist Aesthetics*. Bloomington: Indiana University Press.

Baudrillard, Jean. 1988. *Selected Writings*. Edited by Mark Poster. Stanford, CA: Stanford University Press.

Baudrillard, Jean. 1996. *The System of Objects*. Translated by James Benedict. New York: Verso.

Baym, Nancy K. 2018. *Playing to the Crowd: Musicians, Audiences, and the Intimate Work of Connection*. New York: New York University Press.

Bear, Laura, Karen Ho, Anna Lowenhaupt Tsing, and Sylvia Yanagisako. 2015. "Gens: a Feminist Manifesto for the Study of Capitalism." Accessed May 9, 2023. https://culanth.org/fieldsights/gens-a-feminist-manifesto-for-the-study-of-capitalism.

Beasley-Murray, Jon. 2000. "Value and Capital in Bourdieu and Marx." In *Pierre Bourdieu: Fieldwork in Culture*, edited by Nicholas Brown and Imre Szeman, 100–119. New York: Rowman and Littlefield.

Beaster-Jones, Jayson. 2014. "Beyond Musical Exceptionalism: Music, Value, and Ethnomusicology." *Ethnomusicology* 58, no. 22 (Spring–Summer): 334–40. https://doi.org/10.5406/ethnomusicology.58.2.0334.

Becker, Judith. 2004. *Deep Listeners: Music, Emotion, and Trancing*. Bloomington: Indiana University Press.

Bendix, Regina. 2009. "Heritage between Economy and Politics: An Assessment from the Perspective of Cultural Anthropology." In *Intangible Heritage*, edited by Laurajane Smith and Natsuko Akagawa, 253–69. London: Routledge.

Bendix, Regina. 2018. *Culture and Value: Tourism, Heritage, and Property*. Bloomington: Indiana University Press.

Benjamin, Walter. 1968. "The Work of Art in the Age of Mechanical Reproduction." In *Illuminations*, edited by Hannah Arendt, translated by Harry Zohn, 217–51. New York: Schocken.

Bennett, David. 2005. "Getting the Id to Go Shopping: Psychoanalysis, Advertising, Barbie Dolls, and the Invention of the Consumer Unconscious." *Public Culture* 17: 1–26. https://doi.org/10.1215/08992363-17-1-1.

Boas, Franz. 1891. "Dissemination of Tales among the Natives of North America." *Journal of American Folklore* 4, no. 12 (January–March): 13–20.

Bourdieu, Pierre. 1977. *Outline of a Theory of Practice*. Translated by Richard Nice. Cambridge: Cambridge University Press.

Bourdieu, Pierre. 1984. *Distinction: A Social Critique of the Judgement of Taste*. Translated by Richard Nice. Cambridge, MA: Harvard University Press.

Bourdieu, Pierre. 1986. "The Forms of Capital." In *Handbook of Theory and Research for the Sociology of Education*, edited by J. G. Richardson, 241–58. New York: Greenwood.

Bourdieu, Pierre. 1990. *The Logic of Practice*. Translated by Richard Nice. Stanford, CA: Stanford University Press.

Bourdieu, Pierre. 1993. *The Field of Cultural Production*. Edited by Randal Johnson. New York: Columbia University Press.

Bourdieu, Pierre. 1995. *The Rules of Art: Genesis and Structure of the Literary Field*. Translated by Susan Emanuel. Stanford, CA: Stanford University Press.

Bourdieu, Pierre. 2013. "Symbolic Capital and Social Classes." *Journal of Classical Sociology* 13, no. 2: 292–302. https://doi.org/10.1177/1468795X12468736.

Brown, August. 2016. "Origami Vinyl's Neil Schield on His Echo Park Record Store's Closing: 'It Wasn't Sustainable.'" *Los Angeles Times*, 15 March. Accessed February 21, 2023. http://www.latimes.com/entertainment/music/posts/la-et-ms-origami-vinyl-neil-schield-store-closing-20160315-story.html.

Brown, Shelina. 2018. "Yoko Ono's Experimental Vocality as Matrixial Borderspace: Theorizing Yoko Ono's Extended Vocal Technique and Her Contributions to the Development of Underground and Popular Vocal Repertoires, 1968–Present." PhD diss., University of California, Los Angeles.

Brown, Wendy. 2005. *Edgework: Critical Essays on Knowledge and Politics*. Princeton, NJ: Princeton University Press.

Cakebread, Caroline. 2017. "Radio Thrives as a Place for Music Discovery Despite the Streaming Threat." *Business Insider*, October 9. Accessed February 21, 2023. https://www.businessinsider.com/radio-thrives-as-spot-for-music-discovery-chart-2017-10.

Çalışkan, Koray, and Michel Callon. 2009. "Economization, Part 1: Shifting Attention away from the Economy toward Process of Economization." *Economy and Society* 38, no. 3 (August): 369–98. https://doi.org/10.1080/03085140903020580.

Carah, Nicholas. 2010. *Pop Brands: Branding, Popular Music, and Young People*. New York: Peter Lang.

Carraway, Brett. 2011. "Audience Labor in the New Media Environment: A Marxian Revisiting of the Audience Commodity." *Media, Culture & Society* 33, no. 5 (July): 693–708. https://doi.org/10.1177/0163443711404463.

Chanan, Michael. 1994. *Musica Practica: The Social Practice of Western Music from Gregorian Chant to Postmodernism*. London: Verso.

Cloonan, Martin. 2015. "Managing the Zoeys: Some Reminiscences." In *Organising Music: Theory, Practice, Performance*, edited by Nic Beech and Charlotte Gilmore, 226–35. Cambridge: Cambridge University Press.

"Converse Goes Global with Its Rubber Tracks Music Initiative." 2015. *Creativity*, May 26. Accessed May 9, 2023. http://creativity-online.com/work/converse-rubber-tracks-goes-global/41882.

Davison, Marc. 1997. *All Area Access: Personal Management for Unsigned Musicians*. Milwaukee: Hal Leonard.

Demos, Alison. 2007. "The Limits of Market-Research Methods." *Advertising Age*, October 8, 27. https://adage.com/article/cmo-strategy/limits-market-research-methods/120917.

Dichter, Ernest. 1947. "Psychology in Market Research." *Harvard Business Review*, no. 25: 432–43.

Dichter, Ernest. 1949. "A Psychological View of Advertising Effectiveness." *Journal of Marketing*, no. 14 (July): 61–66.

Dichter, Ernest. 1956. "Scientifically Predicting and Understanding Human Behavior." In *Consumer Behavior and Motivation*, edited by Robert H. Cole, 26–37. Urbana: Bureau of Economic and Business Research, College of Commerce and Business Administration of the University of Illinois.

Di Giovine, Michael A. 2009. *The Heritage-scape: UNESCO, World Heritage, and Tourism*. Lanham, MD: Lexington Books.

Dimock, Michael. 2019. "Defining Generations: Where Millennials End and Generation Z Begins." Pew Research Center Fact-Tank, January 17. Accessed February 21, 2023. https://www.pewresearch.org/fact-tank/2019/01/17/where-millennials-end-and-generation-z-begins/.

Dinerstein, Joel. 2017. *The Origins of Cool in Postwar America*. Chicago: University of Chicago Press.

Douglas, Susan J. 1999. *Listening In: Radio and the American Imagination . . . from Amos 'n' Andy and Edward R. Murrow to Wolfman Jack and Howard Stern*. New York: Times Books.

Durkheim, Émile. 1964. *The Elementary Forms of the Religious Life*. Translated by Joseph Ward Swain. London: George Allen and Unwin.

Durkheim, Émile. 1984. *The Division of Labor in Society*. Translated by W. D. Halls. New York: Free Press.

Erlmann, Veit. 1996. *Nightsong: Performance, Power, and Practice in South Africa*. Chicago: University of Chicago Press.

Fajans, Jane. 1993. "Introduction: Exchanging Products, Producing Exchange." In *Exchanging Products: Producing Exchange*, edited by Jane Fajans, 1–13. Sydney: Oceania Monographs, University of Sydney.

Feigenbaum, Gail, and Inge Reist. 2012. "Introduction." In *Provenance: An Alternate History of Art*, edited by Gail Feigenbaum and Inge Reist, 1–4. Los Angeles: Getty Research Institute.

Fekete, John, ed. 1987. *Life after Postmodernism: Essays on Value and Culture*. New York: St. Martin's.

Feld, Steven. 2012. *Sound and Sentiment: Birds, Weeping, Poetics, and Song in Kaluli Expression*. 3rd ed. Durham, NC: Duke University Press.

Feld, Steven. 2000. "A Sweet Lullaby for World Music." *Public Culture* 12, no. 5: 145–71. https://doi.org/10.1215/08992363-12-1-145.

Finkel, Jori. 2014. "Painting on a Radio Canvas." *New York Times*, February 27, §AR, p. 20.

Fisher, Daniel. 2015. "Radio." In *Keywords in Sound*, edited by David Novak and Matt Sakakeeny, 151–64. Durham, NC: Duke University Press.

Fitzpatrick, Eileen. 1998. "PolyMedia, *Teen* Mag Link." *Billboard*, June 10, 10.

Foster, Robert J. 2013. "Things to Do with Brands: Creating and Calculating Value." *Hau: Journal of Ethnographic Theory* 3, no. 1: 44–63. https://doi.org/10.14318/hau3.1.004.

Frank, Thomas. 1997. *The Conquest of Cool: Business Culture, Counterculture, and the Rise of Hip Consumerism*. Chicago: University of Chicago Press.

Friedman, Josh. 2008. "Movie Ticket Sales Hit Record." *Los Angeles Times*, March 6. Accessed May 9, 2023. http://articles.latimes.com/2008/mar/06/business/fi-boxoffice6.

Frith, Simon. 1996. *Performing Rites: On the Value of Popular Music*. Cambridge, MA: Harvard University Press.

Fuchs, Christian. 2012. "Dallas Smythe Today: The Audience Commodity, the Digital Labour Debate, Marxist Political Economy and Critical Theory. Prolegomena to a Digital Labour Theory of Value." *tripleC* 10, no. 2: 692–740. https://doi.org/10.31269/triplec.v10i2.443.

Gaisberg, F. W. 1942. *The Music Goes Round*. New York: Macmillan.

Gardner, Burleigh B., and Sidney J. Levy. 1955. "The Product and the Brand." *Harvard Business Review*, March–April, 33–39.

Garfield, Simon. 1986. *Expensive Habits*. London: Faber and Faber.

Garland, Shannon. 2019. "Amiguismo: Capitalism, Sociality, and the Sustainability of Indie Music in Santiago, Chile." *Ethnomusicology Forum* 28, no. 1: 26–44. https://doi.org/10.1080/17411912.2019.1622431.

Garnham, Nicholas. 1990. *Capitalism and Communication: Global Culture and the Economics of Information*. Edited by Fred Inglis. Newbury Park, CA: Sage.

Geertz, Clifford. 1973. *The Interpretation of Cultures*. New York: Basic.

Geertz, Clifford. 1983. *Local Knowledge: Further Essays in Interpretive Anthropology*. New York: Basic.

Gibson-Graham, J. K. 2006. *The End of Capitalism (as We Knew It): A Feminist Critique of Political Economy*. 2nd ed. Minneapolis: University of Minnesota Press.

Giddens, Anthony. 1979. *Central Problems in Social Theory: Action, Structure, and Contradiction in Social Analysis*. Berkeley: University of California Press.

Gladwell, Malcolm. 1997. "The Coolhunt." *New Yorker*, March 17, 78–88.

Gloor, Peter A., and Scott M. Cooper. 2007. *Coolhunting: Chasing Down the Next Big Thing*. New York: AMACOM.

Graeber, David. 2001. *Toward an Anthropological Theory of Value: The False Coin of Our Own Dreams*. New York: Palgrave.

Graeber, David. 2005. "Value: Anthropological Theories of Value." In *A Handbook of Economic Anthropology*, edited by James G. Carrier, 439–54. Northampton, MA: Edward Elgar.

Graeber, David. 2015a. "Radical Alterity Is Just Another Way of Saying 'Reality.'" *Hau: Journal of Ethnographic Theory* 5, no. 2: 1–41. https://doi.org/10.14318/hau5.2.003.

Graeber, David. 2015b. *The Utopia of Rules: On Technology, Stupidity, and the Secret Joys of Bureaucracy*. Brooklyn, NY: Melville House.

Graham, Phil. 2019. *Music, Management, Marketing, and Law: Interviews across the Music Business Value Chain*. Cham, Switzerland: Springer.

Greenberg, Karl. 2014. "Mom's Thoughts Feature in LG Appliance Campaign." *Marketing Daily*, May 14. Accessed May 9, 2023. https://www.mediapost.com/publications/article/225836/moms-thoughts-featured-in-lg-appliance-campaign.html.

Greene, Andrew. 2018. "Revolutionary Songs in a Gentrifying City: Stylistic Change and the Economics of Salvage in Southern Mexico." *Popular Music* 37, no. 30: 351–70. https://doi.org/10.1017/S0261143018000429.

Gregory, C. A. 2015. *Gifts and Commodities*. 2nd ed. Chicago: Hau Books.

Griffin, Sharon F. 1995. "Isicathamiya: 'To Tread Like a Cat.'" *ICWA Letters*, July, 1–6.

Gronow, Pekka. 1981. "The Record Industry Comes to the Orient." *Ethnomusicology* 25, no. 2 (May): 251–84.

Grossman, Lev. 2003. "Trends: The Quest for Cool." *Time*, September 8, 44–50.

Gupta, Akhil. 2012. *Red Tape: Bureaucracy, Structural Violence, and Poverty in India*. Durham, NC: Duke University Press.

Habermas, Jürgen. 1991. *The Structural Transformation of the Public Sphere: An Inquiry into a Category of Bourgeois Society*. Translated by Thomas Burger and Frederick Lawrence. Cambridge, MA: MIT Press.

Hahn, Hans Peter. 2008. "Diffusionism, Appropriation, and Globalization: Some Remarks on Current Debates in Anthropology." *Anthropos* 103, no. 1: 191–202.

Hamilton, Colin (Hammy). 1999. "Session." In *The Companion to Irish Traditional Music*, edited by Fintan Vallely, 345–46. Cork, Ireland: Cork University Press.

Hampp, Andrew. 2011. "The Anti-Branding Music Branding Strategy." *Billboard*, December 3, 8–9.

Harris, Deonte L. 2022. "On Race, Value, and the Need to Reimagine Ethnomusicology for the Future." *Ethnomusicology* 66, no. 2 (Summer): 213–35. https://doi.org/10.5406/21567417.66.2.03.

Hart, Keith. 2001. *Money in an Unequal World*. New York: TEXERE.

Hart, Keith. 2014. "Marcel Mauss's Economic Vision, 1920–25: Anthropology, Politics, Journalism." *Journal of Classical Sociology* 14, no. 1: 34–44. https://doi.org/10.1177/1468795X13494716.

Harvey, David. 2010. *A Companion to Marx's* Capital. New York: Verso.

Haselstein, Ulla, Irmela Huiya-Kirschnereit, Catrin Gersdorf, and Elena Giannoulis, eds. 2013. *The Cultural Career of Coolness: Discourses and Practices of Affect Control in European Antiquity, the United States, and Japan*. Lanham, MD: Lexington Books.

Hebdige, Dick. 2012. *Subculture: The Meaning of Style*. New York: Routledge.

Hesmondhalgh, David. 2010. "User-Generated Content, Free Labour and the Cultural Industries." *Ephemera* 10, no. 3/4: 267–84.

Hesmondhalgh, David, and Leslie M. Meier. 2015. "Popular Music, Independence and the Concept of the Alternative in Contemporary Capitalism." In *Media Independence: Working with Freedom or Working for Free?*, edited by James Bennett and Niki Strange, 94–116. New York: Routledge.

Higgonet, Anne. 2012. "Afterword: The Social Life of Provenance." In *Provenance: An Alternate History of Art*, edited by Gail Feigenbaum and Inge Reist, 195–209. Los Angeles: Getty Research Institute.

Hodgson, Thomas. 2021. "Spotify and the Democratisation of Music." *Popular Music* 40, no. 1 (February): 1–17. https://doi.org/10.1017/S0261143021000064.

Horkheimer, Max, and Theodor Adorno. 1990. *Dialectic of Enlightenment*. Translated by John Cumming. New York: Continuum.

Horowitz, Daniel. 1998. "The Emigré and American Consumer Culture: George Katona and Ernest Dichter." In *Getting and Spending: European and American Consumer Society in the Twentieth Century*, edited by Susan Strasser, Charles McGovern, and Matthias Judt, 149–66. Cambridge: Cambridge University Press.

"How Influencing as a Career Has Impacted Today's Economy." 2019. NPR. *All Things Considered*, June 3.

Hyde, Lewis. 2007. *The Gift: Creativity and the Artist in the Modern World*. New York: Vintage.

IFPI (International Federation of the Phonographic Industry). 2012. *Investing in Music: How Music Companies Discover, Nurture and Promote Talent*. Report.

Inglis, Ian. 2003. "'Some Kind of Wonderful': The Creative Legacy of the Brill Building." *American Music* 21, no. 2 (Summer): 214–35.

Irregular Labs. n.d. *The Irregular Report 2: Fluidity*. Los Angeles: Irregular Labs.

Jones, Andrew. 2001. *Yellow Music: Media Culture and Colonial Modernity in the Chinese Jazz Age*. Durham, NC: Duke University Press.

Jones, Michael L. 2012. *The Music Industries: From Conception to Consumption*. Houndmills, Basingstoke, UK: Palgrave Macmillan.

Kaplan, Don. 1997. "Sony Arm Spins Artists into Brands." *Billboard*, April 5, 59–60.

Katz, Elihu, Christopher Ali, and Joohan Kim. 2014. *Echoes of Gabriel Tarde: What We Know Better or Different 100 Years Later*. Los Angeles: USC Annenberg Press.

Katz, Greg. 2016. Lecture. University of California, Los Angeles. Delivered May 23.

Katz, Greg. 2019. Lecture. University of California, Los Angeles. Delivered April 8.

Kaul, Adam. 2009. *Turning the Tune: Traditional Music, Tourism, and Social Change in an Irish Village*. Oxford: Berghahn.

Keane, Webb. 2008. "Market, Materiality and Moral Metalanguage." *Anthropological Theory* 8, no. 1: 27–42. https://doi.org/10.1177/1463499607087493.

Keil, Charles, and Steven Feld. 1994. *Music Grooves: Essays and Dialogues*. Chicago: University of Chicago Press.

Kerner, Noah, and Gene Pressman. 2007. *Chasing Cool: Standing Out in Today's Cluttered Marketplace*. New York: Atria.

Kim, Gooyong. 2019. *From Factory Girls to K-Pop Idol Girls: Cultural Politics of Developmentalism, Patriarchy, and Neoliberalism in South Korea's Popular Music Industry*. Lanham, MD: Lexington Books.

Kirshenblatt-Gimblett, Barbara. 1995. "Theorizing Heritage." *Ethnomusicology* 39 (Autumn): 367–80.

Kirshenblatt-Gimblett, Barbara. 2006. "World Heritage and Cultural Economics." In *Museum Frictions: Public Cultures/Global Transformations*, edited by Ivan Karp, Corinne A. Kratz, Lynn Szwaja, and Tómas Ybarra-Frausto, with Gustavo Buntinx, Barbara Kirshenblatt-Gimblett, and Ciraj Rassool, 35–45. Durham, NC: Duke University Press.

Klein, Bethany. 2009. *As Heard on TV: Popular Music in Advertising*. Burlington, VT: Ashgate.

Klein, Naomi. 2000. *No Logo: Taking Aim at the Brand Bullies*. New York: Vintage.

Kluckhohn, Clyde. 1954. Foreword to David P. McAllester, *Enemy Way Music: A Study of Social and Esthetic Values as Seen in Navaho Music*. Cambridge, MA: Peabody Museum of American Archaeology and Ethnology, Harvard University.

Kluckhohn, Clyde. 1956. "Towards a Comparison of Value-emphases in Different Cultures." In *The State of the Social Sciences*, edited by Leonard White, 116–32. Chicago: University of Chicago Press.

Kluckhohn, Clyde. 1961. "The Study of Values." In *Values in America*, edited by Donald Barrett, 17–45. Notre Dame, IN: University of Notre Dame Press.

Kluckhohn, Clyde. 1962. "Values and Value-Orientation in the Theory of Action: An Exploration in Definition and Classification." In *Toward a General Theory of Action*, edited by Talcott Parsons and Edward A. Shils, 388–433. Cambridge, MA: Harvard University Press.

Kluckhohn, Clyde. 1966. "Expressive Activities." In *People of Rimrock: A Study of Values in Five Cultures*, edited by Evon Z. Vogt and Ethel M. Albert, 275–98. Cambridge, MA: Harvard University Press.

Kluckhohn, Florence, and Fred Strodtbeck. 1961. *Variations in Value Orientation*. Evanston, IL: Row, Peterson.

Kopytoff, Igor. 1986. "The Cultural Biography of Things." In *The Social Life of Things: Commodities in Cultural Perspective*, edited by Arjun Appadurai, 64–91. New York: Cambridge University Press.

Lambek, Michael. 2013. "The Value of (Performative) Acts." In: *Hau: Journal of Ethnographic Theory* 3: 141–60. https://doi.org/10.14318/hau3.2.009.

Lammer, Christof, and André Thiemann. 2023. "Introduction: Infrastructuring Value." *Ethnos: Journal of Anthropology*. https://doi.org/10.1080/00141844.2023.2180063.

Latour, Bruno, and Vincent Antonin Lépinay. 2009. *The Science of Passionate Interests: An Introduction to Gabriel Tarde's Economic Anthropology*. Chicago: Prickly Paradigm.

Lee, Benjamin, and Edward LiPuma. 2002. "Cultures of Circulation: The Imaginations of Modernity." *Public Culture* 14, no. 1 (Winter): 191–213. https://doi.org/10.1215/08992363-14-1-191.

Lee, Hark Joon, director. 2012. *9 Muses of Star Empire* (film).

Lefcowitz, Eric. 2013. *Monkee Business: The Revolutionary Made-for-TV Band*. Port Washington, NY: Retrofuture Products.

Levine, Lawrence W. 1988. *Highbrow/Lowbrow: The Emergence of Cultural Hierarchy in America*. Cambridge, MA: Harvard University Press.

Lévi-Strauss, Claude. 1969. *The Elementary Structures of Kinship*. Edited by Rodney Needham. Translated by James Harle Bell, John Richard von Sturmer, and Rodney Needham. Boston: Beacon.

Levy, Sidney J. 1964. "Symbolism and Life Style." In *Toward Scientific Marketing: Proceedings of the Winter Conference of the American Marketing Association*, edited by Stephen A. Greyser, 140–50. Boston: American Marketing Association.

Lott, R. Allen. 2003. *From Paris to Peoria: How European Piano Virtuosos Brought Classical Music to the American Heartland*. New York: Oxford University Press.

Love, Joanna. 2015. "From Cautionary Chart-Topper to Friendly Beverage Anthem: Michael Jackson's 'Billie Jean' and Pepsi's 'Choice of a New Generation' Television Campaign." *Journal of the Society for American Music* 9: 178–203. https://doi.org/10.1017/S175219631500005X.

Lubinski, Christina, and Andreas Steen. 2017. "Traveling Entrepreneurs, Traveling Sounds: The Early Gramophone Business in India and China." *Itinerario* 41: 275–303. https://doi.org/10.1017/S0165115317000377.

Lundberg, George A. 1950. "Human Values: A Research Program." *Research Studies of the State College of Washington* 18, no. 1 (September): 103–11.

Macchiarella, Ignazio. 2011. "Sauvegarder l'oralité? Le Cas du *canto a tenore*." In *Patrimoine culturel immatériel: Enjeux d'une nouvelle catégorie*, edited by Chiara Bortolotto, Annick Arnaud, and Sylvie Grenet, 167–86. Paris: Éditions de la Maison des sciences de l'homme.

Macchiarella, Ignazio. n.d. "'Anyway, We Just Keep on Singing as We Know': Sardinian *a Tenore* Song after UNESCO's Proclamation." Photocopy.

Mankekar, Purnima. 2015. *Unsettling India: Affect, Temporality, Transnationality*. Durham, NC: Duke University Press.

Martineau, Pierre. 1957. *Motivation in Advertising: Motives That Make People Buy*. New York: McGraw-Hill.

Marx, Karl. 1990. *Capital: A Critique of Political Economy*. Vol. 1. Translated by Ben Fowkes. London: Penguin.

Maurer, Bill. 2006. "The Anthropology of Money." *Annual Review of Anthropology* 35: 15–36. https://doi.org/10.1146/annurev.anthro.35.081705.123127.

Mauss, Marcel. 2002. *The Gift: The Form and Reason for Exchange in Archaic Societies*. Translated by W. D. Halls. New York: Routledge.

Mauss, Marcel. 2016. *The Gift*. Expanded ed. Translated and edited by Jane I. Guyer. Chicago: University of Chicago Press.

McAllester, David P. 1954. *Enemy Way Music: A Study of Social and Esthetic Values as Seen in Navaho Music*. Cambridge, MA: Peabody Museum of American Archaeology and Ethnology, Harvard University.

McClintock, Pamela. 2014. "$200 Million and Rising: Hollywood Struggles with Soaring Marketing Costs." *Hollywood Reporter*, July 31. Accessed February 21, 2023. http://www.hollywoodreporter.com/news/200-million-rising-hollywood-struggles-721818.

McCracken, Grant. 1997. *Plenitude*. N.p.: Periph.: Fluide.

McGuigan, Jim. 2009. *Cool Capitalism*. New York: Pluto.

Meier, Leslie M. 2017. *Popular Music as Promotion: Music and Branding in the Digital Age*. Malden, MA: Polity.

Meillassoux, Claude. 1981. *Maidens, Meal and Money: Capitalism and the Domestic Community*. New York: Cambridge University Press.

Meintjes, Louise. 2017. *Dust of the Zulu: Ngoma Aesthetics after Apartheid*. Durham, NC: Duke University Press.

Merriam, Alan P. 1964. *The Anthropology of Music*. Evanston, IL: Northwestern University Press.

Merriam, Alan P., and Harvey C. Moore. 1956. Review of David P. McAllester, *Enemy Way Music: A Study of Social and Esthetic Values as Seen in Navaho Music*. *American Anthropologist* 58, no. 1 (February): 219–20.

Millard, Andre. 2005. *America on Record: A History of Recorded Sound*. 2nd ed. New York: Cambridge University Press.

Moor, Liz. 2007. *The Rise of Brands*. New York: Berg.

Morcom, Anna. 2020. "Music, Exchange, and the Production of Value: A Case Study of Hindustani Music." In *The Oxford Handbook of Economic Ethnomusicology*, edited by Anna Morcom and Timothy D. Taylor. https://doi.org/10.1093/oxfordhb/9780190859633.013.28.

Morrow, Guy. 2009. "Radiohead's Managerial Creativity." *International Journal of Research into New Media Technologies* 15, no. 2: 161–76. https://doi.org/10.1177/1354856508101581.

Mukerji, Chandra. 1983. *From Graven Images: Patterns of Modern Materialism*. New York: Columbia University Press.

Muller, Carol A. 2004. *South African Music: A Century of Traditions in Transformation*. Santa Barbara, CA: ABC-CLIO.

Munn, Nancy. 1992. *The Fame of Gnawa: A Symbolic Study of Value Transformation in a Massim Society*. Durham, NC: Duke University Press.

"Musician Marketing: Branding." n.d. PsPrint. Accessed February 21, 2023. https://www.psprint.com/resources/musician-marketing-branding/.

Myers, Fred R., ed. 2001. *The Empire of Things: Regimes of Value and Material Culture*. Santa Fe, NM: School of American Research Press.

Myers, Fred R. 2002. *Painting Culture: The Making of an Aboriginal High Art*. Durham, NC: Duke University Press.

Nettl, Bruno. 1956a. Review of *Enemy Way Music* by David P. McAllester and *Songs of the Nootka Indians of Western Vancouver Island* by Helen H. Roberts and Morris Swadesh. *Journal of American Folklore* 60, no. 2 (October–December): 398–99.

Nettl, Bruno. 1956b. Review of David P. McAllester, *Enemy Way Music: A Study of Social and Esthetic Values as Seen in Navajo* [sic] *Music*. *Ethnomusicology* 1, no. 8 (September): 26–27.

Nisbet, Robert A. 1993. *The Sociological Tradition*. New Brunswick, NJ: Transaction.

Novak, David. 2013. *Japanoise: Music at the Edge of Circulation*. Durham, NC: Duke University Press.

Oakes, Jason Lee. 2005. "Losers, Punks, and Queers (and Elvii too): Identification and 'Identity' at New York City Music Tribute Events." PhD diss., Columbia University.

Ochoa Gautier, Ana María. 2013. "Disencounters between Music's Allure and the Expediency of Culture in Colombia." *Latin American Research Review* 48: 12–29. https://doi.org/10.1353/lar.2013.0054.

O'Reilly, Daragh, Gretchen Larsen, and Krzysztof Kubacki. 2013. *Music, Markets and Consumption*. Woodeaton, UK: Goodfellow.

Ortner, Sherry B. 1984. "Theory in Anthropology since the Sixties." *Comparative Studies in Society and History* 26, no. 1 (January): 126–66. https://doi.org /10.1017/S0010417500010811.

Ortner, Sherry B. 1989. "Theory in Anthropology Three Years Later: A Response to Papers." In *Author Meets Critics: Reactions to "Theory in Anthropology since the Sixties,"* CSST Working Paper no. 32, edited by Sherry B. Ortner, 96–116. Ann Arbor: University of Michigan.

Ortner, Sherry B. 1996. *Making Gender: The Politics and Erotics of Culture*. Boston: Beacon.

Ortner, Sherry B. 2006. *Anthropology and Social Theory: Culture, Power, and the Acting Subject*. Durham, NC: Duke University Press.

Ortner, Sherry B. 2013. *Not Hollywood: Independent Film at the Twilight of the American Dream*. Durham, NC: Duke University Press.

O'Shea, Helen. 2006–7. "Getting to the Heart of the Music: Idealizing Musical Community and Irish Traditional Music Sessions." *Journal of the Society for Musicology in Ireland* 2: 1–18. https://doi.org/10.35561/JSMI02061.

Otto, Ton, and Rane Willerslev, eds. 2013. "Value as Theory." Special issue, *Hau: Journal of Ethnographic Theory* 3, nos. 1 and 2.

Packard, Vance. 1957. *The Hidden Persuaders*. New York: David McKay.

Parry, Jonathan, and Maurice Bloch, eds. 1989. *Money and the Morality of Exchange*. Cambridge: Cambridge University Press.

Passman, Donald S. 2015. *All You Need to Know about the Music Business*. 9th ed. New York: Simon and Schuster.

Pergam, Elizabeth A. 2012. "Provenance as Pedigree: The Marketing of British Portraits in Gilded Age America." In *Provenance: An Alternate History of Art*, edited by Gail Feigenbaum and Inge Reist, 104–22. Los Angeles: Getty Research Institute.

Piaget, Jean. 1970. *Structuralism*. New York: Basic.

Piketty, Thomas. 2014. *Capital in the Twenty-First Century*. Translated by Arthur Goldhammer. Cambridge, MA: Harvard University Press.

Polanyi, Karl. 2001. *The Great Transformation: The Political and Economic Origins of Our Time*. Boston: Beacon.

Powers, Devon. 2019. *On Trend: The Business of Forecasting the Future*. Urbana: University of Illinois Press.

Presbrey, Frank. 1929. *The History and Development of Advertising*. Garden City, NY: Doubleday, Doran.

Qureshi, Regula. 1995. *Sufi Music in Pakistan: Sound, Context and Meaning in Qawwali*. Chicago: University of Chicago Press.

Rappaport, Roy A. 1979. *Ecology, Meaning, and Religion*. Richmond, VA: North Atlantic Books.

Raux, Sophie. 2012. "From Mariette to Joullain: Provenance and Value in Eighteenth-Century French Auction Catalogs." In *Provenance: An Alternate History of Art*, edited by Gail Feigenbaum and Inge Reist, 86–103. Los Angeles: Getty Research Institute.

Reiss, Scott. 2003. "Tradition and Imaginary: Irish Traditional Music and the Celtic Phenomenon." In *Celtic Modern: Music at the Global Fringe*, edited by Martin Stokes and Philip Bohlman, 145–69. Lanham, MD: Scarecrow.

Rice, Timothy. 1994. *May It Fill Your Soul: Experiencing Bulgarian Music*. Chicago: University of Chicago Press.

Rockefeller, Stuart Alexander. 2011. "Flow." *Current Anthropology* 52, no. 4 (August): 557–78. https://doi.org/10.1086/660912.

Rogan, Johnny. 1989. *Starmakers and Svengalis*. London: Futura.

Sahlins, Marshall. 1972. *Stone Age Economics*. Chicago: Aldine-Atherton.

Sahlins, Marshall. 1981. *Historical Metaphors and Mythical Realities: Structure in the Early History of the Sandwich Islands Kingdom*. Ann Arbor: University of Michigan Press.

Samples, Mark. 2011. "A Package Deal: Branding, Technology, and Advertising in Music of the 20th and 21st Centuries." PhD diss., University of Oregon.

Sanyal, Kalyan. 2013. *Rethinking Capitalist Development: Primitive Accumulation, Governmentality and Post-Colonial Capitalism*. New York: Routledge.

Schmidt, Eric J. 2020. "Arid Fidelity, Reluctant Capitalists: Salvage, Curation, and the Circulation of Tuareg Music on Independent Record Labels." *Ethnomusicology Forum*, https://doi.org/10.1080/17411912.2020.1755333.

Schnapper, Laure. 2004. "Bernard Ullman-Henri Herz: An Example of Financial and Artistic Partnership, 1846–1849." In *The Musician as Entrepreneur, 1700–1914: Managers, Charlatans, and Idealists*, edited by William Weber, 130–44. Bloomington: Indiana University Press.

Sconce, Jeffrey. 2000. *Haunted Media: Electronic Presence from Telegraphy to Television*. 2nd ed. Durham, NC: Duke University Press.

Seeger, Anthony. 2004. *Why Suyá Sing: A Musical Anthropology of an Amazonian People*. Urbana: University of Illinois Press.

Seeger, Anthony. 2009. "Lessons Learned from the ICTM (NGO) Evaluation of Nomination for the UNESCO *Masterpieces of the Oral and Intangible Heritage of Humanity*, 2001–2005." In *Intangible Heritage*, edited by Laurajane Smith and Natsuko Akagawa, 112–28. London: Routledge.

Seemiller, Corey, and Meghan Grace. 2019. *Generation Z: A Century in the Making*. London: Routledge.

Sewell, William H. 2005. *Logics of History: Social Theory and Social Transformation*. Chicago: University of Chicago Press.

Shipley, Jesse Weaver. 2013. *Living the Hiplife: Celebrity and Entrepreneurship in Ghanaian Popular Music*. Durham, NC: Duke University Press.

Simmel, Georg. 1971a. "Sociability." In *On Individuality and Social Forms*, edited by Donald N. Levine, 127–40. Chicago: University of Chicago Press.

Simmel, Georg. 1971b. "The Stranger." In *On Individuality and Social Forms*, edited by Donald N. Levine, 143–49. Chicago: University of Chicago Press.

Simmel, Georg. 1990. *The Philosophy of Money*. 2nd ed. Edited by David Frisby. Translated by Tom Bottomore, David Frisby, and Kaethe Mengelberg. New York: Routledge.

Simon, Paul. 1986. *Graceland*. Warner Bros. 92 54471 (album).

Small, Christopher. 1987. "Performance as Ritual: Sketch for an Enquiry into the True Nature of a Symphony Concert." In *Lost in Music: Culture, Style and the Musical Event*, edited by Avron Levine White, 6–32. Sociological Review Monograph 34. London: Routledge and Kegan Paul.

Smith, Barbara Herrnstein. 1988. *Contingencies of Value: Alternative Perspectives for Critical Theory*. Cambridge, MA: Harvard University Press.

Smythe, Dallas W. 1977. "Communications: Blindspot of Western Marxism." *Canadian Journal of Political and Social Theory* 1, no. 3 (Fall): 1–27.

Smythe, Dallas W. 1981. *Dependency Road*. Norwood, NJ: Ablex.

Smythe, Dallas W. 1994. *Counterclockwise: Perspectives on Communication*. Edited by Thomas Guback. Boulder, CO: Westview.

Sombart, Werner. 1967. *Luxury and Capitalism*. Ann Arbor: University of Michigan Press.

Souleles, Daniel Scott, Matthew Archer, and Morten Sørensen Thaning, eds. 2023. "Value and Change, Value in Crisis." Special issue, *Economic Anthropology* 10, no. 2.

Spotify. 2019. "Everything You Wanted to Know about Gen Z (but Were Afraid to Ask)." *For the Record*, June 3. https://newsroom.spotify.com/2019-06-03/everything-you-wanted-to-know-about-gen-z-but-were-afraid-to-ask/.

Stamps, Charles Henry. 1979. *The Concept of the Mass Audience in American Broadcasting*. New York: Arno Press.

Steedman, Ian, et al. 1981. *The Value Controversy*. London: Verso.

Stokes, Martin. 2004. "Music and the Global Order." *Annual Review of Anthropology* 33: 47–72. https://doi.org/10.1146/annurev.anthro.33.070203.143916.

Stratton, Stephen S. 1907. *Nicolo Paganini: His Life and Work*. New York: Charles Scribner's Sons.

Straw, Will. 1991. "Systems of Articulation, Logics of Change: Communities and Scenes in Popular Music." *Cultural Studies* 5 (October): 368–88. https://doi.org/10.1080/09502389100490311.

Streib, Gordon F. 1955. Review of David P. McAllester, *Enemy Way Music: A Study of Social and Esthetic Values as Seen in Navaho Music*, and Richard Hobson, *Navaho Acquisitive Values*. *American Sociological Review* 20, no. 6 (December): 770–75.

Suisman, David. 2009. *Selling Sounds: The Commercial Revolution in American Music*. Cambridge, MA: Harvard University Press.

Sylvanus, Nina. 2016. *Patterns in Circulation: Cloth, Gender, and Materiality in West Africa*. Chicago: University of Chicago Press.

Tarde, Gabriel. 1902. *Psychologie économique*. Vol. 1. Paris: Félix Alcan.

Tarde, Gabriel. 1903. *The Laws of Imitation*. Translated by Elsie Clews Parsons. New York: Henry Holt.

Tarde, Gabriel. 1969. *Gabriel Tarde on Communication and Social Influence: Selected Papers*. Edited by Terry N. Clark. Chicago: University of Chicago Press.

Tarde, Gabriel. 1989. *L'Opinion et la foule*. Paris: Les Presses universitaires de France.

Tarde, Gabriel. 2007. "Economic Psychology." Translated by Alberto Toscano. *Economy and Society* 36 (November): 614–43. https://doi.org/10.1080/03085140701615185.

Taylor, Timothy D. 1997. *Global Pop: World Music, World Markets*. New York: Routledge.

Taylor, Timothy D. 2001. *Strange Sounds: Music, Technology and Culture*. New York: Routledge.

Taylor, Timothy D. 2007. *Beyond Exoticism: Western Music and the World*. Durham, NC: Duke University Press.

Taylor, Timothy D. 2012. *The Sounds of Capitalism: Advertising, Music, and the Conquest of Culture*. Chicago: University of Chicago Press.

Taylor, Timothy D. 2016a. "The Hip, the Cool, and the Edgy, or the Dominant Cultural Logic of Neoliberal Capitalism." *Rivista di Analisi e Teoria Musicale* 22: 105–24.

Taylor, Timothy D. 2016b. *Music and Capitalism: A History of the Present*. Chicago: University of Chicago Press.

Taylor, Timothy D. 2017. *Music in the World: Selected Essays*. Chicago: University of Chicago Press.

Taylor, Timothy D. 2020. "Social Class and the Negotiation of Selling Out in a Southern California Indie Rock Scene." In *The Bloomsbury Handbook of Popular Music and Social Class*, edited by Ian Peddie, 59–75. London: Bloomsbury.

Taylor, Timothy D. 2023. *Working Musicians: Labor and Creativity in Film and Television Production*. Durham, NC: Duke University Press.

Taylor, Timothy D. n.d. "In the Factory of Fine Arts: Nickel-and-Dime Capitalism in the First Decades of Television Background Music." In preparation.

Taylor, Timothy D., Mark Katz, and Tony Grajeda, eds. 2012. *Music, Sound, and Technology in America: A Documentary History of Early Phonograph, Cinema, and Radio*. Durham, NC: Duke University Press.

Tedlow, Richard S. 1996. *New and Improved: The Story of Mass Marketing in America*. Boston: Harvard Business School Press.

Tedlow, Richard S., and Geoffrey G. Jones, eds. 1993. *The Rise and Fall of Mass Marketing*. New York: Routledge.

Tenores di Bitti. 1996. *S'amore 'e mama*. Real World LC 2098 (compact disc).

Thall, Peter M. 2016. *What They'll Never Tell You about the Music Business: The Complete Guide for Musicians, Songwriters, Producers, Managers, Industry Executives, Attorneys, Investors, and Accountants*. Berkeley, CA: Watson-Guptill.

Thornton, Sarah. 1996. *Club Cultures: Music, Media and Subcultural Capital*. Music/Culture. Middletown, CT: Wesleyan University Press.

Thornton, Sarah. 2008. *Seven Days in the Art World*. New York: W. W. Norton.

Tortorella, Neil. 2013. *Starting Your Career as a Musician*. New York: Allworth.

Traiman, Steve. 1999. "More Music-Related Projects Using Merchandise Licensing." *Billboard*, July 3, 63–64.

Trapido, Joe. 2016. *Breaking Rocks: Music, Ideology and Economic Collapse, from Paris to Kinshasa*. New York: Berghahn.

Trendera. n.d. *The Trendera Files: The Big Brand Issue*. Accessed May 10, 2023. https://www.trendera.com/trenderareports/thebigbrandissue.

Tsing, Anna Lowenhaupt. 2000. "The Global Situation." *Current Anthropology* 15, no. 3 (August): 327–60.

Tsing, Anna Lowenhaupt. 2005. *Friction: An Ethnography of Global Connection*. Princeton, NJ: Princeton University Press.

Tsing, Anna Lowenhaupt. 2009. "Supply Chains and the Human Condition." *Rethinking Marxism* 21: 148–76. https://doi.org/10.1080/08935690902743088.

Tsing, Anna Lowenhaupt. 2012. "On Nonscalability: The Living World Is Not Amenable to Precision-Nested Scales." *Common Knowledge* 18, no. 3 (Fall): 505–24. https://doi.org/10.1215/0961754X-1630424.

Tsing, Anna Lowenhaupt. 2013. "Sorting Out Commodities: How Capitalist Value Is Made through Gifts." *Hau: Journal of Ethnographic Theory* 3: 21–43. https://doi.org/10.14318/hau3.1.003.

Tsing, Anna Lowenhaupt. 2015. *The Mushroom at the End of the World: On the Possibility of Life in Capitalist Ruins*. Princeton, NJ: Princeton University Press.

Turino, Thomas. 2000. *Nationalists, Cosmopolitans, and Popular Music in Zimbabwe*. Chicago: University of Chicago Press.

Turner, Terence. 1979. "Anthropology and the Politics of Indigenous Peoples' Struggles." *Cambridge Journal of Anthropology* 5: 1–43.

Turner, Terence. 2003a. "The Beautiful and the Common: Inequalities of Value and Revolving Hierarchy among the Kayapó." *Tipití: Journal of the Society for the Anthropology of Lowland South America* 1 (June): 11–26.

Turner, Terence. 2003b. "Class Projects, Social Consciousness, and the Contradictions of 'Globalization.'" In *Violence, the State and Globalization*, edited by Jonathan Friedman, 35–66. New York: Altamira.

UNESCO. 2017. "Urgent Safeguarding List with International Assistance." Form ICH-01bis. Accessed May 9, 2023. https://ich.unesco.org/en/forms/.

UNESCO. n.d. "Text of the Convention for the Safeguarding of the Intangible Cultural Heritage." Accessed May 9, 2023. https://ich.unesco.org/en/convention.

Vazsonyi, Nicholas. 2010. *Richard Wagner: Self-Promotion and the Making of a Brand*. New York: Cambridge University Press.

Vogt, Evon Z. 1951. *Navaho Veterans: A Study of Changing Values*. Papers of the Peabody Museum of American Archaeology and Ethnology, Harvard University 41, no. 1. Reports of the Rimrock Project Values Series, no. 1.

Vogt, Evon Z., and Ethel M. Albert, eds. 1966. *People of Rimrock: A Study of Values in Five Cultures*. Cambridge, MA: Harvard University Press.

Waits, Jennifer C. 2008. "Does Indie Mean Independence? Freedom and Restraint in a Late 1990s US College Radio Community." *Radio Journal: International Studies in Broadcast & Audio Media* 5, no. 2–3 (July 2008): 83–96. https://doi.org/10.1386/rajo.5.2-3.83_1.

Walker, Alan. 1983. *Franz Liszt*. Vol. 1, *The Virtuoso Years, 1811–1847*. New York: Knopf.

Wall, Tim. 2007. "Finding an Alternative: Music Programming in US College Radio." *Radio Journal: International Studies in Broadcast & Audio Media* 5, no. 1 (December): 35–54. https://doi.org/10.1386/RAJO.5.1.35_1.

Waterman, Christopher. 1990. *Jùjú: A Social History and Ethnography of an African Popular Music*. Chicago: University of Chicago Press.

Weber, Max. 1946. *From Max Weber: Essays in Sociology*. Translated and edited by H. H. Gerth and C. Wright Mills. New York: Oxford University Press.

Weber, Max. 2001. *The Protestant Ethic and the Spirit of Capitalism*. Translated by Talcott Parsons. New York: Routledge.

Weber, William. 2004. "From the Self-Managing Musician to the Independent Concert Agent." In *The Musician as Entrepreneur, 1700–1914: Managers, Charlatans, and Idealists*, edited by William Weber, 105–29. Bloomington: Indiana University Press.

Weiner, Annette. 1980. "Reproduction: A Replacement for Reciprocity." *American Ethnologist* 7, no. 1: 71–85. https://doi.org/10.1525/AE.1980.7.1.02A00050.

WHY-Q? INC. n.d. *Introduction to WHY-Q?*. PowerPoint.

Williams, Adrian. 1990. *Portrait of Liszt: By Himself and His Contemporaries*. New York: Oxford University Press.

Williams, Raymond. 1977. *Marxism and Literature*. New York: Oxford University Press.

Williamson, John. 2015. "Artist Managers and Entrepreneurship: Risk-Takers or Risk Averse?" In *Music Entrepreneurship*, edited by Allan Dumbreck and Gayle McPherson, 87–112. London: Bloomsbury.

Wolf, Eric R. 1997. *Europe and the People without History*. Berkeley: University of California Press.

Zandl, Irma, and Richard Leonard. 1992. *Targeting the Trendsetting Consumer: How to Market Your Product or Service to Influential Buyers*. Homewood, IL: Business One Irwin.

Zelizer, Viviana A. 1994. *The Social Meaning of Money*. New York: Basic.

Zelizer, Viviana A. 2011. *Economic Lives: How Culture Shapes the Economy*. Princeton, NJ: Princeton University Press.

Zemler, Emily. 2013. "The National on Their New Documentary and Being the Kings of Leon of Denmark." *Elle*, August 14. Accessed February 21, 2023. http://www.elle.com/culture/music/news/a23549/the-national-mistaken-for-strangers-documentary-interview/.

INDEX

commodification: alienation assessment, 102–9; of audience, 20; circulation of goods and, 176–77; of cultural production, 98–117; exchange and circulation and, 187–88; of goods, 43, 46–48; of Irish traditional music, 141–49; of music, 138–41; performance as value medium and, 152–68; practice as, 35–41; transitoriness and, 4; as translation, 116–17; trendspotters and, 85–86; value theory and, 2

community: Irish traditional music and, 142–49. *See also* enclaved community

competition, value and, 165–68

compositional systems, 193n2

concert music: capitalist marketplace and, 26–31; performer-audience interactions and, 157; radio's impact on, 172–73

consecration of goods, commodification and, 99, 101–2

Consulta del Tenore, 37

consumer capitalism: class stratification and, 72–76; trendspotters and, 97

consumer research: account planning and, 78–85; big data humanization and, 87–89; current trends in, 75–76; ethnography and, 79–80; history of, 76–78; locating subjects for, 81–83; market segments and, 89–94; product improvement and, 85–86

consumption: exchange vs., 184–85; of performance, 162–63; product improvement and, 85–86; scalability and, 63–71

Converse (sneaker company), 86, 91, 131–32, 195n8

convertibility, value and, 13

"Coolhunt, The" (Gladwell), 76

coolhunters, in consumer research, 75–76

coolness: advertising and marketing of, 77–78; corporate patronage and, 131–32; fragmentation of, 83–84

corporate patronage, 131–32

craic (Irish sociality), 145–46

credibility, branding and, 115–16

Criminal Hygiene (band), 121, 125, 127, 175

cultural capital, 73

cultural distribution, power and profit in, 45

culture and cultural production: branding impact on, 113; circulation of, 170–89; commodification of, 98–117, 138–41; ethnography and, 79–80; intangible cultural heritage and, 35–41; money and, 122; non-scalability and, 49–63; performance and, 156–57; popular music and, 44; radio and, 172–75; scalability and, 49–56; supply chains and, 22–42; as symbolic capital, 18; symbolic capital and, 24–42; value theory and, 5–10, 13–14

culture and cultural production, economics of, 19

Davison, Marc, 59

Day, Andra, 69–70

demographics, of Generation Z, 94–96

Demos, Alison, 79–80

Dervish (Irish band), 142

Dichter, Ernest, 77

diffusionism and dissemination, 171

Di Giovine, Michael A., 40

digital technology: consumer research and, 88; Generation Z as digital natives, 95–96; music production and, 170–89

do-it-yourself (DIY) ethic, generalized reciprocity and, 126–28

domestic community. *See* enclaved community

dominance, in Kayapo culture, 158–59
Douglas, Susan J., 173
Durkheim, Emile, 146, 148–49
Dust of the Zulu (Meintjes), 165
Dwight, John Sullivan, 108
Dylan, Bob, 61

Echo Park (Los Angeles): capitalist vs.
    noncapitalist cultural production
    in, 133–36; as enclaved community,
    120–32; indie rock scene in, 118–37;
    informal economy in, 128; radio
    airplay and indie rock scene in,
    174–75; value production and forms
    of exchange in, 126–32
Economic Anthropology, 5
economic value: branding and, 109–16;
    cultural commodities and, 19; per-
    formance and, 152; radio airplay
    and, 173–75; spheres of, 159–60;
    symbolic capital and, 24–26; value
    theory and, 8–10, 12–15, 99
economic world reversed, Bourdieu's
    concept of, 30
Edison, Thomas, 103–4
Eilish, Billie, 95, 97
Elementary Structures of Kinship, The
    (Lévi-Strauss), 128
enclaved community: capitalist vs. non-
    capitalist modes of production in,
    133–36; Echo Park indie rock scene
    as, 119–32; generalized reciprocity
    in, 126–28; money and social mean-
    ings in, 122–25; value production
    and forms of exchange in, 126–32
enemy way ceremony (Navajo ritual),
    5–10
Enemy Way Music (McAllester), 5–9
Erlmann, Veit, 165–68
Esposito, John, 112
ethics, value theory and, 8–10, 168–69
ethnography: on circulation of music,
    176–79; consumer research and,
    75–85; of Echo Park indie rock

scene, 118–37; on Irish traditional
    music, 142–49; market segment
    research and creation and, 90–94;
    product testing and, 86; rise of,
    79–80
ethnomusicology, value theory in, 5–10
Ethnos: Journal of Anthropology, 5
"Ethos, World View, and the Analysis of
    Sacred Symbols" (Geertz), 153
Evans, Jeffrey, 62–65, 69–70
evolution, in music management, 62–63
exchange: capitalist vs. noncapital-
    ist modes of, 133–36; circula-
    tion of goods and, 171, 176–79,
    182–85; concerts and role of, 26,
    172–73; generalized reciprocity and,
    126–28; gift exchange, value the-
    ory and, 3; performance, 163; radio
    and, 186–88; value production and,
    126–32
exchange-value, Marx's concept of,
    138–41

Fajans, Jane, 20, 163, 167, 182–83, 186
fan loyalty: branding and, 115–16;
    building fan base and, 63–68; main-
    tenance of, 68–70; scalability and,
    63–71
fashion sense, music managers and, 59
Feigenbaum, Gail, 32
Feld, Steven, 155, 165
Felix, Eric, 132
feminist theory, value theory and, 3–4
Fétis, François-Joseph, 29
fetishism, intangible cultural heritage
    and, 40
film: capitalism and, 16; music produc-
    tion for, 125
Fiore, Michael, 121–22, 125, 127, 175
flows/fluidity in genres: digitalization
    and, 170–71; Generation Z and,
    95–96
Fluidity report (Irregular Labs), 91,
    95–96

focus groups, 77, 81–82

For the Record (Spotify), 96

Foucault, Michel, 15

Frith, Simon, 2

Frobenius, Leo, 171

Frost, Gabby, 84

Furano, Dell, 111

Gabriel, Peter, 37

Garland, Shannon, 10

Garnham, Nicholas, 45

gas money, importance of, 124–25

gatekeepers, in music industry, 57–58

Geertz, Clifford, 2–3, 6, 141–42, 153, 164–65, 169, 182

generalized reciprocity: indie music and, 126–28; performance and, 157

generation labeling, demographics and, 94–96

Generation Z: demographics of, 94–96; market research on, 91–94, 194n11; product testing and, 85–86

genreless music, Generation Z and, 95–96

Gibson-Graham, J. K., 3, 15, 120

Giddens, Anthony, 10

Gide, Charles, 178

Gift, The (Mauss), 2–3

Gladwell, Malcolm, 76, 86

globalization: circulation of culture and, 20, 170–71, 176–79; commodifica-tion and, 73–74; cultural produc-tion and, 151; public culture and, 185–86

glorymeter, Tarde's concept of, 180

goods: careers of, 4; circulation of, 99, 179–82; commodification of, 16; as commodities, 43, 46–48; music per-formances as, 26

Gordon, DeeDee, 76

Gorne, LeeAnn, 145

Graceland (Simon album), 165, 168

Graeber, David, 3–6, 10, 13, 15, 39–41, 43–44, 140, 150, 154–55, 158–69, 192n5

Grateful Dead (band), 112

Gupta, Akhil, 40–41

Habermas, Jürgen, 178

Halford, Rob, 61

halo effect, of masterpieces, 35–41

Harris, Deonte, 10

Hart, Keith, 3, 122

Hau: Journal of Ethnographic Theory, 5

Heine, Heinrich, 28

Herz, Henri, 30–31

Hidden Persuaders, The (Packard), 77

Higginson, Henry Lee, 108

Higonnet, Anne, 33–34

hipness, fragmentation of, 83–84

Holguin, Peri, 144

home music-making, expansion of, 27–28

honor, M. Weber on status and, 72

Hot Sheets (Zandl group), 91–94, 97

"How Influencing as a Career Has Im-pacted Today's Economy" (NPR, *All Things Considered*), 84

human capital, labor as, 113–16

humanism, value theory and, 2

Hummel, Johann Nepomuk, 27

hyper-nichification, 89

ideas: exchange of, 183–85; transmis-sion of, 178–79

image management: branding and, 111–13; for musicians, 56–63, 66–70

income stream, establishment of, 66–67

increase, narrative of, 76–78

independent (indie) music: branding and, 115–16; capitalist vs. non-capitalist modes of production and, 133–36; corporate patronage and, 131–32; in Echo Park (Los Angeles), 118–37; enclaved communities and, 120–32; informal economy in, 128;

structuralism, practice theory and, 10

subcultural market doctrine, 74–76; Echo Park indie rock scene and, 119–20

subjectivism: capitalism and, 15–16; practice theory and, 10

Suisman, David, 106–7

Summer Bummer label, 129–30

supplementary cultural analysis, consumer research and, 82

supply chain capitalism: branding and, 109–16; bureaucracy as, 35–41; commodification and, 99–102; cultural production and, 22–42; mass reproduction and, 104–9; music performances and, 26–31; provenance of symbolic capital and, 32–35; value creation and, 19

surplus value: capitalism and, 16; commodification of music and, 138–41; in cultural production, 44–45

Suyá (Kisêdjê) people, 156, 162

"Symbolic Capital and Social Classes" (Bourdieu), 73

symbolic capitalism: bureaucracy as supply chain, 35–41; circulation and, 180–82; cultural production and, 24–42; market forces and, 41–42; money's symbolic value and, 124–25; provenance as supply chain of, 32–35; radio and, 188; value theory and, 18, 22; virtuosi and money and, 26–31

tact, sociality and, 147–48

Take Me Apart (Kelela album), 96

TAKE ME A_PART: The Remixes (Kelela release), 96

talent, musicians' focus on, 120

Tarde, Gabriel, 20, 177–81, 183–86

Tarr, Delaney, 84

team building, music management and, 60–63

Teen magazine, 112

television, mass culture and, 173–75

Thall, Peter, 59, 62

"Theory in Anthropology since the Sixties" (Ortner), 11–12

Tinder, 88

Tomemitsu, Martin, 132

Totally Integrated Music Marketing (TIMM), 111–12

Touma, Joseph, 84–85

tournaments of value, 16–17, 43

traditionalist workers, transit to labor, 44

translation of value, 74–76, 116–17; circulation and, 179, 181–89

Trendera (consumer research firm), 80–85

trendspotters/trendspotting: big data and, 87–89; consumer research and, 77–78, 97; cultural capital and, 74–76; evolution of, 79–85; Generation Z and, 96; product improvement and, 85–86; search for, 83–84; value theory and, 18–19; work of, 85–96

Tsing, Anna: on accumulation and capitalism, 134; on circulation, 185; on commodification as translation, 116–17; on cultural production, 44, 46–47, 49; on global capitalism, 171; on indeterminacies of encounter, 61; on noncapitalism, 74, 120, 187–88; on project inputs, 60–63; on scalability and non-scalability, 49–51, 70; on supply-chain capitalism, 18–19, 22, 25–26, 99–102; on translation of value, 181–82; on value theory, 5, 15

Tumblr platform, 90

Turner, Terence, 4–5, 73–74, 154, 158, 161, 163–64

twelve-tone composition, 193n2

Twitter platform, 90

www.ingramcontent.com/pod-product-compliance
Lightning Source LLC
Chambersburg PA
CBHW031930020625
27599CB00017B/131